"Mary Ellen Doyle has given us what we have long needed: a sensitive, sophisticated, and meditative study of Gaines's artistry. She smartly points out the myriad ways his subject—Louisiana, its people, and the interaction of the state's complex cultures—generated his methods; she also offers a new critical vocabulary to use as we begin to read his magnificent fiction as a system of interbraided voices. No student of African American, Southern, or American studies can afford to miss this provocative and inspiring reading of the works of a writer who has few peers in contemporary letters."

—John Lowe, editor of *Conversations with Ernest Gaines*

"Graceful, courteous, courageous, honest, unselfish, mutually appreciative and respectful approaches to the problems of life seem to have Gaines's approval. Doyle's very fine analysis and appreciation of these and other aspects of Gaines's complex, humane genius is well worth reading."

—*Virginia Quarterly Review*

Southern Literary Studies

Fred Hobson, Editor

Voices from the Quarters

The Fiction of Ernest J. Gaines

Mary Ellen Doyle

LOUISIANA STATE UNIVERSITY PRESS

Baton Rouge

5/14/07
Lan
$ 15.95

Louisiana Paperback Edition, 2003
12 11 10 09 08 07 06 05 04 03
5 4 3 2 1

Designer: Amanda McDonald Scallan
Typeface: Goudy
Typesetter: Coghill Composition Co., Inc.
Printer and binder: Thomson-Shore, Inc.

Library of Congress Cataloging-in-Publication Data

Doyle, Mary Ellen, 1932–
        Voices from the quarters : the fiction of Ernest J. Gaines / Mary Ellen Doyle.
            p.   cm.—(Southern literary studies)
        Includes bibliographical references and index.
        ISBN 0-8071-2729-9 (cloth); ISBN 0-8071-2910-0 (pbk.)
        1. Gaines, Ernest J., 1933—Criticism and interpretation.   2. Southern States—In
    literature.   3. African Americans in literature.   4. Louisiana—In literature.   I. Title.   II.
    Series.

        PS3557.A355 Z654   2001
        813'.59—dc21   2001029630

Portions of this book appeared previously in different form as "Ernest Gaines' Materials: Place, People, Author"
in MELUS, volume 15 (fall 1988); and "The Best of Bloodline: 'Camcorder' Narration in Two Stories by
Ernest Gaines" in the Journal of the Short Story in English, volume 18 (spring 1992).

The paper in this book meets the guidelines for permanence and durability of the Committee on Production
Guidelines for Book Longevity of the Council on Library Resources. ∞

*In honor and in respectful memory of "the People" who lived
and told the stories and passed on the lessons.*

Contents

Illustrations

Acknowledgments

AS THIS STUDY of Gaines's work has progressed over a span of years, portions of it have seen print and have now been expanded and updated. I thank the editors of *MELUS* and the *Journal of the Short Story in English* for permission to reprint material that first appeared in their pages.

Personal acknowledgments must begin with Ernest Gaines himself. After we met in 1983, he put me in touch with his brother Lionel, with whom I toured the area of Oscar and New Roads and met their great-uncle, the late Horace McVay. Mrs. Madeline Caillet then welcomed me to River Lake plantation, where I interviewed her and the elderly people then living there. From the gracious and open conversations of all these people, I gleaned the liveliest portions of the *MELUS* article, now included in chapter 1. Since that time, Ernest Gaines and his wife, Dianne, have been most helpful in answering questions, providing photographs, and offering interest and friendship while honoring my independence as critic/writer. I thank them sincerely.

Every writer of literary criticism needs other critics, not just of her subjects' works but of her own; she needs their insights, evaluations, and suggestions for fresh thought and improved style. For these benefits, I acknowledge my debt to colleagues, students, family, and community members—friends all. I note especially those who read and commented on portions of my work-in-progress: David Estes, Robert Butler, Mary Helen Washington, John Callahan, John Doyle, Mary Doyle Springer, and the readers for Louisiana State University Press, Fred Hobson and J. Lee Greene. For numerous, patient responses to questions and for many encouraging words, I thank John Easterly, Executive Editor of the Press, Nicola Mason and Sarah Doerries, most helpful editors.

A writer also needs working space and research assistance, for which I thank the staff of Spalding University Library, Louisville, Kentucky. If she is also an electronic troglodyte, she has exceptional need of ready and good-humored assistants, such as Kevin Peers, Reference Librarian, and especially Lee Morrison, Manager of the computer lab, who rescued my disks from a virus. Without these folks, I would still be at my task in frustration and distress. For them, no amount of thanks can be too much.

Finally, my deepest debt, as always, is to my community, the Sisters of Charity of Nazareth. They, especially the leadership, recognized this work as an expression of our priority to combat racism and promote justice and humane values. Their recognition has been conveyed through interest and encouragement over the years and through provision of the practical necessities: time, tools, and daily bread. My debt here is matched by my gratitude.

Abbreviations

Works of Ernest Gaines

Titles are omitted in citations unless needed for clarity. After a first citation, the following abbreviations or short titles are used:

"Sky"	"The Sky Is Gray"
"LDN"	"A Long Day in November"
"Bl"	"Bloodline" (the short story)
"TM"	"Three Men"
"CS"	"Chippo Simon"
"Auntie"	"Auntie and the Black Experience"
"Ink"	"Bloodline in Ink"

Collections of Interviews and Essays

CEG *Conversations with Ernest Gaines*, edited by John Lowe

CRF *Critical Reflections on the Fiction of Ernest J. Gaines*, edited by David Estes

PT   *Porch Talk with Ernest Gaines: Conversations on the Writer's Craft*, by Marcia Gaudet and Carl Wooton

Voices from the Quarters

Introduction

ERNEST GAINES DENIES concern for the opinions of literary critics, saying he just tries to "write a book that I think is true. . . . nobody tells me how to write."[1] That statement might give pause to one trying to write a book of criticism of his work. Yet Gaines acknowledges to interviewers the heavy influence of his editors, and especially his agent, who have critiqued his works-in-progress; he explains and affirms the changes they demanded and he accepted. He has been very open to interviews, over many years discussing all aspects of his work and often enough saying with good humor that the interviewers have explained something better than he could have or told him something he didn't know himself. A critic may hope to write a book that is "true" to his fiction, offering such helpful insights and explanations—not necessarily to him, but to readers who relish his stories.

If Gaines does not feel constrained by critics, he does want readers. When pressed to identify those for whom he writes, he named "the black youth of the South . . . the white youth of the South" (CEG, 151). What his books can offer

---

1. John Lowe, ed., *Conversations with Ernest Gaines* (Jackson: University Press of Mississippi, 1995), 79 (hereafter cited in the text as CEG).

to these young people is a matter of his often-expressed concern. He also acknowledges the pleasure he has taken in letters from older readers who offer him their feelings and thoughtful responses (CEG, 314). Be they academics and teachers of fiction, or the many who haunt libraries and search bookstores for fiction of quality, such readers are apt to find Gaines's work deeply satisfying.

This book is also designed for these various readers: students reading Gaines by choice or assignment and wanting to grasp his artistry; teachers wishing to share a colleague's insights; and any readers who simply enjoy fine fiction and the pleasure that derives from a better understanding of its topics, themes, and techniques. People in all those groups have contributed immensely to this book. It grew out of years of the author's pleasure in reading and teaching Gaines, reading others' assessments, and discussing his work with students, family, and community members—and friends who agreed to share his stories and also got "hooked" enough to want to share their own excitement and opinions. Many of them will no doubt recognize their opinions, though I have long since absorbed them and made them mine. Some will find themselves in the footnotes.

An eclectic audience calls for an eclectic approach. Malcolm Cowley, one of Gaines's teachers, has called literary criticism a "many-windowed house." Whatever angle of approach to the fiction seemed likely to illuminate it, wherever the light shone, through that window I have looked as intently as I could. I was guided in large part by my desire both to focus on Gaines's own chief concerns in his fiction—those that most show his processes and progress as an artist—and to use those critical methods that have proved most fruitful over years of reading and teaching.

No critic of Gaines can avoid form criticism and still be true to his works. Over and over, he has stressed his conviction that form and structure turn the doughy mass of possible plot lines, characters, and themes into a work of art. Because his characters are drawn consistently from the people of his Louisiana territory, they embody his thematic statements about its racial history. Because he intently explores black manhood in all its definitions and relationships, his themes also enter the arena of feminist criticism. How, and how convincingly, his people express these themes in speech and action can often be discovered by mimetic and psychological analysis of character.

Even more than they act, Gaines's characters speak. The creation and effects of voice, in both dialogue and narration, are perhaps that aspect for which his fiction is best known. Certainly "the sound of [his] people talking" has been his preoccupation as an artist. He wants to capture their voices on paper, to let them tell the tales of life and labor and love, on the plantations and in or around his fictive Bayonne. A critic must listen closely to all voices and gauge their sounds, understand who is saying (or thinking or simply perceiving) what, why, and to what effect.

Though Gaines may revisit similar concerns from story to story, novel to novel, his artistry has never been static. From his first brief tale, "The Turtles," which follows two boys compelled into "manhood," to the stunning achievement of manhood by two men in *A Lesson Before Dying*, his command of his craft and its modes has grown. And so his work invites chronological and comparative study to see the course of his development. It is the purpose of this book to make such a study, interweaving information on the purposes and production of his texts with interpretation and evaluation of their developing meaning and methods.

I intend to demonstrate that Gaines's evolution as an artist has been a process: he has refined his own conception of his major themes, honed his storytelling skills, and melded the two. Through his use of oft-repeated themes and character types, he created more complex and volatile characters and situations in more varied and suitable formal arrangements. He found ways to manipulate the short story form to create the novel. And his varied, sophisticated, and distinctive "voices" fused with his themes and revealed his characters—"voices" here understood in three ways: as dialogue, modes of narration, and the implied or explicit expression of meaning and value by that persona known as the implied author. As the first two voices became more diverse and suited to their subjects, the third became richer, deeper, and more resonant.

Real "listening" to Gaines's voices equates with close reading, the closest possible, with attention to details, to their nuances and suggestions. That is what is offered in this book, to the best of its writer's ability. This study is meant to be an instrument by which the "Voices from the Quarters" can be clearly heard.

1

——◆——

Place, People, Personal Experience
"This Louisiana Thing"

SOUTHERN LOUISIANA . . . CAJUN Country . . . Pointe Coupee . . . New
Roads . . . Oscar . . . River Lake plantation . . . False River . . . pecan trees and
live oaks . . . fields of sugarcane and cotton . . . bayous and "parishes" . . . "galleries" on plantation homes . . . cabins in "the quarters": these compose the place
of Ernest Gaines's fiction. Speakers of French, Cajun patois, or black English . . .
black workers who cut cane and drive the mules that haul it . . . Cajun overseers
who drive the cutters . . . black children who play in lanes, work like adults, and
hide their toothache and hunger . . . old men who fish and hide their fears and
resentful memories . . . young militants and the old folk who raised them, who
both admire and fear them, who tell the oral history that has nourished their
dreams and demands . . . Creoles who struggle between the whites who despise
and displace them and the blacks they despise and will not join . . . landowners
who "possess" all these people yet slowly lose possession in a world of cultural
and economic change: these are the people who populate Gaines's fictional yet
intensely realistic world. To read his books is to enter and learn this world; yet
to read with understanding, one must, in some measure, already know it, know
this territory, its varied folk, its cultural demands and taboos, know the author
and "this Louisiana thing that drives [him]" (CEG, 87). Despite all comparison

by critics, Gaines's parish is not the same in terrain, history, or culture as other parts of the South of modern literature, especially not Faulkner's Yoknapatawpha County; nor is his fictional re-creation of it truly comparable in content, style, or tone.

A geography lesson on the landscape Gaines has made his own would begin with a map of south-central Louisiana. On Interstate 10 between Baton Rouge and the Atchafalaya River, one would trace an irregular triangle with the town of New Roads as the northern apex and the Mississippi River on the eastern side. Curving along Route 1, from New Roads down to the hamlet of Oscar, is the new-moon False River, actually an oxbow lake left by the Mississippi when sedimentation and erosion changed its ancient course. Close by Oscar is River Lake plantation—the heart of the Gaines world, where he himself was born and reared—which he has re-created, book after book, in all its phases of life.

This triangle, essentially, is Pointe Coupee Parish, renamed St. Raphael in Gaines's fiction to honor his stepfather, Raphael Norbert Colar. Baton Rouge retains its name, but many a frustrated reader has searched a Louisiana map for Bayonne or St. Adrienne (the latter named for his mother); both are actually New Roads, the seat of the parish. The False River, renamed for his brother, has become the St. Charles River of his old-man and boy fishers; and River Lake plantation is surely Marshall's, Hebert's, Sampson's, and every other plantation where Gaines's people live out their poverty-stricken yet emotionally rich lives.[1]

The character of this land, the people who lived on it, and the way they lived can be initially discovered by a drive out of Baton Rouge, west and north up Route 1 to New Roads. Guidebooks, local manuscripts, and Gaines's stories become real as one sees the largely flat, dark, fertile soil, the immense pecan and live-oak trees hung with Spanish moss, and, if the ride is in summer, the intensity of heat that so shapes the moods and even the decisions of many of Gaines's characters. On the left appear the extensive fields of cane and cotton; these were the large land grants of the early French settlers, who built the parish's economy first from tobacco and indigo, then cotton and sugarcane, and from related industries at the cotton gins, sugar mills, and saw mills. On the right is the False River, wide and lovely, indented by numerous modern piers, inviting the Gaines reader to imagine the Cajuns out in boats, to imagine also the disastrous floods recorded as late as 1927, for which the levees were only a partial solution until the modern

1. Charles H. Rowell, "That Little Territory in and around Bayonne: Ernest Gaines and Place" (paper presented at the annual meeting of the Modern Language Association, Los Angeles, December 1982), 2–3; CEG, passim.

spillway poured excess water into the Atchafalaya Basin. The shore of False River is dotted with small stores but mostly is a grassy plot, again inviting imagination of Gaines's characters gathering for fishing, baptisms, and sermons. Across the river, one sees the "Island," the land within the moonlike curve of False River, settled chiefly by the later French arrivals, who received much smaller land grants, and by the Acadians, the tragic French deportees from British Nova Scotia and ancestors of the modern Cajuns.[2] Here is one source of the social stratification that so clearly marks this Louisiana parish—in reality and in fiction, in former and in present times—that is such a motivating force in Gaines's stories and is made visible in the distinctive types of houses that face False River or are hidden away at a distance from it.

The most notable of these houses are the large, white French-style plantation homes, with front steps rising to a main entrance on the second floor and a gallery projecting over the lower rooms, where family or servants sought cool and shade to eat or work. These are the "big houses," "at the front," the legacies of various Gaines characters, some troubled by the total heritage they symbolize. River Lake plantation itself tells the story: an 1803 U.S. patent shows it owned by Antoine Descuirs; by 1823 his purchases had brought it to a length of more than a mile and a depth of nearly three miles. Circa 1845, his daughter Antoinette married Arthur Denis, grandson of French aristocracy, and the house was altered, made larger and more stylish. A nineteenth-century court record lists these buildings at River Lake: a two-story house, two sheds, a cotton gin and press, blacksmith shop, corn mill, kitchen, hospital, two pigeon houses, four corn houses, thirty "negroe huts," and some other armory buildings.

More numerous along Route 1 are smaller frame houses, perhaps with outdoor stairways on the side; these the explorer learns to identify as Cajun architecture, with the outdoor stairway leading to the *garçonnière*, a room for the boys or the yet-unmarried but increasingly independent young men of the family.[3] These houses seem to have only garden-sized land attached, to be the homes of those who work elsewhere in farming, fishing, or small business.

If one turns left off the main route and drives down a long lane near one of the big houses, one will see the "quarters," the area where formerly as many as thirty or forty cabins gathered black slaves or tenants into a culturally united

2. Idolie Olinde David, "Historical Sketch of Early Pointe Coupee" (New Roads, La., Public Library, n.d. Typescript), 2–5.

3. Drury Tallant, "French Influences on River Lake Plantation" (Private collection of Madeline Caillet, n.d. Typescript), 1–3; Rowell, "Territory," 1–2.

community, where now perhaps a dozen old people live out their lives in a few remaining weather-beaten houses, even raising a patch of cotton or cane for memory's sake, along with the flowers and grass plots they try to hold against the weeds encroaching from empty lots.

Thadious Davis, quoting Gaines, asserts that his initial writing came less from a concern for character or incident than from his strong sense of this homeplace. It is true that characterization and the moral quality of actions become more prominent in Gaines's later works; nevertheless, these too retain the force of that initial desire: "I wanted to smell that Louisiana earth, feel that Louisiana sun, sit under the shade of one of those Louisiana oaks, search for pecans in that Louisiana grass in one of those Louisiana yards next to one of those Louisiana bayous, not far from a Louisiana river."[4]

It is evident that the labor and culture sustained on this land were shaped not only by its soil, its waterways, and its sky—blazing in July and chilly in November—but even more by the kinds of people who settled it, from the first French *coureurs des bois* to the modern oil merchants, from the first owners of plantations to the remaining black dwellers in the quarters. Gaines has somehow known them all, depicted most of them; the traveler in Pointe Coupee today will meet, in some real way, their ghosts or their living selves.

Gaines's earliest fictional persons appear in story time about 1863, but Pointe Coupee history from its beginnings in about 1700 is in his characters' blood. French Canadians were hunting and fishing there in 1708, and the post of Pointe Coupee was established in 1717 northeast of New Roads, in an area now engulfed by the Mississippi River. Since slavery was introduced as early as 1719, the land grantees must have begun almost at once to establish the plantations. By 1860, a census listed sixty-three "large owners" of fifty or more slaves. These possessors of land and human labor were French, some of them aristocrats, or their children. They were Catholic; by 1728 they had a missionary, and by 1738, a church. They infused into southern Louisiana culture elements of language, faith, and lifestyle that outlasted competition from later Spanish colonists and, after 1803, American settlers who poured in, bringing several nationalities, the English language, the Episcopal and various Protestant faiths. In Pointe Coupee, the French landowners prevailed. Names such as Poydras, Marioneau, Jarreau, Buonchaud, Patin, and Lebeau far outnumber in the records the Stewarts and Deans.[5]

---

4. Thadious M. Davis, "Headlands and Quarters: Louisiana in *Catherine Carmier*," *Callaloo* 7 (spring/summer 1984): 1.

5. Bernard Curet, *Our Pride: Pointe Coupee* (Baton Rouge: Moran, 1981), 4; David, 1–8.

River Lake's line of owners tells the story. In 1893, the aristocratic Denis family sold the entire estate to Purvis Major. He eventually divided it among his three sons, John, George, and Joseph. John and George had the portion with the big house, on the right of the lane to the quarters; this eventually was divided among their nieces and nephews. Joseph owned the land on the left side of the road and built a home on it; today it is the possession of his granddaughter, Mrs. Madeline Caillet. In her childhood, social stratification was still very obvious. No one was very well off, not even the landowners, but status was distinct and codes were definite; the child Madeline could play with the blacks on the plantation but not with the local "poor whites," i.e., the Cajuns.[6]

The French plantation owners probably would have fixed the French influence in Louisiana even without the influx of the Acadian population in the 1760s; today, however, the Cajuns are the most distinctive cultural group in the Pointe Coupee area, the most apt to be sought by the tourist or cultural historian. Descendants of refugees, the Cajuns were French but not "quality." In the nineteenth century, they were fishers and independent farmers, *paysans*. Their primary and absolute values were and are religion, family, land, and hard work; education comes after these. In the twentieth century, when large plantations were necessarily broken up for lack of heirs or money, the Cajuns became the principal tenants on the large acreage and used their racial connection with the owners to get the best lands "near the front," nearer False River and farther from the swamplands "at the back." With that advantage in the soil, they could produce more, reap more profit, then buy modern equipment, and so continue a circle of wanting yet more land, leading to more production and profit.[7]

Obviously, the losers as the Cajuns advanced were the blacks and the Creoles, those who had been slaves, then sharecroppers and tenants on small lots. Lionel Gaines shared his memory of the system at River Lake in his boyhood: "In Mr. George's time, the black tenants might have a piece of land even near the front, but when he died, Mr. John was not one to see to the land; it was run by an overseer, Mr. Jarreau. He would request a piece of front land from Mr. John and just get it. . . . They went where they wanted to work; you went where they didn't want to work, toward the back, almost in the woods."

The relations of blacks and Cajuns form one of the most distinctive features of Gaines's fiction, the one that has most often raised either puzzled questions or charges of bias. He has defended his posture toward Cajuns with some effective-

---

6. Lionel Gaines and Madeline Caillet, interviews.
7. Bruce Turner, interview; Davis, 5; CEG, passim.

ness. He knows well that they have also been the victims of a caste system and an unequal economic structure, trying by hard work and acquisition to shake off the restrictions and deprivations of their own past. They are not villains but competitors. Since they cannot fight the plantation owners, they can progress only at the expense of the Creoles and blacks. Like these people, they also see their young shaking off the old ways and values, leaving the land to go to college and to industry. If the Cajuns are objects of anger, symbols of terror, loss, and lynching, they are also, in the oral black tradition, the objects of jokes, of the comic relief that defuses anger.[8]

Alvin Aubert has said bluntly that the French legacy so distinguishing Gaines's fiction from that of other southern black writers is derived from the French settlers' uninhibited sexual alliances with blacks. The resultant society comprises whites (landowners and Cajuns), blacks, and Creoles; it also has issues with fair and dark skin unique to Louisiana and more severe than anywhere else in the South (CEG, 229–30). Gaines, according to Aubert, depicts the Creole not as the old tragic stereotype but as an archetype, a metaphor of the disunity created in the black community by "sexploitation." Michel Fabre also notes that Gaines's Creoles are more comparable to a dying dynasty in Faulkner than to the classic "tragic mulatto." The latter suffers from being unable to identify in either race; the proud Creoles refuse to do so and maintain an "aristocracy," a proud subculture more refined that that of the Cajuns, who nevertheless systematically displace them.[9]

Creole "superiority" to blacks is founded in the old *Code Noir* of 1724, which gave citizenship to "free persons of color"—almost inevitably Creoles, whose various shades of *couleur* were classified in colonial and antebellum records. These persons had the same rights as all citizens of French Louisiana, except for marriage to and legacies from whites: they were privileged as neither they nor any other part-blacks would have been in any other state. In French, Spanish, and American Louisiana, the Creoles continued to see themselves as a third caste, with customs predicated on separation from both blacks and whites. Certain

8. CEG, 9; Ruth Laney, "The Last One Left," (*Baton Rouge*) *Advocate,* Sunday Magazine (October 30, 1983): 6–7; David C. Estes, "Gaines's Humor: Race and Laughter," in *Critical Reflections on the Fiction of Ernest J. Gaines,* ed. David C. Estes (Athens: University of Georgia Press, 1994), 229. This collection will be cited hereafter as *CRF*.

9. Alvin Aubert, entry for Ernest J. Gaines in *Contemporary Novelists,* ed. James Vinson (New York: St. Martin's Press, 1976), 483; Aubert, "Ernest J. Gaines's Truly Tragic Mulatto," *Callaloo* 1 (May 1978): 69; Michel Fabre, "Bayonne or the Yoknapatawpha of Ernest Gaines," trans. Melvin Dixon and Didier Malaquin, *Callaloo* 1 (May 1978): 117–8.

families and their homeplaces became well known; the Metoyers of Isle Brevelle on the Cane River are probably the source for Gaines's Creole Place and several fictional families. But the tragedy of these Creoles is that any status of their privileged ancestors is long gone; now they are simply rural, uneducated sharecroppers and tenants, clinging to empty, ancient forms, refusing to ally themselves socially or politically with blacks. Their daughters are as much barred by their own code from marrying a black as they are prevented by the white code from marrying a white. They will not recognize change or join the blacks bleeding to win it. "Creole" may, in fact, be used as a badge of security and thus add to the existing resentment and disunity. And so the Creoles are isolated in a community that grows smaller and more strangulating as the South inexorably divides into simply black and white.[10]

The Creoles are African and French in origin, Catholic in religion; the blacks who inhabit the quarters and constitute the main body of Gaines's characters are African and Protestant, usually Baptist. They are the descendants of the slaves who built the big houses; they are Gaines's people, who in his childhood still planted the cotton and cut the cane, told the stories in the language he absorbed and transmitted, and transformed the quarters from a place to confine and control subservient laborers into a source of political unity, common striving, mutual protection, friendship, folk education and culture, a place to generate leadership and change. These blacks are influenced by the French and Creole legacy around them; they may have French names, use French words amid their own black folk English, and argue about the relative efficacy of Baptist or Catholic prayers. But they are distinctly their own people, struggling with their own tensions as they lose land, lose their young, and grapple with the changes forced on them by owners and Cajuns or by their own children, whom they have raised to be restless and aware. If the quarters are marked by heat, dust, dying plants, and encroaching weeds, they are, or they were, also the "ritual ground of communion."[11] In Gaines's fiction, the tragedy is less the confinement of life and aspiration to the quarters than the disappearance of the quarters and the community it formed.

The reader who wishes to see both Gaines's places and people with deeper understanding and empathy can do so best by visits to two places: Burden Research Plantation at the Rural Life Museum, Baton Rouge, and, if possible, River

10. Davis, 7–8; CEG, 230.
11. Charles H. Rowell, "The Quarters: Ernest Gaines and the Sense of Place," *Southern Review* 21 (1985): 750.

Lake plantation, the site of Gaines's boyhood in the quarters. At the Burden plantation may be seen a typical commissary, rural church, Cajun house, and several cabins of the typical "double pen, saddle-bag" (i.e., duplex) construction, with fireplace and chimney in the center and a door between the two rooms, so that two families might live there, each with its own "firehalf." Also visible is an overseer's house with its *bousillage* walls of cypress insulated with mud and Spanish moss, its cowhide chairs and pewter ware—all indicative of just that social and economic distinction that cut the essential gap between a Cajun overseer and a black leading workman, no matter how much they might associate in labor, in conversation, and in mutual understanding. The cane-grinding operation (many of Gaines's events occur in "grinding time") is made real as well: the mule-drawn, two-wheel carts that pulled the cane to the mill, the mule-pulled crusher pole that ground the stalks, the juice flowing into the huge vats and emptied into open kettles in the sugarhouse.[12] Any pulling and hauling not done by the mules was, of course, done by the people and was still done by them in Gaines's boyhood at River Lake. There, only the one-room church/school remains; the last of the old people are gone, those who willingly shared memories of the old times and of Ernest Gaines himself, the boy who now returns regularly to draw again from the living memory they embody.

From these people's experiences, in their memory and honor, Gaines constructs what Rowell has called his "myth," his "symbolic geography" and "center of meaning."[13] To an interviewer Gaines stated, "I'm very very proud of my Louisiana background, the people I come from—my uncle and the people we drink with, the people I talk with, and the people I grew up around, and their friends" (CEG, 42). About these common, nonhistorical but heroic people he wants to write with all the imagination, creativity, and passion in him.

Who were the specific people who thus shaped Ernest Gaines's own life and attitudes? What early experiences inform his fiction and, if known, can make it more vitally understood? What was it like to live, work, go to school, and be part of the people on River Lake plantation from 1933 to 1948? Why did he leave, and what is it like to return, educated beyond any opportunity available in the homeplace? Why does that place still so move his heart and creative imagination? What has made him a writer about Pointe Coupee, Louisiana, who chose for many years to live and work chiefly in San Francisco, California? Numerous interviewers have presented these questions to Gaines and found him both a

12. "The LSU Rural Life Museum" (guidebook), 15–6.
13. Rowell, "Quarters," 735.

man of intense privacy that compels respect and a cooperative partner in the effort to make his background and his books accessible.

Ernest Gaines's ancestry includes a maternal great-grandmother who was half black, half Native American; his maternal great-grandfather, Jimmy McVay, "looked like Faulkner," enough that Gaines's picture of the author was once taken for that of the ancestor. His paternal grandmother was "much darker." With all three strains, Gaines calls himself a black, also simply an American (CEG, 323). He was born on January 15, 1933, at River Lake plantation, then known as Cherie, on the portion belonging to Mr. John Major. His paternal grandfather was the yardman, his maternal grandmother the cook at the big house; his parents, Manuel and Adrienne Jefferson Gaines, worked in the fields.

By the age of nine, Ernest was in the field himself, picking cotton, digging potatoes and onions, and pulling corn for fifty cents a day. As the oldest child, he assumed such duties as getting the well water and going into the swamps to cut wood for the stove and fireplace, a "twelve-year-old kid trying to pull a saw for half a day . . . about the most cruel thing you can do to somebody" (CEG, 286). Many of Gaines's experiences, of work and play and schooling, of hardship and discipline, of serving, listening to, and learning from the old people, have been transferred to his child characters. Incidents affecting young James in "The Sky Is Gray," for instance, were drawn from Gaines's own youth: toothache and going to the dentist, traveling to New Roads in the back of the bus, walking a mile to the back of town to a cluttered blacks' waiting room, killing birds for food, and caring for younger siblings. (Gaines has eight brothers and three sisters; five children were born in Louisiana, the younger seven in California.)[14]

These younger children, in their turn, joined in the work. An older boy or girl might "advance" to the cutting of cane. Lionel Gaines recalls that in his boyhood there were no machines for either picking cotton or cutting cane; the work was simply "rough" in a climate either "too hot or too cold." Ernest's fiction deals more often with the heat as symbol of the workers' oppressed condition, but Lionel spoke vividly of cutting cane from November to January, when workers often had to pick ice off the cane before loading it.

Some of this work was done to assist their mother's uncle, Horace McVay, then a tenant of forty acres. During a ride through an area originally of large, solely owned plantations, then divided into leased acreage, Lionel Gaines ex-

14. Laney, 7; CEG 12, 82; Marcia Gaudet and Carl Wooton, *Porch Talk with Ernest Gaines: Conversations on the Writer's Craft* (Baton Rouge: Louisiana State University Press, 1990), chapter 4 (hereafter cited as *PT*).

plained how the tenant system worked at that time: those on "Mr. John's" land "worked on a quarter"; those on "Miss Lillian's" (daughter and heir of Mr. Joseph) "worked on a half," i.e., a quarter or a half of the crop they "made." As for the method of payment:

> "You see, a tenant used that land, but everything he made, all his checks, had to go to the big man, the man who owned the place, until 'settle up time.' Just before Christmas, you'd go up to the big office, and the man'd tell you how much you made, and how much you used of his stuff, how much grain he had to buy for you. Then if you have something left, he'd give it to you; if you don't then he'd loan you something for the next year."
>
> "You just took what he said?"
>
> "Oh yeah! You had no other choice but take that or don't take anything."

At Cherie, tenants received two checks at the gin after the cotton and seed were separated; they could keep and spend the smaller check for seed; the other was given to Mr. John, and at Christmas the usual settlement was made. A similar arrangement worked with the cane cutting: a train picked up the cane and brought it to the sugar mill. In this case, "You didn't see no check. Mr. Wilkerson mailed your check back to Mr. John. Whatever they say it was, that what it was. What they gave you at the end of the year, that what you had. They say 'You broke even' or 'you still owe me two hundred dollars,' that's the way it was. 'You want to borrow. . . ?' "

A final slip of the bolt lock on these sharecroppers was payment in the form of plantation money, old samples of which can be seen at River Lake today. Coins marked with the plantation name were minted in values of ten cents to a dollar. Workers had to spend these coins at the plantation commissary, which of course could charge whatever the owners wanted—"Yep, whatever they wanted!"

Both Lionel Gaines and the older people at River Lake gave assurance that a child's life there was not all heavy labor. During their "plenty of play time," the boys would shoot marbles or play with a ball made from a marble wrapped in rags, cord, and a cloth cover sewed for them by the old people. "Anywhere we could get it wide enough and big enough, we played ball." According to Lionel, however, when he was shooting marbles, Ernest would usually be "somewhere doing something" else, chiefly reading for his own pleasure, reading or writing letters for the old people, or going to the store for them, "whether they gave him a nickel or not." Rosie Ruffin, at River Lake before Gaines's birth, said he went "down the quarter" often for her: "a nice boy, raised up nice." Here the interviewer begins to grasp the chain of circumstances and people that connects "EJ" or "J" the plantation child with Ernest J. Gaines the writer, that forms a plausible explanation of his and his characters' development.

The first link is the story of his education. According to Willie Aaron, lifetime resident of River Lake and another of its elderly storehouses of memory, the children of his generation went to school only at night: "they used to give school down here in the house; I went to that." By the time "J" was in school, classes were held in the little church in the quarters. Teachers, "Mr. Paul and Miss Ada . . . Miss Green," who were paid a fraction of white teachers' salaries, commuted from New Roads or came from Baton Rouge and lived with someone in the quarters. One teacher lived about five years with Gaines's grandmother. The school had benches; the children used their laps for desks or knelt and wrote on the pews; they had "slate on the wall, but they had paper, too." Books were supplied by the state; the students or the teacher went to New Roads to get them. A white superintendent visited once or twice a year, talked a few minutes, and left. The school year was officially six months; students were lucky if it lasted five, from late October to early April. About thirty children attended, those who could get away from the fields. Ernest and Lionel were among them any day they were not sick.

The school at the quarters ended with grade six; then children had the choice to go to St. Augustine's Catholic School in New Roads or quit; Pointe Coupee Parish had no high school for blacks. A school bus ran to New Roads; it would come into the quarters when the road was good enough; when bad, the children made the long walk to the front to meet it. Lionel recalls a little bus that went from Port Allen to New Roads. A Trailways bus from the quarters to New Roads cost fifty cents, this little one only twenty. Children could take the school bus home as far as Bigman Lane, then walk the long remainder of the way. Under the circumstances, the temptation to quit was not small, but Ernest and Lionel were among the five or so children from the quarters who went to St. Augustine's. He stayed there from grades seven through nine.[15]

Ernest's response to education in this system was attested by all who remembered him: his uncle, his brother, the old folks in the quarters. He was "pretty smart," "a scholar," "pretty high up in every respect"; "look like he always wanted to be somebody, learn something"; "he loved school—yes, indeed!"

15. Lionel Gaines, Willie Aaron, and Rosie Ruffin, interviews; CEG, 217–9.

Their accounts begin to take the dimensions of myth. According to Lionel, Ernest would "cry all day" if he had to miss school; he would not go to bed until a lesson was mastered and might often be up till two o'clock studying by kerosene lamp. Sometimes Lionel would go to bed, wake up at five, and find Ernest still at the lamp. If his studies required the whole night, he would use it—then go to school. Both his uncle and his brother told the "thorn story," apparently now a family legend: "EJ," who ran often, got a thorn deep in his heel. Lionel pulled it out, put fat meat on the foot and tied it up; and Ernest went hopping to school rather than miss a day. He was about twelve at the time.

On Sundays, of course, the schoolhouse in the quarters served its first purpose—Baptist church services. Ernest and all the other children were expected to attend, to learn their Bible, and, in due time, to experience conversion and baptism in False River. He has acknowledged that he and presumably others underwent this public experience more to satisfy their elders than from any real spiritual impulse. From this amalgamation of Baptist upbringing and education in the quarters and Catholic education at St. Augustine's, Ernest derived the attitude toward religion that pervades his work: respect for any sincere belief that issues in worthy action, and an equally sincere belief that no particular denomination or form of church attendance is necessary. He feels that formal religion has not succeeded in bringing about the moral changes so desperately needed in society, especially changes in American racism and its devastating impact on black families and communities.

Of all that devastation, nothing more deeply affected Gaines or appears more movingly in his fiction than the impact of racism on black men, especially as husbands and fathers. The source of this concern he noted tersely in an interview: "My mother and father split up early—and it is a theme that enters everything—and I don't know where the fathers are" (CEG, 21). Manuel Gaines went into the service when his oldest son was about eight or nine; his children had no further contact with him, and the separation from his wife was final by the war's end (PT, 68–9). She and their children moved to nearby Parlange Lane (now LA 78), where she owned some land and where she met Raphael Norbert Colar. After a few more years back at Cherie, she married him, and they found work in New Orleans. Colar joined the Merchant Marines and was transferred to California, where first Ernest, in 1948, and then all the older children except Lionel eventually joined them. To Norbert Colar's memory Gaines dedicated *The Autobiography of Miss Jane Pittman*. From this and from everything he has said in interviews, it is clear that he received from Colar a father's affection and guidance and that he gave in return an equal affection and profound respect.

The disruption of the family, however, had one result that Gaines clearly considers the most positive influence of his life: he and the older children came under the care of his mother's aunt, Miss Augusteen Jefferson. About this woman Gaines will speak with a love and reverence and fullness that suggest she has taken almost mythic stature in his memory and imagination. Nor is her reality diminished when one interviews the old folk at River Lake, who well remember "Aunt Teen" and the way "she raised them children." The outstanding physical fact about her is that she was crippled from birth or very early childhood; Gaines says he never knew anyone who remembered her walking. Yet she "could do anything she wanted to" by crawling about the cabin or outside and down the steps to her garden. She raised flowers and vegetables, chickens and hogs; she sat on a bench to hoe or to cook or wash clothes in the water hauled by Ernest or the other boys, and occasionally to apply the switches they were required to cut and bring her. She encouraged, taught, and disciplined them by her presence and personality, perhaps most by the fact that she was never heard to complain. To the oldest of her nephews, the indelible lesson was "Just do the job, do it as well as you could, but don't complain."[16] Leaving her when he went to California was the most wrenching separation Ernest had yet known; she has remained the strongest moral influence in his life. In the dedication of *The Autobiography of Miss Jane Pittman*, he summarized that influence: she "did not walk a day in her life but [she] taught me the importance of standing." Miss Augusteen died in the quarters at River Lake and was buried there on Carnival day, 1954, five years after Ernest's departure. In 1994 he, his wife, and friends began a continuing effort to save the cemetery where she and others were buried in unmarked graves (CEG, 298).

Augusteen Jefferson was the moral model of Jane Pittman and other older women in his fiction; like Jane, she embodied that element of life in the quarters that chiefly caused "J" Gaines to become Ernest J. Gaines the writer—oral tradition. Because Miss Augusteen could not walk, the folk came to her for the visits and long conversations that were their principal recreation. J served them tea or lemonade; he also sat and listened to them talk of old times. He talked and listened when he ran their errands and wrote their letters, when he accompanied another aunt on her rounds to sell Avon products, when he sat on the ditch-

16. Ernest Gaines, "Auntie and the Black Experience in Louisiana," in *Louisiana Tapestry: The Ethnic Weave of St. Landry Parish*, ed. Vaughn B. Baker and Jean T. Kreamer (Lafayette: Center for Louisiana Studies, University of Southwest Louisiana, 1982), 21 (hereafter cited in text as "Auntie").

banks with men telling stories. As an adult, he heard from Walter "Pete" Zeno, an old man who had known five generations of Gaineses, of the storytellers in his own family, all "great liars." Listening and listening, Gaines absorbed the stories, the speech patterns in which they were told, and the values and feelings they expressed. And these older folk—Zeno, Reese Spooner, Rosie Ruffin, Willie Aaron, Carrie Hebert—became, under various names, the characters who populate his novels. To them he insists he must return, not merely as an observer, but "to absorb things," to be with the land and people, to go to the fields and towns and bars, eat the food, and listen to the language (CEG, 86). The labor of his life is to translate their oral forms into written, to create on paper their sounds, gestures, and syntax, to turn into sentences their speech and its meanings.

Even though Ernest's love of study and his success with books made him special in the quarters of River Lake, his creative writing there was limited to early efforts at dramas, which he directed and produced in the church. He recalls a mock wedding he performed as the minister, with his script on the Bible and his back to the audience, since he did not know his own part. He grew up with radio and on Sunday nights listened to plays and imagined whole scenes. He has noted the influence of radio on his dialogue, his use of first-person narration, his writing works to be read aloud, and his own frequent public readings. He has also said that had he moved to New York instead of the West, he might well have become a playwright, given his penchant for a scene in a small space and for dialogue (CEG, 54, 179–80, 224).

The impetus that made him a fiction writer was the transplantation to California when he was fifteen years old. He would later say it occurred at just the right time for his future as a writer: he had lots of memories, knew all the religions, ethnic groups, and the problems back home. Five years earlier, he would have lacked enough experience; five years later, he "would have been broken—in prison, dead, insane" (CEG, 279).

In Vallejo, where Norbert Colar was stationed, Ernest became part of the heterogeneous population of a California military base. His awareness and outlook expanded as he heard the languages and life experiences of Japanese, Chinese, Filipinos, Latinos, American whites and blacks. But though Vallejo was not Watts or Harlem, its variety did include local teenage gangs, and Colar forestalled trouble by counseling Ernest forcefully to "get the hell off the streets." The lad found his way first to the YMCA. He had no experience with basketball, but he assumed a "country kid" could box. After one severe punch in the mouth, he decided to try the library ("Auntie," 22). What followed there, like the story of his early schooling, has the qualities of which legends are made.

Ernest Gaines, a black youth in Louisiana before 1948, had never seen the inside of a public library. In Vallejo's, he was astounded to discover that a simple card entitled him to temporary possession of more books than he had ever seen, all he had time enough in life to read. At first, he tried all subjects and borrowed armloads at random according to the attraction of the covers. Eventually, he settled into the fiction section and, to alleviate the homesickness that haunted him, sought stories about the kind of people he knew and intensely missed. He found none. At the time, Richard Wright was the only black author with a national reputation, and Gaines had yet to learn the names of white authors who at least attempted to portray the rural black South. None of these was much in public demand in Vallejo, California, in 1948. He did, however, find stories of rural people and peasants—the works of John Steinbeck, Willa Cather, Anton Chekov, and Ivan Turgenev. He read and he read and he read; he saw that these authors understood rural people. Still, "none of them had Auntie" ("Auntie," 22). And so, at about the age of sixteen, he began to write. If no one else had told the stories of his people, he would do so himself.

The tale of that first attempt at a novel has a decided comic flair as Gaines tells it. He wrote in longhand until his mother, "to keep me quiet," agreed to rent a typewriter on which he pecked out "what I thought was a book." Startled by Ernest's self-imposed task and his persistence at it, his stepfather, home on leave, voiced within his hearing the opinion that "that boy going crazy there, yeah." His friends tried to lure him out to sports. Most laughed at the idea of his writing a book; others advised him to write about California—or at least New Orleans, but not "that plantation stuff everybody's trying to forget." But Ernest had already tried in his early Vallejo days to pass himself off as an urbanite from New Orleans; when sufficiently ridiculed for his inability to name any street but Canal, he had abandoned the pretense. His experience was the quarters at River Lake and the Friday-night cowboy movies in New Roads; he would write what he knew—and loved. So his first "novel," titled *A Little Stream*, was typed on both sides of half sheets of paper, bound together like a book, and sent off to New York in 1949. The young author waited for the fortune he would send back to Auntie. What he received, of course, was the rejected manuscript, which he promptly took to the yard and burned. But he still wanted to write ("Auntie," 22–3).

A long road remained before Gaines the young author could return to his "little stream" and give its ideas both form and flow as *Catherine Carmier*. After graduation from Vallejo High School in 1951 and an A.A. degree from Vallejo Junior College, he spent 1953 through 1955 in the army. After basic training at

Fort Ord, California, in 1953, and six months at Camp Chaffee, Arkansas, in 1954, he went to Guam for a year. There he won two prizes and a total of twenty-five dollars for a short story, as well as a new determination to write.[17] At the end of his tour of duty, friends urged him to stay in the army for the security of income, food, and three beds—one each in the barracks, hospital, and stockade. He was bright and got along well; he could go to officer's school ("Auntie," 23–4). What more could he want? He still wanted to write.

With that goal and his claim on the GI Bill, he mustered out and went to San Francisco State to study English literature and creative writing. But, junior college notwithstanding, he was behind in general education requirements and found himself in Expository Writing 110, the only black in a class of about twenty-five. His experience there, analogous to Faulkner's with freshman English, might well make faculties question the value of the course to potential creative writers. Gaines's first three essays received D's, each followed by a conference with the teacher, Stanley Paul Anderson. This man, second only to Augusteen Jefferson and the people of Pointe Coupee, seems to merit credit for Ernest Gaines's becoming a fiction writer. He gave him permission to try explaining himself in that form rather than in essays. The result was a short story, "The Turtles," that Anderson liked enough to pass around to other faculty. In 1956 it was published in *Transfer*, the college's literary magazine, which also published, in 1957, "Boy in the Double Breasted Suit." Two more results followed: Dorothea Oppenheimer, a former editor about to open her own literary agency in San Francisco, noted Gaines's work, and he won a creative writing fellowship to Stanford University ("Auntie," 24). With his B.A. (1957) and his new access to some of the best teachers in his field, he was on his way to becoming a writer.

Gaines is often asked about the influences on his formation as a writer: teachers, books, other art forms, other writers—especially black writers. Who or what influenced his persistent choice of Louisiana as subject? From earliest to latest interview, his answers are utterly consistent.

His principal teachers were Stanley Anderson and Mark Harris at San Francisco State, and Wallace Stegner, Richard Scowcroft, and Malcolm Cowley at Stanford (1958–1959). All "great critics," they offered him singular encouragement and taught him technique; they made no demands on his subject matter. He was to write what he wished and bring it for discussion of its literary achieve-

17. Ernest Gaines, "Bloodline in Ink," *College English Association Critic* 51 (winter 1989): 7 (hereafter cited in text as "Ink"); Ernest J. Gaines to Mary Ellen Doyle, February 1990. In possession of Mary Ellen Doyle.

ment. Although he tried some California subjects, they never fired his creative imagination or produced work he wanted to publish. Louisiana and its multi-ethnic people filled his head and heart; they would be his subject, and he always knew it. What else he needed to know, what his classes and critics taught him, was *how* to write, and what authors would give him the best examples of technique: the Greek tragedians, the Russians, Guy de Maupassant, James Joyce, Ernest Hemingway, F. Scott Fitzgerald, Eudora Welty, and William Faulkner.

Gaines has always insisted that no black writer influenced him. By the time he went to San Francisco State, Richard Wright and James Baldwin were available, and *Invisible Man* had just been published. But neither these nor any other earlier black writers were taught in the classroom or recommended for his reading. That may or may not be regrettable: the reading of black writers might have fogged his vision of his own subject matter and goals; from the white authors, he knew he was learning skills of narration, not a way of seeing his own world. Jean Toomer's *Cane*, he says, would have influenced him, had he known it, with its subject (the rural black South) and its structure (short pieces combined into a novel). But he did not know *Cane*, and any resemblance now is coincidental or due to the authors' similar experiences (CEG, 221–2).

At Stanford, the "little stream" flowed again; *Stanford Short Stories* for 1960 published "Mary Louise," whose characters and themes would reappear in *Catherine Carmier*. Ernest was also advised that to make his living as a writer, he would need to tackle a novel again; as a writer of short stories only, he would starve. So he set himself to become a novelist and gave himself ten years to "make it" (CEG, 222–3). He wrote in the morning, worked in the afternoon; his jobs included shining shoes, washing dishes, driving cabs, clerking in the post office, and delivering mail in an insurance office. He lived on $175 a month in a one-room apartment with a Murphy bed in the wall and no phone; he used a table in the hallway for writing and for eating his hot dogs and pork and beans. "Here I was, the first male in my family to go to college, and I was living like a bum" (CEG, 280). At the insurance company, as ideas occurred to him, he would sneak into the bathroom and make notes on scraps of paper towels; a draft of "Long Day in November" was written on 250 pieces of paper towel in about three weeks. When his boss kicked the door and yelled, Gaines once replied, "Don't you know there's a genius at work in here?"[18] The full irony of this story is felt when one recalls that forty years later Gaines would receive the Mac-

18. Anne K. Simpson, *A Gathering of Gaines* (Lafayette: Center for Louisiana Studies, University of Southwest Louisiana, 1991), 21; CEG, 293–5.

Arthur "genius grant." After each day's work and ideas, next morning he wrote again—and again—on his Louisiana subjects ("Ink," 9–10). And all the time he followed his teachers' advice; he read and reread the authors who could teach him technique. Each showed him "one route you can take"; he absorbed all they could give him, then moved beyond them to his own style (CEG, 44, 52–3).

The labor to write and publish was, at best, up-lift and down-drop. Between 1963 and 1966, four more stories were published in noteworthy literary journals. In 1959, he began reconstruction of the book he'd burned; as a draft of *Catherine Carmier*, it won the Henry Jackson Literary Prize for best novel-in-progress. He thought the rest would be easy and finished in a year; instead he said he had to struggle with unreal plot, untrue dialogue, and forced action by cardboard figures. "So everything I wrote one day, I destroyed the next day. Wrote and destroyed, wrote and destroyed."[19] Gaines has admitted that "those first ten years of writing were hell" (CEG, 84).

That he persevered and found his peak skills is partly due to the influences of others, living and dead. In those first ten years, if ever, the courage he learned from Miss Augusteen and the encouragement of his college teachers stood him in good stead. As advisors, Anderson, Harris, and Stegner were replaced by his editors, E. L. Doctorow and Bill Decker at Dial Press, and especially by his agent, Dorothea Oppenheimer. This woman, who offered her services to the collegian Gaines, gave him until her death in 1987 what he counts as his most valuable literary relationship. She offered not only many helpful critiques of his writing, but also a related cultural education. With her, he attended symphonies or listened to classical music on the radio, as well as jazz and blues, and so learned more about the use of motifs, repetition, and understatement. He viewed paintings in galleries, prints in bookstores, and great foreign films, and saw that a few significant details could create a scene. She kept him going with extra food and encouragement; she told him honestly when his work was not yet ready for the "big city"—and when it was. "She was there when no one else was."[20]

His chief supports came from inside: his own awareness of his talent; the discipline and repetition of effort he had learned at River Lake and in college track and field; and above all his independence of character, the haunting memories of his own place and people, and his determination to be loyal to them as his subject. A turning point came in 1962. Friends were going to Mexico to write;

19. Simpson, 28, citing an undated speech by Gaines.
20. CEG, 213–4; "Ink," 10–1; Ernest J. Gaines to Mary Ellen Doyle, February 1990 (in Doyle's possession).

one invited Gaines to go along. He was considering it when James Meredith went through fire into the University of Mississippi. Meredith's courage called Gaines to take his own chances in order to write about his home state. In January of 1963 he went to Baton Rouge for a six-month stay and experienced the indignities of segregation and police questioning. That stay "definitely saved my writing and quite possibly my life. . . ."[21] This trip and subsequent annual returns enabled him to know the experiences of young and old in a society changing from sugarcane to oil, from rigid segregation to limited integration, from oppression and fear to activism and assertion. He realized anew what he has often said since: that he need never change his basic subject; it holds more than he could exhaust in a lifetime.

In 1964, six months after his stay in Louisiana, *Catherine Carmier* took final form and was published. But it did not sell. A modest book contract in 1966 gave him some independence and more work time. In 1967 he was able to publish *Of Love and Dust*, and in 1968 three of his magazine stories and two new ones made the collection *Bloodline*. These books earned few and mixed reviews; most critics who noted his work at all saw its strength and potential, especially in the short stories. But publication brought no royalties, no fame, and no clear hope of ever making his living at his craft. In addition, his loyalty to his subject was now being severely tried.

Publishing in the militant sixties subjected Gaines to the demand on black authors to write for social and political goals. Resistance was not easy. California especially was seething with hippies and protests; other young writers thought him out of touch at best and, at worst, an Uncle Tom. Gaines has recognized that had he stayed in Louisiana throughout the civil rights era, he might, like one of his characters, have died on the streets of his hometown. But militant words and acts were not what he had experienced "at home"—not even demonstrations. And he believed that the way to force reluctant white recognition of black humanity was to "do something positive . . . to use the anger in a positive way, to create a lasting punch, one that will have a longer effect than just screaming" or calling obscene names (CEG, 84).

So, as the violence escalated, he kept writing. On a day of bad news, he would sit till he had written a perfect page. He would prove to the George Wallaces, Bull Connors, and Orval Faubuses of the South that he could take the words given by *their* ancestors and use them better, could do more with them to help his race than they could do to destroy it ("Auntie," 26). And he would do it his

---

21. Simpson, 30–1, citing undated speech.

way. He would "write black" indeed, but *his* black, that of his people; and he would write not only about the black people in the quarters but the multi-ethnic people, the Creoles, Cajuns, and landowner whites—all their interaction as he knew it, as it had been seared into his memory and carved onto his heart for the first fifteen years of his life. Eventually, of course, Gaines did begin to include in his fiction the '60s and '70s, the traumas and triumphs of the civil rights movement, but only as he had learned its effects on his people during his return visits to Louisiana. For his choices of subject, the heart had its reasons, which no political or aesthetic movement could shake. He was already free, free as any artist is, to write "what he wants, when he wants, and to whomever he wants."[22]

To whom, then, does he write? Gaines has insisted without deviation that he writes for no particular audience but to satisfy his own impulse and standards. He has half-joked, however, that if he were required at gunpoint to name an audience, he would say first the black youth of the South, and second the white youth of the South. To the former he hopes to convey a sense of proud and free identity, to the latter a sense of the essential unity of all human beings (CEG, 151). If his intuition of his audience and goal is correct, it may explain why children and young people are so much a part of his fiction, why his earliest works choose them as protagonists and even as narrators, and why his stories are so eminently teachable, so appealing and successful as classroom texts.

It was the most teachable and often taught of all his novels that finally brought him success—almost on his appointed ten-year deadline. *The Autobiography of Miss Jane Pittman* in 1971, along with three awards from Louisiana, California, and the Black Academy of Arts, dozens of laudatory reviews, and especially the teleplay in 1974, made Ernest Gaines a famous writer.[23] Even so, fame carried its lingering ironies. The novel was nominated for both the Pulitzer Prize and the National Book Award but received neither. The television production made the story and its star more famous than the author; however, it also caused private readings and classroom assignments (and thus sales) to soar. In 1974 Gaines received a Guggenheim grant and began his next novel.

That novel, *In My Father's House*, represents seven years of grappling with his sooner-or-later, painful but inevitable theme: the missing father, the search of son and father for each other. It received mixed reviews, and a limited income from writing needed the supplement of public readings and short stints of teach-

22. William E. Grant, entry for Ernest J. Gaines in *American Novelists since World War II*, vol. 2 of *Dictionary of Literary Biography* (Detroit: Gale, 1978), 171.

23. Valerie Melissa Babb, *Ernest Gaines*, Twayne United States Authors Series, no. 584 (Boston: Twayne, 1991), xiii (hereafter cited as Babb, *EG*).

ing, such as he had begun in 1971 at Denison University in Ohio. Then came the invitation from the University of Southwestern Louisiana (now the University of Louisiana at Lafayette) to teach creative writing for a full semester. Though reluctant to leave San Francisco for so long, he tried it in 1981. In 1983, the university gave him tenure and a house on campus; his presence as writer-in-residence has since attracted would-be regional writers to the school and revitalized its annual Deep South Writers Conference (CEG, 189–90, 280, 283). The year 1983 also saw the publication of A Gathering of Old Men, another success and the subject of a second television production.

If 1971 and 1983 were years of acclaim, they could hardly compare with the flood stage in 1993: the PBS documentary Ernest Gaines: Louisiana Stories, a tribute to his years of achievement; the publication of A Lesson Before Dying, which won the National Book Critics Circle Award and universal critical praise; and finally the "genius grant" of $355,000 from the John D. and Catherine T. MacArthur Foundation, an award of value even beyond the money, since the recipient neither applies nor is recommended but is selected solely by the foundation's own evaluation (CEG, 277). Beyond all the vicissitudes, the high and low points of a career to which he had dedicated his life, Gaines's reputation as a major American—and black—writer was now fully secure.

Other awards, numerous interviews, and international invitations to conferences, readings, and visiting professorships have followed Gaines's fame. The latest honor is the National Humanities Medal received from President Clinton on December 20, 2000. Neither money nor fame, however, has essentially changed Ernest Gaines the writer and teacher. He has not forgotten nor wished to escape the symbolism of the unmarked graves at River Lake. He once overheard a young woman in a bookstore ask, "If he's so important, what's he doing here?" His answer is his drive to continue writing about a place and people who consider themselves unimportant, to show their significance (CEG, 298–9). New writing projects are in progress, probably several novellas. But the goal remains the same: to be remembered simply as one who "tried to write as well as he could and tried to be fair. Fair toward my characters and fair to other people. I just want to write as well as I can about the people I know" (CEG, 71). The essential and compelling elements of his work also remain the same: in the fiction, his place and his people; in the author, a sense of vocation to be the last witness to their way of life before it passes: "Who will write about the way my people talk, the way they sing, the way they feel about God, the way they work, their superstitions? There are so many things that can be said."[24]

24. Simpson, xi, citing a Gaines notebook.

2

Experiments in Theme and Technique
The Uncollected Short Stories

"I THINK THEY are pretty good stories, and they show the ideas of the young writer" (CEG, 158). So the mature Ernest Gaines evaluated his "college stories," those written at San Francisco State and Stanford. Like most authors learning the craft of fiction, he began with short stories. Many of these remain unpublished in his papers at the archives of the University of Louisiana at Lafayette; they are not yet available for study. Other stories saw print in college magazines and then in reputable journals. Of these, three were later selected for inclusion in *Bloodline*; four others were excluded.

Those four stories, published before *Bloodline*, deserve to be studied as a group, as an important segment of Gaines's oeuvre and as significant indicators of his future as a writer. In them, he begins his study of manhood, shown emerging in child or adolescent protagonists. He introduces themes found in his later works: father-son relationships; the role of women, the church, and preachers in the formation or distortion of men's characters; the personal qualities desirable in a man; and the experiences likely to encourage or hinder a boy's growth into self-awareness, adult values, and authentic manhood. These early stories are also tentative forays into the characters and experiences of women as they try to shape their own lives. All the tales have the wit, the sympathetic insight into folkways, and the finely tuned folk dialogue of Gaines's better-known stories. Not all, however, are as well focused and technically developed as the later collected stories; none is as mature, as wise and deep in its thematic insights. Speculation on the reasons for their exclusion from the collection offers some insight into Gaines's progression as a writer.

Gaines's first published works of fiction, the two "Max stories," are obviously influenced by Hemingway and his Nick Adams. Hemingway's short-story cycle about a boy's progress to manhood and the author's formal structure and character-drawing by terse dialogue served as useful models for the undergraduate writer. Though the influence is clear, so is Gaines's early independence in establishing his own driving theme—to be explored in his own locale through his own questions and tentative answers.

"The Turtles" was written at San Francisco State and published there. Gaines gives it the affection due any "very first" publication and describes its focus as "the introduction to manhood sort of thing" (CEG, 53). The key question of story and author is "What makes a man?" The protagonist, fourteen-year-old Max, accompanies his friend Benny and both their fathers on a fishing trip, at which the grown men catch "about a dozen each." Max's father catches a two-foot trout, but the boys hook only turtles. The walk home is interrupted by a stop at the home of the local prostitute, to whom Max goes at his father's command, while Benny resists in tears his father's order to follow suit. The story ends with Benny's father still trying to force him, while Max's "old man" pronounces him now "a man."[1]

What, indeed, makes a man? The potential, it seems, is tested by participation in men's activities, such as fishing; the defining achievement is having sex. Benny is totally inadequate as a fisherman: he crawls over a log, afraid to get his clothes wet; he cannot handle the line properly and loses both his own and Max's catch; when he hooks a turtle, he is afraid to unhook it; when frustrated at his lack of success, he merely gives up. At the call to sexual experience, he resists by poking a stick in the ground and crying like a child. Max, by contrast, walks the log, wishing he'd fall in; he knows how to fish and is not afraid to unhook and kill a turtle. He is obviously inexperienced in sex, though he has a sense of what is involved in his father's order. He, too, is very reluctant to obey

---

1. Ernest Gaines, "The Turtles," p. 9. The short stories in this chapter are cited by page numbers referring to the first or only publication, as listed in the bibliography. Only "The Turtles," as far as I know, has been reprinted in an anthology.

and does so only to maintain his "partnership" with his widower father (6–7). Though unafraid, he, like Benny, is essentially forced into the encounter, and his father has to interpret his experience for him as the achievement of manhood. What distinguishes Max from Benny is that he is not easily frightened or frustrated. What makes this boy into a man is not merely sexual experience but courage, a willingness to try the new and frightening, emotional as well as physical balance, and the ability to relate well to an older man. That sentence might stand as an acceptable statement of the story's theme.

Readers, however, especially women, may be excused if they find elements of the theme repugnant. The implication is plain enough that while sexual experience is not the only mark of manhood, it is a necessary one, and that using a prostitute is one customary and acceptable way for a boy to achieve it. Thus the role of some women, at least, is to make themselves available. Amy has clearly offered her services before; she knows what is wanted, looks at the boys, and goes into the house to await them. Girls like her, willing to be used to make "boys" into "men," are a sort of commodity. The fathers, unabashed at using her, have brought the boys to see her on the day her aunt goes to town.

Manhood, it is further implied, extends beyond sex into other relations with women, and the fathers themselves have different degrees of achievement. Max's mother has been dead "a long time" (7); no suggestion is made either that her husband did not love her or that he greatly misses her. His son is now his "partner." The father exerts strong authority without physical punishment, but "our friendship and our partnership" is conditional on the boy's obeying: "When I didn't it would end" (7). It is not unthinkable that his partnership with his wife had similar patterns. Benny's father, by contrast, has surrendered control to his wife and is not apt to cross her to assert himself or the boy's wish to spend Sunday elsewhere than in church (1, 2). Max is his father's boy; Benny is his Mama's. Being a man, it is implied, is being unafraid of women in any circumstance, being able either to use or to control them.

One may, however, see a tension within the story about that theme. As emphatic and seemingly affirmative as is the father's pronouncement at the end—that the boy is now a man—Max himself had not assumed it, nor had he responded to his experience with Amy as anything but an exercise in obedience. It is the "cool dust" under his bare feet that "felt good" at the end—suggestive of an overall positive experience but not a great sexual thrill or a view exactly like his father's. Gaines, the young creator of both characters, may have shared either or both views. In any case, he was later to create Munford in "Three Men" and to give that old and much-experienced jailbird a speech on the limits of sex in the making of a man.

The theme of "The Turtles" may be uncertain, but the early skill of its author is not. Short as the story is, it is neatly (almost too neatly) structured by parallel actions and characters. The first part, the group's fishing, serves to introduce the central issue of fear and the secondary related motifs of frustration and aptitude, all amplified and made forceful in the visit to Amy, all essential parts of the definition of manhood. Both boys are frustrated in their fishing, but only Benny is impatient and inept as well as fearful. Only Benny loses his line, while Max puts his pole securely in the ground. The men are successful fishers, Max's father more so than Benny's. What the boys catch is useless, good only to play around with, destroy, and leave behind; what the men catch is nourishing, pleasurable food. At Amy's, Max "goes in" and ends up feeling good, at least about his father's satisfaction with him; his satisfied father has again caught "the big one." Benny ends up in tears, until his too-easygoing father reaches maximum frustration and presumably will force him for "one day" to "do what I say" (9). Though the symbolic parallels of sex to a fishing expedition and a prostitute to a snapping turtle are among the distasteful aspects of the story, they do, admittedly, work. The "men" and the "boys" have been regrouped at the end.

"The Turtles" begins Gaines's experiments with modes of narration. He seems intuitively to have chosen his most successful mode, the first-person narrator. Max's stance as narrator seems a bit uncertain. His past-tense verbs are less immediate than the present tense of Gaines's later work, yet the account is more immediate in details of posture, small gestures, facial expressions, and looks than might be expected in either reflective "porch talk" or the memory of a writer telling his own story. The narration, in fact, is nearly all objective, a staging or reporting of scene, action, and dialogue. Max makes concise notation of his awareness of his father's moods and his own feelings; he reflects briefly on the "partnership." But those notations are all within story time; no after-the-fact reflections are offered. Ultimately Max parallels Gaines the young writer, both remembering and creating, transmitting his insights only as far as they had developed by age fourteen. Any evaluations by Max as older narrator must be deduced from the objective data. That is partly why the theme intended by Gaines is not perfectly clear.

Max's voice allows for presentation and implied evaluation of the other three characters. Without contempt, he records Benny's weakness; without loss of respect for an elder, he implies a negative judgment on Mr. James's softness as a parent and submission as a husband. His own father's severity is recorded in conjunction with the son's obvious respect and affection. The three supporting characters are essentially flat, befitting a very short story. The narrative role, however, serves to give Max himself a fuller character and to reveal the variety of traits that have contributed to his essential manhood. He is perceptive, imaginative, active, and intuitive. He perceives the beauty of the lake and the "few leaves" that "slept on top of it like cocoons on a twig" (1). He intuits that Benny's fear of falling in the river and getting his clothes wet is actually fear of his mother's reaction to such an accident; Max's own hope that his "feet might slip so I could fall in" reveals both his pleasure in sensation and his awareness that such things do not rouse his father's anger. Yet he is equally sensitive to what *does* anger or please or express a paternal wish, and he reveals that by a series of notations of his father's observations of him, Benny, and Amy. When he says, "My old man looked at" any of them, we know he is very aware of what that means. From a fully objective narrator, those looks would merely be physical action; noted by Max, they reveal as much about him as about his father. He knows his father; he knows himself and can manage himself in their relationship.

Gaines said that his early teachers spotted his "sense of place, using small areas and then a lot of dialogue and that my whole scenes were place and then dialogue, place and dialogue" (CEG, 224). This earliest story is an illustration of that manner; each setting is briefly described; what follows is almost all dialogue, brief exchanges in short, simple, or truncated sentences. This pattern, however, does well to reveal characters and their interaction. The first setting is Mr. James's house, symbolically at some little distance from Max's; there, dialogue and gestures reveal the heat and the contrasting personalities of the fathers: Benny's resting and fanning, Max's dictating the time to start. The relation of both husband and son to Mrs. James is hinted at in their simple exchange about the need to inform her of their departure; they are bound by more than simple courtesy.

At Gilman's lake, Max's observations place all the physical details; the boys here are literally out on a limb, as they will be symbolically at Amy's. Dialogue reveals the essential differences in their situations and maturity. Max's father gives commands (terse, yet the only three substantial speeches in the whole story); Max follows them with little question and no demur. Benny reveals his lack of confidence in his father's authority by a bit of dialogue:

"Why don't you ask Mr. James?"
"Ma'll never let me go." . . .
"Why don't you ask Mr. James?"

Benny looked at his old man down the lake.

"Shucks," Benny said. (2)

The boys' brief yet all-revealing dialogue ends when Benny has displayed so much ineptitude and fear that Max doesn't bother to answer him.

Finally, the location of Mrs. Brown's place two miles from any other house indicates the social and moral isolation of Amy and her aunt; the minimal dialogue required to set up the sexual encounter reveals the character of Amy and the relation of Max to his father. In Amy's hot, airless room, details of the motionless curtains and of her grinning under the bedspread create a sense of the boy's uneasy suspense. This is followed by the back-and-forth dialogue of Max and Amy, Max and his "old man"—the minimum required to get Max to stay there and to reveal his motives for doing so. Only at this point of transition to manhood does the boy question a command—but not yet refuse it.

If independence of personal moral choice is a true signal of manhood, then Max's achievement is less than his father's declaration implies. The unyielding control of the "old man" over Max may be as detrimental as Mr. James's flabby authority over Benny. Gaines, at this point, seems to have a theme-in-progress; it will be many fictions hence before "boys" of advanced age become "men" and manhood is recognized as true humanity, beyond gender. Nevertheless, "The Turtles" is a remarkable first story. Quarrel as one may with elements of it, it displays unusual skill. It explains how the young writer's talent caught the attention of his teachers and won him both a scholarship and an agent.

"Boy in the Double Breasted Suit," Gaines's second story published in the San Francisco State literary magazine, is another tale of Max, suggesting an intention to create a story cycle. This time, Max is only eight or nine years old, getting his first suit with long pants. His mother died when he was seven, and his father, who now has a name, Oscar Wheeler, began courting a widow, Mrs. Adele, "about a year later" (3). The boy is childishly naive about relationships, sexuality, and the ways people manipulate each other. He cannot evaluate their behaviors except by their immediate impact on himself, but he does have a sense of the value of family life and love. He very much wants Mrs. Adele to be his stepmother. In this story, before Max can become a man, he must learn about relationships within the adult community of influence: parents, church and preacher, men and women, any or all of whom may be in conflict, may abuse each other, and may build or shatter his hopes.

This phase of Max's education is worked out among three such influential adults: his father, Mrs. Adele, and the preacher. Oscar Wheeler's character is essentially what it was in the first story, that of a man whom nobody hits, nobody insults with impunity, and nobody controls, but who controls his son with a command—roared if repeated. He is capable of quick rage and severity: in one scene he assumes that Max has sneaked in on him and Adele and wants to whip him. She has to stop him from hitting both the boy and the preacher in another scene (4, 8). In some ways, Oscar foreshadows the mother in "The Sky Is Gray"—harsh (or perhaps merely strong because alone), equally given to fierce independence and to issuing tough and unexplained orders. He takes out on Adele and Max the anger he can't vent directly at the preacher. Oscar is a man who lets no woman think or decide for him; to Adele's "I thought it was best . . ." he replies, "I'll do my own thinking from now on" (6). In this story, as in the first, Max reports his respectful obedience to his father; however, he displays less spontaneous affection or admiration and more of a small child's caution around a powerful adult. Description and the child's reactions imply rather clearly that the author behind the boy narrator thinks that Oscar, however manly, may be too harsh for his own happiness or his child's good, that gentleness is necessary for both and is quite compatible with genuine manhood and fatherhood.

That gentleness is embodied in the widow Adele. This story shows, as the first did not, a positive role for a woman, a mother figure. Adele, of course, has not been smart in thinking it was best to turn the preacher onto Oscar; Reverend Johnson and his style of religion have fooled her into unwise, shortsighted behaviors and may have spoiled her chance for renewed happiness as wife and mother. But she is Max's needed loving balance to his father's severity and authoritarian manner. She is also the needful, softening influence on Oscar. She is able to talk to him after the preacher's blow and to get his permission for Max to keep the suit she has given him (8–9). That outcome suggests the boy will also retain the cultivation and good manners he has learned from her, the "Sunday connection" to the community, all symbolized by the suit. But if she does not regain Oscar's affection and regular contact with his son, the boy, it is implied, may grow up equating harshness and an unbending spirit with manly dignity.

Though the church may be the gathering place of community, Reverend Johnson is the first of Gaines's rather numerous preachers who are either fools or abusers of power—or both. The story opens with the preacher's hitting Oscar in the middle of blessing the meal and in the presence of his son. He uses the meal to scold and threaten even as he stuffs himself. This chicken-eating, Bible-beating preacher with a huge watch and gold chain shows the young author's descent into pure stereotype; he is a man under the influence of women, dependent on them for food and for support of his preaching and his church. The preaching is described as "hollering," probably, like his table talk, all irrationality and spiritual threats (4). Unlike Mr. James in "The Turtles," Reverend Johnson leans on his own authority; yet he, too, is a foil to Oscar and conveys the same thematic idea: a true man is independent of women and earns respect by his control of himself, his circumstances and choices, and other people.

The narrative style in this story is no more oral "porch talk" than that in the first; nor is it consistently that of a nine-year-old or an older boy able to recount an incident. Its tone is reminiscent and explanatory, that of an adult writer (the author, in fact) deliberately mixing adult control of narrative and sentence structures with childish style and diction. Only an adult would carefully interrupt an active scene to describe the preacher in detail and to interpolate an organized account of how the "relationship between Mrs. Adele and me came about" (3). He sounds very adult in this description of the preacher: "his teeth that looked almost like horse teeth were very strong, and it was said around Wakeville that he could pick up a fifty-pound sack of rice with his teeth and swing it like a pendulum for a minute every weekday, and go to church on Sunday and preach two full hours without stopping as long as the sisters of the church kept wiping his face with the towel and supplying him with ice water" (3). But some of the long sentences are those of a child's mind, running on, item to barely connected item: "And she liked me too, because I looked so much like Oscar—that's my old man—as she put it, and she told me she would teach me how to keep my shirt inside my pants and keep my face clean, and if I were a good little boy she would buy me a double-breasted suit with long pant legs, and I could stay with her sometimes" (3). The child's need and desire for maternal affection and training, his positive and hopeful sense of his father's romance, and his anticipation of new clothes and a new place all run together, with the suit taking priority of importance. Other sentences run on repetitively to create the way sensory impressions register with a child:

> Then he raised his head and looked at my old man, and got himself a piece of chicken off the platter, and passed the platter around to Mrs. Adele, right in front of my face, but Mrs. Adele passed it over to my old man, and he took off a piece, then he passed it back to her and she let me take off a piece by myself, and smiled her very wonderful way of smiling at me, then she took off a piece and we began to eat, trying not to look at my old man because he was still red where the preacher had hit him twice on the hand when he had reached for a piece of chicken without first saying his blessing. (2)

It takes multiple verbs, phrases, and clauses for the child to see the platter passed around the circle of angry adults and to intuit their moods. Again, a single detail is registered in the choppy and repetitive manner of a child: "He had eyes that set far back in his face, close together eyes, gray eyes" (3); there is no command of parallel syntax, as in a series of adjectives; the noun is simply repeated. Still other sentences mix the verb tenses: "I don't know what he was talking about, but I nodded my head" (8); this mixes the immediacy of the child's reaction with the more knowing narrator's use of the past tense. Soon to come were stories in which Gaines would use sentence structures and verb tense to create an immediacy so total it would constitute an original and potent use of a child's viewpoint on the world.

As in "The Turtles," narration is objective; physical descriptions, facial expressions, and acts of striking, eating, talking, or keeping silence are reported. Dialogue is even more brief and clipped because the adults are in sharp, angry exchanges, and Max is so young and can have so little to say. The force of the story is in the child's inner feelings, which he can voice and interpret only within the limits of his age. He notes and interprets only what he knew at the time the story took place: his father's feelings ("he was mad") and his character ("nobody ever hit him and got away with it"), his own feelings (happiness at seeing Oscar and Adele playing, grief at parting from her). He says no more than he thought at the time: that the wedding didn't occur as soon as he thought it should, that he wondered if his angry father was thinking of going off or maybe even shooting himself (6). But no interpretations are offered from the viewpoint of an older narrator.

Nevertheless, in using Max as the narrator of this story, Gaines was significantly developing his ability to convey and comment on adult behavior through a child's experience and language. Max notes in detail the preacher's manner of eating a piece of chicken: putting it in his mouth, tearing it away, putting it back in, pulling it out bone-clean, and cleaning up the last bit in his mouth, all the while haranguing Oscar; he also notes his father's delay in starting to eat and then his silence as he continues to eat, with both hands on the drumstick—to keep them off the preacher. The gross unrestraint of one man is thus contrasted to the control of the other, though the boy cannot fully evaluate either.

The pragmatic elements of the Oscar-Adele courtship are conveyed as the child knows them: his father was "lonely for a lady" and wanted "someone to kind of look after me"; the widow needed someone "big and strong" to cut wood and do other chores. The issue of sincere, deeply felt personal affection is beyond Max's power of reflection; only a reader senses that the "relationship between

Mrs. Adele and me" may be stronger and more durable than his father's with her. Again, Max overhears the preacher and Mrs. Adele plotting to work on Oscar but registers this conversation as less important or interesting than his teasing a little girl (4–5); the reader senses that it may portend disaster to the child's hopes of a new and loving mother.

Max's slight observations reveal the subtle racism that he does not yet understand as the ambiance of his life: his father and Adele are pleased that his suit is a perfect fit; the socially aware reader knows that had to be chanced, because blacks could not try on clothing in the store nor return it later. The sidewalk near the church, Max says, is "too grassy"; either it is in town, where the black area gets no upkeep, or in the quarters, where a "sidewalk" is merely an overgrown track. To prepare for his coming adulthood in two worlds (black and white), Max needs two parents with complementary strengths of mind and emotion; what he tells us offers no assurance he will have them.

The ending of the "The Turtles" is ambivalent; Max may have reached a level of manhood, but the means are dubious. This story's ending is clear about what would be good for Max but quite ambiguous about his getting it. Adele's "Still am" (going to be his stepmother) and "He will" (Oscar will come back to her) are reassuring words (7). Yet at the end she tells Max "to always remember that I want to be your—your step-mother," and that "it still might happen" (9). Oscar leaves without a farewell or sign of reconciliation, and Adele is crying. If this ambiguity is purposeful, its value is the stress put on Max's continuing to possess the suit. He is following his angry father but carrying with him what he has gained from a woman's gentleness and love. That is an important progression toward manhood.

The two Max stories must be read as independent of each other, yet they are clearly about the same boy. They were written in reverse order of Max's age, probably for no more significant reason than the timeline of Gaines's ideas for plots. If they are read in order of Max's age, however, important thematic questions emerge more clearly. Max at eight or nine is a close observer and keen interpreter of adult behaviors, but he can respond only emotionally. He is controlled by them and initiates no action of his own to shape the outcome of an event. He gets the suit, so his father is not all hard; but Adele is crying as if her final conversation with Oscar had destroyed her hope of a future with him. The last words are, "I followed him." At fourteen, Max knows and can accommodate his father's moods; he values his "partnership" enough to do all he must to preserve it. He is not ready or able to make independent decisions, yet he is without fear, willing to "fall in" to the waters of life. His dignity is in not being a crybaby and in obeying without being physically forced; he has a readiness to learn. But he is still motherless. He will have to clean the fishes when he gets home; there is no truly loving woman in his life now, no Mrs. Adele to model women's best gifts and roles, no woman to both affirm and modify his father's model of masculine strength.

And so the questions remain: Who thinks Max is now a man? His father, yes, but Max himself? Ernest Gaines? Is becoming a man only in following a strong (tough) male role model? Is being a man only or chiefly in being able to command women and children? The young Gaines, veteran and collegian, was still exploring these issues. His next story of manhood would move toward action— action initiated by a boy to right a situation unfair to a woman out of his own sense of order and ethics.

To trace this exploration of manhood, the discussion must deviate from the order of Gaines's early publication. At Stanford, he was writing short stories and working on the revisions of *Catherine Carmier*; one part of the novel was published in 1960 by Stanford as "Mary Louise." The short stories, however, were still focusing on boys learning to be men.

The early 1960s saw the publication of three of Gaines's best stories, "Long Day in November," "The Sky Is Gray," and "Just Like a Tree." In the first two, set in the 1940s, the time of Gaines's own boyhood, the strong parent is now the mother; it is she who either strengthens the weak or replaces the absent father and, in so doing, teaches manliness and responsibility to her very young son. The boy observes life within the quarters and, for the first time, is taken outside it to learn how he must conduct himself in the face of discrimination or condescension. The third story brings the outside world into the quarters, where the civil rights movement forces the community to deal with a young man protesting injustice at a risk to everyone. But he is one of their own, and it is the strong, older woman who has most formed his manly courage. All these motifs—of men and women, the development of children, and responsive action in two worlds— would be the stuff of Gaines's later work.

These three stories were the first published outside his colleges' literary magazines; later they would be selected for republication in *Bloodline* (see chapter 3). The same period produced another story also published in an academic journal (later than the other three, in 1966) but not selected for the collected works. Its theme and its quality invite comparison with the Max stories and speculation as to why Gaines did not choose it for *Bloodline*.

This tale, "My Grandpa and the Haint," published ten years after Gaines's first story, is longer, more developed, more imaginative and humorous, more positive and consistent in tone than the Max stories. Though the protagonist/narrator, Bobby, is a teenager, like Max in "The Turtles," his values are much clearer. He has neither parent, but he has known love and stability through his grandparents, and he knows that he must preserve these values, in them and for himself. Though he is as obedient to adults as is Max, he is much more proactive for their sake and his own. Fooling around with a prostitute is not acceptable here. To stop it, he sees what he has to do and takes his moment to act. The tone, however, is comical; Miss Molly Bee and her business do not arouse the repugnance Amy does. Molly is not necessarily old (she has "jet hair"), but she is not young; she is more for the entertainment of old fools than for serious "use." It requires a wise woman to resolve the issue after the boy has initiated a solution. Though readers may well be doubtful about the hoo-doo, they cannot be about the story's ending. The tale has moved steadily to confront a threat to a valued relationship, has saved it, and has made a boy grow toward manhood by his own reflection and action. Where the Max stories were somewhat ambivalent about father-son and male-female relationships, "My Grandpa and the Haint" reverses the roles of mature and boyish males, gives the woman power with compassion, and thus ends with two "men," a saved marriage, and a family.

Bobby, as the "man" narrating this story, obviously is glad of his action and its outcome. It is not clear how long after the central event he is telling the story, but he was twelve then; clearly he is old enough now to have reflected on the actions he recounts, to have seen their meanings and relative importance. He can distinguish between the "little boy" of eleven who thought the cause of Molly Bee's giggling "sure wasn't any of my business" and the boy of twelve who "thought it was my duty" to act to preserve his grandparents' union (151, 153). He is now distant enough to view the story with some pride in his own motives and clever plans, with affection for both grandparents, with humor at the folly of his Grandpa and Miss Molly Bee, and with admiration for his grandmother's wit and tolerance.

He also tells the story with an art richer than the Max narrators were capable of. He begins at the central action, the visit to Miss Molly Bee en route home from fishing; then he flashes back to the "first time I went over there"; the "next time"; the "third time," when he watched the play in the kitchen (151–2); and the "three or four times more," which finally made him tired of the game and concerned about the ethics of it. Then he returns to the time of the story's main event, reflects on his motives for taking action, and narrates what he did to stop the foolishness and the unfairness to his grandmother. When the corrective hoo-doo event has occurred and Pap is mumbling in delirium, Bobby inserts Pap's own later account so that readers will grasp the meaning of his repeated "Get him away from me" (158). This flashback structure gives a distinct sense of composition, of arrangement for meaning and impact, for implied evaluations, and not merely a sequence of events reported as remembered to an audience, especially not to one of teenaged peers.

The style, too, is rather composed, not a boy's spontaneous talk with a group of buddies. In later books, Gaines would achieve in his narrative voices some fine distinctions of immediacy, after-the-fact recollection, and oral and written storytelling. In this story, the mix of composition and free memory or quotation works well if the question of Bobby's audience is simply suspended (as one suspends disbelief in the hoo-doo). His sentence patterns may be carefully arranged: "For the past couple of months I had been trying to think of a way to let Mom know without Pap thinking I was the one who told her. And that day while I was up there getting that egg, it all came to me" (152). Mostly, the narration employs the oral style Gaines was perfecting. The phrasing, grammar, and idioms are those of an older teenager in the quarters community: "I knowed five minutes later they was going to be back in the kitchen. . . . I could break me a piece of cane or pick me some pecans. . . . They wasn't on the gallery where I'd left 'em" (151).

Narrative in this story is more ample than dialogue because Bobby is telling mostly what he saw; the speeches he quotes are carefully selected for effect and sound natural. His own words reveal his boyish satisfaction in managing the "snitch" to Mom and coaching Lucius: "I didn't say 'at' neither, Lucius. I said, 'going.' 'Going' make her wonder little bit. Now say it" (153). The shifting of the grandparents' voices reflects the maneuvering that begins as soon as Mom knows why Pap chooses his fishing spot:

> "They biting out in the river right smartly," Mom said.
> "They biting better back in the field," Pap said.
> "Talking to Aunt Lou this morning," Mom said. "Told me she caught
> a big mess few days back."
> "They still biting better back in the field," Pap said. (154)

She has given him his chance to change place and behavior; now she must act, and he must pay. When he does, Gaines makes his fullest use of folk voice so far, in Pap's account of his run from the snake: "I stop. Thing stop. I break at him. Thing break back. . . . Faster I run, faster that haint run. Haint right behind me, going 'Ciss-ciss.' Getting close to the gate, haint get right side me, going 'Ciss-

ciss.'" (158–9). The reversals and repetitions voice Pap's boyish satisfaction in this remarkable, endlessly repeatable "lie tale" of the adventure he has sustained.

Narrative style is part of Bobby's self-revelation as a character. By his way with words, he shows himself able to deal with people of various ages with ethical sense yet without harsh judgment, mingling ironic awareness of folly with affectionate tolerance: "I heard that little grunt again. Then about a half a minute later two more little grunts. Then a little while after that, the giggling. Well, that'll be another hour or so, I told myself" (149). Though only twelve, Bobby already has the intuitive and reflective qualities of the later narrator. He has seen connections: the grunt-giggles precede visits to Molly Bee; his egg gathering rids her and Pap of his presence; their fooling will hurt the wife at home if it continues. Like Max, Bobby can speak up to authority without fear, but he backs quickly into respectful silence and obedience at a word or look. He shows no apparent resentment or sadness at the absence of his parents, makes no explanation of it. He is fully devoted to his grandparents and calls them by parental names, which practice also signals their total acceptance of that role and the stability they have given him. Knowing he is "their only little grandchild," he believes in and accepts his duty to preserve their union and happiness (153). Though he has very limited understanding of what is going on in Molly Bee's kitchen, he senses it is unfair to his grandmother; he carefully thinks out his motives and plots his action, first to inform Mom of the visits and then to seal their victory by letting Pap know Molly is still enjoying life without him (153, 160). Whether or not he believes Pap's tale of the haint, he credits the old man's belief and ability to tell it the same way every time; he never diminishes his elders' dignity.

Max loved his father despite the man's rather hard character; it is no obstacle for him, nor, presumably, for most readers. The "old man" is still the solid rock and best influence in his son's life. Bobby's grandparents must be revealed in proportion to their importance to him—Pap just enough to serve as a lesson, Mom more so, as she is the most solid and influential person in his life. Pap is no crass adulterer. He is much more a boy/man, "feeling sporty" and giggling in anticipation of his play; Molly has given him a child's name, "Toddy" (150). He plays like a child/man, giving Molly Bee her jollies; but, Bobby tells us, "one thing about Pap, he knew when to stop" (152). That means more than Bobby knows, apparently even now; he says Pap stopped before she laughed so much "she might hurt herself." The reader sees that he stops before he has irreparably hurt his wife, his fidelity, or his marriage; obviously he has no intention to reject or leave Mom or Bobby. Nor is he resentful when he discovers their plot; he merely lets

Bobby know he has caught on to it. Like his fishing pole, Grandpa and his marriage are "bent at the end, but . . . strong as iron" (149).

Mom, in turn, is a typical Gaines mother, as powerful as Max's father: no one talks while eating her food; the boy can "feel her eyes on the back of [his] neck" (154); she doesn't welcome certain questions, and she answers none she doesn't wish to; she decides whether Bobby goes with Pap or not; and the neighbors don't argue with her, either. However, she is tolerant, knows how to correct both her boys. She controls and teaches Bobby by brief commands and "that mean way she got of looking when she wants me to pay attention" (156); there are no hints of physical force except Lucius's thinking Bobby will get a whipping (and Bobby only *thinks* that Lucius thinks this). Bobby is explicit about his love for his grandmother (153).

With her wayward husband, she is a mixture of toughness, tolerance, and tenderness. Once informed, she creates no explosion, only takes action to right the situation. She admits, "I hate what I'm doing. . . . But I can't help it"; she has to stop his "Letting that yellow woman make a fool of him like that" (157). Her concern, then, is more for his dignity and good name than for the indignity and shame to herself. After getting him out of the barbwire fence, she sits in the bed of the wagon holding him in her arms, whispering, "It's all right" (158). She sits up all the first night, bathing his cuts, feeding him soup; she insists on caring for him herself. At the start of his account of the haint, she requires the truth: "From where? . . . From where? . . . You know? . . . I know" (158). Having truth between them again, she requires no revenge.

Why does she involve Bobby in the hoo-doo work? Since she could have told him to stay home or let him go once more with Pap to avoid his knowing of her visit to the woman, she clearly wants him to know. She could have watched the woodpecker herself, gone in the wagon without the boy, pretended she had done nothing but find her husband accidentally. She involves him presumably to teach him the lesson of a "real" man's fidelity and how to correct a situation without separation or killing. This must not be Bobby's first lesson. Before Mom knew of this situation, Bobby had already acted in her manner, more by action than by words. He had already learned from Mom the "ability to stand," to take a position and action in a cause, which, in all Gaines's stories, is the mark of manhood (and eventually of universal achieved humanity).

This story is not inferior to the three that were written at about the same time and included in the *Bloodline* collection. Why, then, was it not included? The protagonists of the stories chosen were small boys, six and eight years old, and young men of nineteen or in their early twenties. Bobby would have seemed to fit in between them as an adolescent protagonist. In addition, "My Grandpa and the Haint" has a comic tone that might have balanced the seriousness of the other stories. Unless the answer is simply that the publisher limited the number of stories in the collection, Gaines's reason for exclusion may have been the similarity of the plot to "Long Day in November"—saving a marriage by resorting to a hoo-doo woman—or reluctance to use a fully comic story in a collection with serious purpose. "Long Day" is kept fairly serious by real threats to the child's future; here the threat is much much less severe, and the tone is always warm and humorous, even when tinged with Bobby's disapproval or impatience.

Another motive suggests itself. This story, as noted, is narrated as an after-the-fact event, in the past tense. In the stories chosen for *Bloodline*, Gaines has developed a mode of narration that makes thought and action immediate. It gives those stories a power that not even this latest one has. One must wonder if he sensed the difference and chose accordingly.

At the same time that Gaines was producing his short stories about boys moving toward manhood, in the 1960s, he was also reworking his "Little Stream" into "The Comeback," then into *Catherine Carmier*. Part of his process apparently was experimenting with narration, giving segments of stories to various narrators. One such segment was "Mary Louise." It was published as a distinct story in a 1960 Stanford collection. If ever the story was meant for inclusion in the novel, Gaines must have realized that it would not fit, that so much attention could not be given to Mary Louise's love for Jackson as seen from her own viewpoint. He must also have realized that her internal struggle with her hopeless love had an interest of its own, not merely as a phase of Jackson's drifting. With conscious intent or not, he shifted for a time from his focus on young males to the parallel issue of young females: What makes a woman—a happy, humanly fulfilled woman?

Mary Louise represents a type of young woman from Gaines's South, one left in the quarters without hope of finding love or family of her own. As the young men leave the plantation, pulled by education or more opportunity for work, the young women must either take their lesser chances of similar opportunity, or stay as props for the old people who must remain, becoming separated from their peers. Mary Louise lives in near solitude as servant to her father and to the white family on the plantation. Girls her own age are competitors for the few young men left, especially now for Jackson. Her only hope is that he will renew their childhood love and either remain with her or take her away. But they are alienated by all the changes that cut off the educated man from the girl who never finished school. The central interest of the story is this character-in-situation.

Can she escape it or survive in it? In the world of the quarters, can she find "life" only as the gift of a man? If not, then how else? Gaines depicts her problem and answers the story's questions through setting, structure, narration, and dialogue.

Setting, in all its grim detail, is what a reader must first notice. It functions admirably to establish Mary Louise's life situation and her sensitivity to it. Her sunrise waking hour is marked by the sights and sounds of a neighbor feeding his hogs from a "bucket of slop," another calling her chickens and "hollering" insults at the neighbor's "old trifling dog" and "his old trifling master" (27). The tensions of the quarters are revealed, followed by the poverty and tensions within her own house: without running water, with only corn cobs for stove fuel, she fixes her father's meager breakfast of salt meat then goes to her room so as to hear "no more of his squabbling" (28). When Jackson comes to talk with her, she is acutely conscious of the weeds her father has not bothered to cut down; the yard, like her life, has gone to ruin through her father's indifference (35). Her observations of people stepping out onto their porches and peeping through their curtains to watch her walk with Jackson indicate the lack of privacy and plenitude of gossip in the quarters, which she can combat only by a public conquest of her man (37). Like her hopes and her life ahead, the fields stretch out, one crop after another, beyond the houses, beyond any life except one of hard labor (36). Jackson will be like the bird she observes hitting a frail stalk "pretty hard" and bending it with him, resting there briefly, then flying away again (40). The green pecan falls between them like the childish love that did not, cannot, ripen; her hope turns into the bit of dirt she rubs between her fingers and weeps over (40, 41).

Structure reinforces setting to reveal Mary Louise's character and situation. Parts 1 through 3 might be called "False Hopes." In Part 1, less than two pages, Mary Louise is glimpsed alone at home, in tension with her father over her yearning for Jackson. Part 2, six pages, elaborates her only inner life, the memory of her childish "sinning" with Jackson in the loft and their severe punishment. She exaggerates this "thing me and him done gone through" into a commitment that "can't be changed" (34); it is her flimsy basis for hope. In part 3, four pages, as she and Jackson walk to the fields, she remembers others' realistic but cruel undercutting of her hope and tries desperately to reassure herself. Part 4, equal in length to part 2, constitutes the disappointment of hopes. There, Jackson lets her know that his change is an insuperable destroyer of her dreams. Her final, desperate self-assessment, "All my life I had been nothing but a fool for people" (42), implies clearly that all her life she will continue to be. Her situation offers no chance of happiness; she does not and cannot choose it freely out of love or concern for others. She will merely settle into it and feel herself defeated.

The structure of meaning is paralleled by the structure of the narration: Mary Louise's alternating mental ruminations and dialogue. Part 1 has no dialogue; the young woman is a pathetic solitary. She sees and hears; she acts to start another deadening day; she thinks of nothing except to avoid her father's disturbance of the only thought she wants. In part 2 she recalls her choice to pass up the opportunity to go to the city and her fear that Jackson may choose Lillian; these silent thoughts briefly frame the long memory of the childhood event on which she is fastening her current hope. In that remembrance the dialogue is abundant, simple, rapid, and repetitive; the word "sinning" moves from referring to a moral act to simply "having sex," which is no more to the children than a forbidden, exciting way to play grown-up. Their speech is comic by virtue of their ignorance. Yet the length and detail of the narrative and dialogue reveal the importance Mary Louise continues to give the episode. To a reader, it is pitiful due to the excess of their punishment then and her continued self-punishment now. It is all she got, will ever get, of life and love. Part 3 reveals how little all that means now; Jackson and Mary Louise can engage in only a bit of banal talk to get them out on their walk, then she must retreat again into her mental fabrications of life as she wants it. Finally, part 4 counterbalances the childhood "love talk" with shattering adult reality. In youth, the "lovers" tentatively came together, not knowing what they were doing; now their dialogue is only his effort to ease the pain of separation, hers to avoid and then block the sound of his pronouncement: "It can't ever be like that again" (41). Once she has heard those words, as if from far away, she hears nothing else he says to soften them or comfort her. Her questions are all in her own mind: "Did he think . . . Did he think . . . Did he think . . . ?" A last attempt to assert her dignity in words turns into futile blows; then her voice fades back into the silence of part 1. But Jackson's speech remains the second "worst whipping" of her life, which also makes her cry and ends in self-condemnation (42).

One might pity Jackson a little in this scene; he is posing reasonable questions—Why didn't you go to school in the city? Why didn't you marry?—to a girl whose heart knows only one reason to do anything and wants only one thing, beyond any rational discussion. He may be insufficiently sensitive to Mary Louise's pain, but he cannot be blamed entirely. Though the lifestyle of the quarters impinges on the freedom of a girl like Mary Louise, the finality of her situation depends on her self-sentencing—she chooses to stay in it. In that sense, it is "all in her mind," and the first-person narration is appropriate, as is the heavy focus on her inner ruminations. She mulls over her memories, over reasons for her every act and thought; she imagines everyone else's thoughts and motives; she fantasizes an impossible future. In the end, she can neither speak nor act. Her life will now return to the silence and avoidance of part 1. Her despair is not of Jackson, nor of her situation, but of herself; it must be believed because it is self-imposed.

"Mary Louise" is a sad story but a well-written one. It could not become a chapter of *Catherine Carmier* chiefly because the novel focused on Catherine, whose situation is so like Mary Louise's and whose solution to stay home and be a lifeless prop in the quarters is the same. Mary Louise could be a minor character, a reflection of a general problem, but her story could not be developed without distracting from that of the heroine.

By his experiments in the four stories he published but did not select for *Bloodline*, Gaines progressed significantly in the techniques of fiction. Thematically, the stories move from a narrow view of manhood as a boy's achievement of male-oriented outlook and skills, to a greater awareness of the balancing and needful qualities of women and of men's responsibility to develop, respect, and be faithful to relationships with them, and finally to a presentation of a woman's need for a sense of her separate self, for development of full humanity by her own free choices. Technically, Gaines learned to focus on one character as carrier of theme, to develop greater density of characterization, revealed by structuring action supported by physical details.

Above all, the young author progressed in his use of voice in narrative modes and in dialogue. The four stories offer a mix of mental ruminations and oral storytelling, varied degrees of emotion appropriate to the different narrators, and a progression from Max's nearly objective reporting to the engaged, consciously self-revealing narration of Mary Louise and Bobby. As the narrators become more engaged and self-revealing, their own and others' voices are increasingly heard in dialogue. Max and the others around him speak but little, just enough to suit their limited needs. Mary Louise has plenty to "holler" about in her childhood, and Miss Charlotte, the voice of adult female authority, has plenty to say about what she had coming to her. Later diminishment of dialogue in this story suits the diminishment of all relationships—and life itself. In "My Grandpa and the Haint" (written after "Mary Louise"), dialogue becomes nearly as rich as in the best of Gaines's later work. It is richly varied in length and style, from Pap's intended cunning-yet-transparent "permissions" to Bobby, to Bobby's precise verbal instructions to Lucius, to Mom's tender assurances and tough interrogations of Pap, and, above all, to Pap's long tale of the haint, as fine a folktale as any Gaines would later create. In this, the last written of the uncollected stories, all folk voices are heard in the quarter.

Speaking of his "pretty good" college stories, Gaines added, "One day I should hope that a 'small press' or a university press would take an interest in [them]" (CEG, 158). His assessment of these works is quite accurate; some are limited in significance of theme and development of plot, but his potential and developing talent are clear. Especially if the stories still in the archives in Lafayette offer the same evidence of worth and of coming achievement, another edited collection would seem to be a very desirable addition to his body of published work.

3

Sketching the Line, Sounding a New Voice

Bloodline

"I ALWAYS FELT that the *Bloodline* stories were going to make my name." So said Gaines; to which Carl Wooton replied, "I think . . . there are some things that you do in the *Bloodline* stories that you don't do better anywhere else" (*PT*, 111). Examination of those excellent "things" suggests not only that it includes masterpieces of the short-story genre likely to become permanent classics of American literature (especially the first two stories)—but also that they reveal noteworthy, even innovative, short-story techniques, especially in narration. Such techniques would become the hallmark of Gaines's best work as he translated them into the novel form.

Most criticism of *Bloodline* has canvassed Gaines's themes—authentic black manhood; the changing order of racial, gender, and generational relationships; and the conflict or mutual support of individual and community—together with the situations and characters that embody the themes. Gaines initially explored these subjects and themes in his college stories (see chapter 2), and he has continued to assert their importance in his work. The three early stories selected for *Bloodline* and the two he wrote to complete the collection have, without question, richer substance of meaning than those he omitted. That richness, however, is attributable as much—perhaps more—to his maturing thought as to his growing mastery of technique and creativity in employing it.[1]

Though less attention has been given to the techniques of *Bloodline* than to its themes, Gaines himself has always insisted that technique is the central fact of literary creation. Good technique, he says, imposes order, essential to a work of art. The writer may go through hell to get order; he may create a picture of hell. But with order and shape, his work will be art. His teachers discussed his work "from a technical point of view"; he now teaches the same way (*PT*, 16–7, 34–5). Though he is chiefly acclaimed as a novelist, Gaines has recognized that his talent for technique is especially released in the short story or in those novels whose segments most resemble short tales, and possibly in the novella, which he has used only once.[2]

Inherent in the short story are economy and focus: limited pages, limited numbers of characters, problems, and settings. Like water forced through a narrow channel or light intensified by focus, the feeling channeled and focused in this limited form gains power and impact. All five stories in *Bloodline* offer interconnected techniques for economy and focus, each powering greater intensity of reader response to the fictional situation, characters, and theme. These techniques include focus on a single critical episode, which is acted out, or mostly *thought* out and *spoken* out, in one small locale or a few even smaller settings within that locale. Limited setting is complemented by sufficient yet purposefully terse dialogue, along with a few choice symbols to imply thematic interpretation. Above all, these short stories use a special mode of narration that balances the economies of the other techniques with intensified focus in the minds of crucial characters.

No aspect of Gaines's short stories seems to fascinate his readers more than his modes of narration. Yet we might say that the *Bloodline* stories have no "readers" because they cannot have "writers." The boy narrators and the adults of the three later stories either could not or surely would not record their experiences in writing; most would not even be apt to tell them to an audience. Yet all the stories, to secure the focus, theme, and impact of other techniques, require narration through a participating character in some mode that creates the immediacy

1. For related discussion of writing process and technique, see Barbara Tomlinson, "Characters Are Coauthors: Segmenting the Self, Integrating the Composing Process," *Written Communication* 3 (1986): 421–48.

2. *PT*, 124. "Long Day in November" is, I think, properly a novella, having many characteristics of that genre. But it has so far been considered one of a collection of short stories, and the formal qualities of the short story discussed here apply to it.

and intensity of that character's perceptions and feelings—a sense of "happening now" and "happening within." That effect could not be achieved either by third-person limited narration, which distinguishes narrative voice from character, nor by the usual first-person, autobiographical modes of written or oral storytelling after the fact. Gaines has therefore developed a mode that, if not demonstrably unique to him, is rare enough to warrant a name of its own and to be cited as the remarkably original source of some of his best effects establishing character and meaning.

This discussion of *Bloodline* will look first at the five individual stories in related groups. The first two explore from the child's point of view a small boy's experience learning how to be a man. The next two look at young men in confrontation with old men who have been subjugated by "the system" yet learned from it. The fifth story brings old and young together in a community confronting the challenge of the civil rights movement, each member seeking to understand, express, or limit the expression of freedom. Finally the chapter will examine the book as a unified collection.

The first two stories present one central episode crucial to the life and future of a child—far more crucial than he can know. Each episode has implications for the adults in the stories, of course; they are obviously affected by racism, poverty, and marital instability. But all the ramifications of the immediate situation are omitted except as they impinge on the child's well-being, safety, learning, and happiness.

In "A Long Day in November," Sonny Howard, six years old, is threatened by the rupture, possibly permanent, of his parents' relationship and, in turn, his family structure. The rift is mended by his father's ability to change, to perceive and live up to his own dignity as husband, father, man. Critics debate the extent and quality of Eddie's change as revealed in his agreement to burn his car and then to beat his wife, as she demands.[3] Gaines said that the story is his early

---

3. See William Burke, "*Bloodline*: A Black Man's South," *College Language Association Journal* 19 (1976): 546–8; Todd Duncan, "Scene and Cycle in Ernest Gaines' *Bloodline*," *Callaloo* 1 (May 1978): 86–8; John W. Roberts, "The Individual and the Community in Two Short Stories by Ernest J. Gaines," *Black American Literature Forum* 18 (1984): 110–1; Frank W. Shelton, "Ambiguous Manhood in Ernest J. Gaines's *Bloodline*," *College Language Association Journal* 19 (1975): 203; Barbara Puschmann-Nalenz, "Ernest J. Gaines: 'A Long Day in November' (1963)," in *The Black American Short Story in the 20th Century: A Collection of Critical Essays*, ed. Peter Bruck (Amsterdam: Gruner, 1977), 163–6; Herman Beavers, *Wrestling Angels into Song: The Fiction of Ernest J. Gaines and James Alan McPherson* (Philadelphia: University of Pennsylvania Press, 1995): 162–4; and Craig Werner, *Paradoxical Resolutions: American Fiction since Joyce* (Urbana: University of Illinois Press), 37.

effort "in a comic way" to bring the black father and son together (*PT*, 57–8) and that Amy demands the beating to forestall mockery of her husband (*CEG*, 157–8). Since Amy has earlier assured her mother that Eddie does not beat her, one may see a discrepancy within the story and suppose that, in any case, today's sensitivities would lead Gaines to find another way to restore a positive marital balance.

The story's focus, however, is not on the adults but on Sonny, on his "unbearable lightness of being" affected by their heaviness, which threatens to crush his childish happiness, secure (until now) in his family and the community of the quarters. This story could be called "One Day in the Life of Sonny Howard," not of the Howard family; it is the story of how he sees and hears that day, feels it, suffers from inability to grasp its meanings, and how in the end he finds reassurance, and probably memories, that will constitute a permanent lesson in manhood.

The story of "The Sky Is Gray" is even simpler: James, age eight, is taken to town by his mother to have an infected tooth pulled; during the long morning, he encounters blacks and whites of varying personalities and attitudes. For James, the event is a striking, early, perhaps primary encounter with severe pain, with the limits of alleviation available to the very poor and black, with the rules for endurance and survival, and with the etiquette for dealing with others so that they also survive with dignity. As in the first story, there is a puzzle about his parents' future and a debate about the manner and quality of maternal instruction.[4] But the focus is again on the child's learning, extended from the quarters to the world just outside, a world of some kindness but much more discrimination.

Sonny's "one day" is localized inside the quarters; at six years old, he may never have been outside them. For Sonny, however, confinement to the quarters means not limitation but security, affection, and encouragement. Within that limited area, he moves among five settings that illustrate the meanings of his life and of this particular day: his own home, his grandmother's, the tiny church/school, the field of labor, and the house of the hoo-doo woman. Only two, his home and the school, are usual and frequent settings for his daily life. Most likely he has been to his grandmother's infrequently, given the tensions there. He has

4. See Duncan, 89–91; Roberts, 112–3; Babb, *EG*, 27; W. Burke, 550; Shelton, 203; Werner, 37; Mary Helen Washington, "Commentary on Ernest J. Gaines," in *Memory of Kin: Stories about Family by Black Writers*, ed. Washington (New York: Doubleday Anchor Books, 1991), 41; Mark J. Charney, "Voice and Perspective in the Film Adaptations of Gaines's Fiction," in *CRF*, 127–9; and Gaines's own explanation, *PT*, 64–5.

been to the fields, for him a place yielding joints of sugarcane, not demanding labor. Now, however, the disruption of usual patterns and the injection of confusion and insecurity into his life are symbolized by the transfer to his barely loved or loving Gran'mon, his embarrassment at school, and his half-day absence while he treks with his father into the fields of adult labor, seeking with fatigue and frustration the way to restore their family. The house of Madame Toussaint aptly symbolizes all his fears, though, ironically, it is there that he will overhear the most important instruction for his future. There, and in the far field where the car is burned, he will learn what must be done to restore him to his own home. He barely understands it all now; yet he is unlikely to forget it or fail to mull it over later in life.

A text for James's initiation into manhood might be titled "One Day in Town." The preliminary rites occur in the quarters, but those episodes are cast as his memories while he waits for the bus. Against the harsh yet somehow supportive reality of the quarters is set the cold, gray, indifferent, or easily threatening town. It is a larger setting, seemingly more varied, but that impression only reinforces the reader's awareness of how small and small-minded the town really is, and how limited is the access of black people to what little it offers. The small subsettings are a bus, a dentist's office, a general store, a café, the Cajuns' store/home—and the street. The bus reinforces the boy's awareness of segregation; the office promises him only pain and a confused awareness of white indifference to it, of the potential for education but also for conflicts and violence among his own people. The store and the café are places where a bit of indoor warmth may be had—if one pretends to have the means to buy or uses one's pittance to stave off serious hunger—and where a woman must use a knife to stave off a man of her own race. Between each place, threatening or barely helpful, a poor black mother and son must return to the seemingly endless, sleet-driven streets. It is in the home of the woman who should be frightening, Helena the Cajun, that James learns the humanly warm side of the wider world. All these lessons he must learn if his mother's final assertion of his manhood is to be verified in the future; all are contained within the narrow setting of the story.

Given Gaines's famous talent for dialogue, it is noteworthy that in these stories most characters speak with great brevity and often maintain a determined silence. Only a few speak at length, when they choose to deliver speeches. Brevity, silences, and speeches all serve Gaines's expository and thematic purposes.

In "A Long Day in November," nearly all the dialogue is terse, consisting of brief questions and replies or short, sharp comments and commands, as Amy and Eddie lose their relationship and Sonny grasps for the little he can comprehend.

Eddie pleads; Amy rejects. Mama or Miss Hebert question; Sonny says yes or no. Eddie pleads; Gran'mon threatens. Eddie begs advice or money, gets both in small amounts. When a marriage is falling apart, what is there to say? When a child is in misery watching it happen, how can it be explained? Only three people speak at any length: Gran'mon harangues Amy against Eddie, Madame Toussaint counsels him on his second visit, and Eddie subsequently rambles aloud to himself about her advice. By giving them the gift of speech, Gaines positions the two women as representatives of the two possible solutions, highlighting each. Eddie, who must make the saving decision, explores it within his son's hearing. In Sonny's presence, his wife accepts it, eventually going with them to see the car burn. Again dialogue is reduced to a minimum: virtual silence in the car; around the fire, "Gran'mon the only person talking; everybody else is quiet." She speaks briefly to reverse her previous judgment: "He's a man after all"; then several "somebodies" express their surprise that "that was in Eddie," and "he must love her more" than his car.[5] When in a single public moment a "boy" becomes an adult, a genuine lover and parent, what else is there to say? But Sonny, son of his father, will remember.

In "The Sky Is Gray," the sparse dialogue reflects the severity of life as James's mother sees it, responds to it, and teaches him to respond. When words are useless and ameliorate nothing, why use them? James at eight has fluency for taunting a little girl on the bus; but though he acknowledges his frequent wish to say something to his mother, "I keep my mouth shut. 'Cause that's something else she don't like. She don't like for you to say something just for nothing" (88). Silence is defensive; it is also a sign of the loneliness and near defeat Octavia feels without her husband. Before he went into the army, the family used to sit up late, presumably talking; now after eating, she goes straight to bed, preparing for a day of labor to stave off their starvation. In supporting her family and in raising James, she "don't talk much," often not at all (95). She counts money aloud to Auntie to show that "I do the best I can" (87). She doesn't explain to James the poverty that requires him to kill birds for food; she beats him into doing it. She answers questions from adults usually in two or three words, their comments not at all. She acknowledges the Cajun Helena's kindness with genuine gratitude but does not speak what she really knows of her generosity. In this whole story, only one person speaks (harangues) at length, the student in the

---

5. Ernest J. Gaines, "A Long Day in November," in *Bloodline* (New York: Vintage Books, 1997), 71–2. All citations are from this edition. (Abbreviated titles of the stories will be used when needed for clarity.)

dentist's office. He offers his "cold logic," his powers of analysis, his commitment to action, his ability to "take it" from the preacher (97). But he says finally that "words mean nothing" (101). On the contrary, Octavia's words mean something when she uses them, especially at the end: "You a man" (117).

Though dialogue is sparse, these two stories as wholes might be called extended monologues. They seem to be long oral reports by two boys about experiences important to them. But the style of narration is only in part what children of their ages could or would use in recounting a tale to classmates or friendly adults. Nor can the boys be simply talking to themselves. Here a technical dilemma for the author is revealed. In an effort to resolve that dilemma, John Callahan noted that the *Bloodline* narrators lack an "immediate audience," that they do "talk to themselves, out loud perhaps as they remember and prepare their stories."[6] This might explain the "interior voices" of the later adult narrators, but not those of children like Sonny and James.

In both stories the central conflict is the child's; the important impressions, therefore, of settings, actions, and dialogue must also be the child's. To make sure the adults' issues did not steal the central focus, nor their impressions and feelings become more important than the child's, Gaines had to keep the story out of their minds. So the narration also had to focus on the child. But how could a child tell all when he understood so little? Gaines found a way. The stories are told not so much *by* as *through* the children, in what may be some of the most subtly nuanced points of view in American fiction. Consider the opening paragraph of each:

> Somebody is shaking me but I don't want get up now, because I'm tired and I'm sleepy and I don't want get up now. It's warm under the cover here, but it's cold up there and I don't want get up now. ("LDN," 3)

> Go'n be coming in a few minutes. Coming round that bend down there full speed. And I'm go'n get out my handkerchief and wave it down, and we go'n get on it and go. ("Sky," 83)

This is not ordinary first-person, after-the-fact narration. The use of the present tense creates a "now" effect and an instant immediacy and engagement with the child and his situation. Ordinarily, this sense of the present, of the action happening before our eyes, is achieved by use of the third-person limited viewpoint

6. John F. Callahan, *In the African-American Grain: The Pursuit of Voice in Twentieth Century Black Fiction* (Urbana: University of Illinois Press, 1988), 190–3.

(à la Henry James or James Joyce), especially if the viewpoint is a child's. But the third-person narrator is then distinct from the child; authorial presence is much more evident. In Gaines's stories, the children seem to speak in their own voices; readers are absorbed into their views, diction, limits of perception and explanation. Thus engaged, readers' emotions can be focused and sustained.

These first paragraphs present only the outer, physical environment, well within a child's ability to comprehend and describe. If the viewpoint of the child is to be maintained, however, it must present everything that he would perceive—and nothing more—in his random and largely unreflective manner of perception, in a chronology dictated by events as they happen around him or by his own limited ability to remember the past, and within his limited ability to interpret or evaluate. Yet through this heavily restricted child's view, readers must observe adult actions and dialogue and be made to grasp a significance totally elusive to the child himself. Hence the dilemma for the writer: how to record all that a small child could not fully register, remember, or report, yet sustain the engagement of this "now" narration.

Gaines accomplishes the feat by what I call "camcorder narration." It is as if a video camera had been placed in the child's mind. From that vantage, everything the child is aware of is reported, primarily his external sensory impressions, actions, and words, including his own movements; these are not thought out but simply registered in his consciousness: "I look out the window and I can see the smoke flying. . . . Bill comes up to the heater and I look up and see him. . . . I look in my book. . . . We go up to the front and sit down. . . ." ("LDN," 23). This camera in the mind also records inner vibrations of thought and feeling— brain waves and heart waves—as if they were in progress and caught on tape for instant projection: Sonny's wandering thoughts on Bill's fire-making, Juanita's prettiness, the dogs in his reader and in the quarters, and his fear and shame at not knowing his lesson. "I feel warm. I'm wet. . . . I'm crying. . . . My clothes's wet. Lucy and them go'n laugh at me" ("LDN," 23–4). Sonny and James tell their own stories, and yet they do not; these are not memories but records of the inner camera.

The camera also registers all they see and hear but could never understand, remember, or repeat: Eddie Howard's discussions with male friends, the preacher, and the hoo-doo woman about how to regain his wife; Gran'mon's comments about Eddie and her efforts to get Amy into the arms of Freddie Jackson ("LDN"); the entire dialogue in the dentist's office about the existence of God and about civil rights ("Sky"). Sonny's vulnerability to a disrupted family and James's to a divided, hostile society strike the reader all the more painfully because the two children do not and cannot yet understand what is being said around them or done to them.

The focus of this immediate narration from a child's perspective is intensified and nuanced by Gaines's selection of detail. Some details are those which adults would not care about or notice at all. A sensitive child would immediately note them but would not necessarily remember or repeat them years later as an older narrator: "[Spot] runs down the steps at me and I let him smell my pot"; "Uncle Al gives me the little stick and I throw it back in the fire"; "I unhook my coat and drop it on the bench till I put my cap on"; "I look in the hole and I see my poo-poo . . . but I don't see any spiders" ("LDN," 17, 19, 29, 38). As one reviewer noted, the egocentric child reports his bodily functions as fully as he does his parents' quarrel,[7] making all the more evident to the adult reader his susceptibility to injury by parental childishness.

Perspective is further nuanced by the age of each of the two children. Many small, forgettable details are recounted in "Long Day in November," in the swiftly passing awareness of the six-year-old. At eight, James tells what he could remember and repeat in detail for a day or two but not much longer: the directions and sequence of his walks through town, the moments of his mother's looking or not looking at him or others, the time the church bell rang or the sleet increased, the color and quality of the shoes on the mannequin in contrast to his own ("Sky").

In addition, James can mentally register the present in relation to his past experience; Sonny never does so, beyond an expectation of his grandmother's continued fussing. The six-year-old's entire story, like his life, is in present time and present tense, whereas James at eight easily shifts tense and slides into the relevant remembered past: Madame Bayonne's efforts to cure his pain, his own killing birds for food, and the happy time when his father was home. These events, however, are recalled in connection and comparison with his intensely felt present, to which he quickly returns. And, with two years' seniority over Sonny, he can begin to offer some explanation: "I know now; I know why I had to do it" ("Sky," 90).

The narrative camcorder records dialogue exactly as it is spoken, with all the nuances of diction. Most adult speech would be beyond a child narrator's vocabulary: "laughingstock," "misunderstanding," "blasphemous," "intelligent," "ignorant," "cold logic," "rights granted by the Constitution." James admits he doesn't understand what he's hearing; Sonny knows not that he knows not. But

---

7. Review of "A Long Day in November," *Hornbook* 48 (1972): 153.

since the narrative is restricted to the boys' level of observation, it repeats *what* the adults speak but rarely *how*: "Mama says. . . . Daddy says. . . ." but no sophisticated narrative indicators of tone of voice, pauses, facial expression, gestures, movements. However, this technique, too, is nuanced by the boys' maturity. Sonny notes his own motion and motive: "I start crying and stomping so Mama'll let me go" ("LDN," 66); James occasionally notices the mood that accompanies another's speech: " 'You hungry?' she says. She says it like she's mad at me, like I'm the cause of everything" ("Sky," 106). The boys' own impressions, distinct from what they hear adults saying, are recorded in their own juvenile diction: "dummies" for mannequins ("Sky," 93), "wee-wee" or "water" for urine (again revealing a nuanced age difference). Their strongest impressions are simply repeated for emphasis: "I don't know my lesson," six times in one paragraph ("LDN," 24); "little bitty old bathroom, but it's clean, clean" ("Sky," 115); "sleet's coming down heavy, heavy now" ("Sky," 117).

When one has admired the skill and achievements of this "now" or "camcorder" narration, one must still ask, What is its relation to short-story form? The answer is simply that its intense focus can be effectively maintained only for a short time. It is hard to imagine this viewpoint used unremittingly throughout the length and complexity of a novel.[8] In addition, when children are the means of narration, it follows that few narrative explanations and comments are possible. Yet interpretation still inheres in a story that is art; theme must then be subtly implied in the narration and by any other economical means available. Authorial interpretation in these two stories is delivered by the sheer impact on an adult reader of what vulnerable children see and say, and also, especially, by a few significant symbols drawn from weather conditions, natural or mechanical objects, and human gestures or acts.

Both stories are set in late autumn or winter; both are pervaded by the bitter cold of cabin rooms, town streets, sleeting skies, or gray skies and river, cold severe enough to penetrate to the children's bones.[9] In Sonny's world, the cold symbolizes the quarreling of adults, his family's instability; for him, however, it is not wholly bitter. He still has the warmth of the bedcovers under which he hides, and the warmth of various fires around which are gathered the important people in his life. For James, the cold represents the outer world, materially or spiritually impoverished and segregated, in which he must learn to survive, from which there is no shelter except when dignity occasionally meets with kindness.

8. Gaines does use the camcorder effectively in *parts* of novels. See especially chapter 8.
9. Cf. Rowell, "Territory," 14.

Cold poverty is the need to calculate exact amounts for the bus and the dentist and see if meat can still be paid for, the need of every half-day's fieldwork, the necessity to kill and eat birds and to wear two sweaters instead of a coat. Poverty, above all, is the absence of a father's warm love and support and the exclusion from dignity and comfort, from food, warmth, shelter, and education imposed by the buses, cafés, stores, and schools of Bayonne. Poverty, life itself, is the need to keep walking in the cold.

"Long Day in November" includes numerous signs of poverty and segregation, but they are not stressed in the narrative, because they have not yet imposed their evil on Sonny's consciousness. His trouble is instability; during the long day of drifting about the quarters, his consciousness registers fixed points, such as a fence, a pecan tree, and the stars.[10] His most serious needs are physical and emotional support, symbolized in leaning on his uncle or holding his father's hand and riding on his back, and in the sweetness of candy and sugarcane provided by his father. The luring but threatening world outside his family nest is symbolized by the car, a false symbol of masculine freedom and control; when it is destroyed in the biggest communal fire of all, genuine masculine maturity, responsibility, presence, modeling, and support return to Sonny's life. The great comic symbol of the story that outlines its plot and theme is the bedsprings. At the beginning of the story, when his mother is alone, Sonny barely hears them; in the middle, he senses their threat as Freddie Jackson sits down on the bed where Amy is resting; and at the end, when his parents are reunited, "I hear the spring on Mama and Daddy's bed. . . . I hear the spring. . . . I hear it plenty now" ("LDN," 79). And he snuggles back into the warmth of his covers.

Life for Sonny is restored to warmth and security by a return to his most limited and protected space; in time he will have to move, like James, outward to the places of risk, pain, and self-assertion. The stories make that intensely clear by absorbing readers in the two boys' immediate experiences. They also require readers to face their own world, if they, like Sonny and James, are to mature and survive with their dignity, integrity, and humanity intact.

The next two stories, "Three Men" and "Bloodline," reveal the moral characters and grim prospects of two young men—virtually destroyed by "the rules" of the old plantation and its allied legal system—in confrontation with old men who have barely survived. Even more than "A Long Day in November" and "The Sky Is Gray," these stories depend heavily on authenticity and credibility of voice.

10. Babb, *EG*, 21–2.

These two older narrators, one tough, the other tired out, might be deceptive, with or without intent. So the "camcorder" is used to capture the episodes accurately, to define aspects of authentic (or inauthentic) manhood, and then, as the young men move tentatively toward it, to encourage readers to understand and care about these otherwise morally unattractive and unsympathetic characters.

Proctor Lewis, protagonist and narrator of "Three Men," is young, brash, and black in Louisiana. He has killed another black in a brawl that he himself caused but his victim made violent. He is therefore defensive about his crime. The story covers his first two nights and one day in jail, during which, goaded and instructed by an old convict and moved by the plight of a boy, he comes to some self-awareness, a new sense of values, and a tentative decision to pay like a responsible man for his action rather than accept bonded-out slavery on a plantation and a future in and out of jail. The focus of the episode is the internal change of a nineteen-year-old in the face of a society that will not alter its expectations of him. Proctor's drama, however, is not complete at the story's end; he is still living it hour by hour, trying to convince himself to end it well. He is not telling his story to anyone, really, and has no motive to do so; since it is unfinished, he cannot assert or brag. His inner camera, therefore, records his drama only as far as it has progressed, up to his final "wait and see."

In "Bloodline," the central interest is the situation itself, embodied in a trio (not just a pair) of antagonists, all maintaining a claim to dignity they will not relinquish. Copper Laurent, son of deceased landowner Walter Laurent and a black woman, has returned to claim a right of inheritance from the present owner, his very ill uncle, Frank Laurent, who will die before he will defy the system he actually detests. It is a no-win situation, with no end occurring in the story or promised with assurance of fulfillment. Given the principal antagonists, no resolution is possible.[11] Nor can the two antagonists record their confrontation, which is prepared for yet delayed throughout the story. Both Copper and Frank must be understood, not merely observed, but neither has direct access to the other's words or actions until they finally meet; each has partial understanding of the other's position and feelings but little sympathy and even less motive to recount them. Even if they had motive and audience, both are too emotionally unstrung to be reliable. Similar limitations rule out Copper's distressed great-aunt, the old family servant Amalia, as a vehicle of narration.

11. Cf. Werner 38–9; Keith Byerman, *Fingering the Jagged Grain: Tradition and Form in Recent Black Fiction* (Athens: University of Georgia Press, 1985), 90.

So the story runs through the vision and hearing, the mind and emotions, of the elderly servant Felix, observer and friend of all yet also a nonviolent participant in the conflict. He is not impartial so much as aware of the hopeless goals and methods of both antagonists.[12] Between Frank and Copper, Felix represents a third way to act in the immediate dilemma, the way of one old enough and wise enough to foresee change and gauge the possible speed and cost of it, one courageous enough to maintain his own dignity and integrity while living his late years according to the rules of behavior even as he speaks up against them and passively resists subjugation by them. Felix is too old "to be joining up with anybody," but he asserts that "I do what I do from respect" (201). Felix and Copper are two versions of black manhood. Blend them, and Gaines's other young activists will appear, explaining that they have joined public protests in response to the stories and rules of spirit learned from Felix's generation. Felix, therefore, unlike Proctor Lewis, would have incentive to retell events later. But Felix has never "written a letter in [his] life," so would hardly write a story (169). The theme requires revelation of his present experience; the story must be told from his perspective.

Both these stories have purposeful "camcorder" narration in the style of the first two stories in the collection, with similarly significant effects. Despite their almost consistent use of past-tense verbs, both have features of the whirring camera capturing the now-moments of an engaged protagonist and of a spectator and peripheral participant.

The first indication of the camcorder technique in both tales is that they begin *in medias res*, just after the precipitating event and without the lead-in of a storyteller. Not, "Last time I was in jail was for killing" or "Last summer Copper Laurent showed up here," but, rather:

> Two of them was sitting in the office when I came in there. One was sitting in a chair behind the desk, the other one was sitting on the end of the desk. They looked at me, but when they saw I was just a nigger they went back to talking like I wasn't even there. They talked like that two or three more minutes before the one behind the desk looked at me again. That was T. J. ("TM," 121)

12. Cf. Robbie Walker, "Literary Art and Historical Reality: Ernest Gaines's Portrayal of the South in Transition," *Griot* 2 (summer 1983): 2–5; Jack Hicks, *In the Singer's Temple: Prose Fictions of Barthelme, Gaines, Brautigan, Piercy, Kesey, and Kosinski* (Chapel Hill: University of North Carolina Press, 1981), 121.

I figured it was about time she was coming to work, so I went to the door to look out for her. There she was, pushing the gate open and coming into the yard. . . . she raised her head and looked toward the tool shop. She knowed I'd be standing there. ("Bl," 159)

It might be asserted validly that an author can write as if jumping into the middle of an oral tale, as one who came onto the porch while the story was in progress. But that new listener would either miss essentials already presented or have to interrupt to get them retold. In these stories, all information is embedded and progressively revealed. The first quote above presents the start of Proctor's incarceration at the moment it occurs. Only in ensuing dialogue do we learn exactly why he has turned himself in; if he were telling the story, the information would almost surely come in his narration, and come early. "Bloodline" also requires two sections, one of Felix's thoughts and one of his dialogue with Amalia, before the reader knows Copper's identity and the kind of crisis he has precipitated. In both cases, beginning in the middle of a crisis plunges the reader into the intense emotional conflicts that are the stories' central issues.

In a similar pattern, both these conflicts come to no clear resolution. Proctor may or may not be man enough to go to the penitentiary; the crucial point is that he now sees the difference between the real freedom of a responsible but jailed man and the psuedofreedom of dependency on a contemptuous white liberator. If he were telling the story after whatever action he took, he would let us know it. But then the story would not convey the ambivalence of every young Proctor in that society. It needs to end where and how it does, in the immediacy of his struggle to decide. Nor is it necessary to know whether Copper Laurent fulfills his closing promise to return and "take" his "birthright." If he comes, he and his "soldiers" will die in the attempt; more likely, few will follow him. There is no solution to his dilemma or to Frank's; both stop where they are, in Felix's awareness.[13]

While the inner tensions rage, they are felt first in the way the narrators relate to their outer world. Given the limited powers of voice in both narrators, Proctor's and Copper's stories heavily depend for articulation on the visual powers of the camcorder to follow setting and to focus in on symbolic objects. These symbol-laden settings are the principal factors in story structure. In the preceding stories, Sonny had to become James, to go out from the safe limits of the quarters

---

13. Babb sees a switch in tone from farce to pessimism created by Copper's ambiguous ending (*EG*, 36).

to the harsh world of Bayonne and see the variety of its dangers. Now Proctor Lewis, having first chosen to live dangerously in "rough joints," must move back into confinement, "plantation or pen," one symbolizing a hell of real and lasting condemnation, the other an excruciating but redemptive purgatory. The setting for his choice is therefore a symbolic place of confinement—the brutal, claustrophobic local jail. That makes the structure of this story suitably simple: entry through the outer office kept by its Cerberus, the sheriff, into a cell as crude and limited as the lives of those who inhabit it—bars that cannot be shaken down, smelly bunks, open toilets, closed window. Through that window, however, Proctor can see "a few stars," "the stars going out in the sky," the star he finds again without cheating, and, at his moment of breakthrough, a "million little white, cool stars" (127–8, 148, 151). In that cell he finds two men, one who represents everything he despises and is sure he's not (a "freak," a "sad woman"), the other—an old razor-scarred repeater—what he will be if he chooses a false redemption. And he is given the boy who is what he once was, who also has a future dependent on choice, who precipitates Proctor's own choice and is called on to support it, for whom the almost-man feels "some kind of love" (153). In that response, Proctor breaks out of his own most harsh and confining cell.

A series of symbolic settings also structures "Bloodline," the second longest story in the collection. The action begins in the yard of the big house, moves through its back door and kitchen into the dining room, and then, after Felix's short trip to the quarters, advances into the library, the inner sanctum of southern gentility and intellectual culture, where Felix has never before sat down. There the elderly servant is made foil to the failing old owner. They, with Amalia between them, confront each other with half-spoken, wholly understood truths, which become more and more explicit as Felix and Amalia grow bolder and Frank's power to control is exposed as weakened and false. When Frank knows all his orders and rituals of compulsion will never bring Copper through the back door, he is reduced to ordering Felix into the living room to await more orders. In this room, sunless even with open curtains, Felix has previously sat down only for wakes—the rituals of a family and code that are slowly dying out. Now he sits contemplating the family portraits, "soldiers everywhere," and especially the picture of Walter Laurent on the stallion Black Terror, who finally dragged him to his death; Walter Laurent who left behind only one rapacious white daughter and one son, a black who calls himself "General" and is spreading terror among his own people with his plan to have soldiers overrun the plantation. "They the same two. . . . It's Walter back" (193). The symbolism of this room may be a bit obvious, but it works. From the living room, museum of the old lifestyle, Frank, the general who knows he "ain't got no more army," orders Felix to drive him to the quarters. Action and symbolic meaning move to Amalia's cabin, the new, temporary big house, where "General Christian Laurent," to the manner born, greets "Uncle," offers chair and beverage, and then engages him in a confrontational discussion of rights, of the means and timing of change. That discussion simply makes the impasse explicit and ends the story—for the moment.

Within the symbolic settings, the characters and their dilemmas are depicted by the immediacy of their observations, impressions, and interpretations. These are conveyed by minute, multiple sensory details, the kind a person notes on the spot but rarely remembers later. Proctor Lewis records the precise motions of the two policemen, the cell-block guard, and Unc' Toby with his food cart. He notes the ashen color of T. J.'s eyes, Munford's bad breath, the scar on his sweaty face, and the gritty sound of his hand on his beard. He observes T. J.'s every look at him, and how cellmates Munford and Hattie eat their bread and baloney and drink their coffee, how one smokes and the other blows his nose. Not only are such details easily forgotten, they seem irrelevant. Proctor himself would find little reason to recall or report them later, but the "camera" records them as the sensations of prison life he must accept now to avoid reliving later.

Similar "irrelevant" detail is used in "Bloodline" to render the situation of "poor Amalia." Felix observes her long gray dress, blue gingham apron, yellow straw hat, and white head rag, and especially her walk, "slow and tired, like any moment she might stop and go back. When she came in the shade of that big pecan tree, she raised her head. . . ." (159). Later Felix notes that the head rag is no longer required of house servants; Amalia still wears it, the sign of her "place" and her security there as long as Frank is "master." Felix's own position between Frank and Copper is seen in details of facial expression, posture, and motion: "[Frank] kept his eyes on the note another second, then he looked up at me. 'He calls me "Dear Uncle."'' I shifted my feet a little, but I didn't say anything. Frank squinted up at me . . . then he looked down . . . again" (169). At the eventual confrontation of uncle and nephew, Felix observes Copper looking down on Frank calmly, while Frank shifts his eyes up and down a tree, waiting for a face-saving reason to look up at the young man again. Felix recognizes the symbolic inversion of mastery; the servants look down on the dying aristocracy.

Character and theme are further rendered by the absence of dialogue. In "Three Men" and "Bloodline," as in the stories about young boys, there is a sense of high orality, as if someone were always talking. In fact, actual dialogue is sparse. In all four stories, the only ready talkers are the children or the hefty men-children who self-identify with expected stereotypes. Other adults are restrained by mature wisdom or the stresses of their situations; only one or two characters in each story engage each other or deliver speeches of substantial length.

When Proctor Lewis turns himself in, the verbal exchange is sharp and clipped: T. J. gives orders; Proctor keeps his mouth shut or answers on demand. Sentences are short—long enough only to reveal Proctor's motive for being there, T. J.'s brutal instincts, and Paul's role as buffer and protector. Proctor's dilemma is clear even before he's in a cell: Medlow or T. J., one form of beating or another. In the cell, Proctor at first speaks scarcely a sentence of more than three words. The essence of his situation is in his one-word replies: "Fighting" . . . "Uncle" . . . "No" [lawyer] . . . "No" [money] . . . "Nineteen" (128, 135, 142).

In contrast, Munford—long winded and vulgar but wised up—consumes nearly six pages for his speeches on personal history, social and racial analysis, preachment against preachers, and exhortation on the pen as the way to manhood. Like any preacher, he ends the sermon without knowing if he has effected a change in his listeners—probably not, but just maybe.[14] After Munford leaves, Hattie self-defensively tries to elicit a response from Proctor—without success. Proctor thinks about Hattie but says not a word until the boy is thrown into the cell; then he speaks only four sharp variations on "Leave him alone." Hattie speaks *about* the boy but says nothing *to* him, except "Shhh now" (149–52). He communicates by physical comforting, a body language that Proctor interprets unhesitatingly. Given the boy's beaten condition, that interpretation is not necessarily accurate. Though not "manly" by Proctor's definition and contrasting behavior, Hattie's action is not necessarily abusive; it remains ambiguous. Proctor speaks to the boy in the same line of questions, warnings, and exhortation that Munford so lately gave him. The parallel is ironic: Munford had never done what he urges Proctor to do—go to the pen and come out a man. Proctor does not do what he orders the boy to do—pray. The story seems to suggest that some blend of tenderness and toughness is the truly manly way to speak and behave.[15]

Because "Bloodline" is a much longer story, with older, more articulate characters, it offers more flow of dialogue. The most unrestrained speech is from the fearful, servile, childish jabberers, comic foils to both Felix and Copper. The four

14. Cf. Babb, *EG*, 29–30; Beavers, 27–9; Duncan, 93; Hicks, *Singer's*, 119, for analyses of Munford's character and speech.

15. Cf. W. Burke, 551–3; Beavers, 30–1; Shelton, 206.

real grown-ups speak with purpose. Felix speaks up to Frank, but briefly, with irony they both recognize ("You the authority"), even as he refuses to keep his "place" and do his "job" as expected (184, 179, 210). He sees through Frank's rationalizations and spunkily turns his irony on him: "Now, the Cajuns there . . . wouldn't mind lending [dogs] to you. We ain't had a good lynching in a long time" (198). He tells Frank forthrightly why the blacks don't fear him and how Copper's behavior resembles that of his white father.

It is instructive to read their dialogue without Felix's narrative interpretations. Omit "He must 'a' been. . . . He didn't believe that. . . . He said it because. . . . He knowed. . . . but he wanted me to believe . . ."; without those interpolations, Frank's speeches sound mostly like orders meant to be obeyed, old-fashioned assertions of racial authority to which an old servant gives ironic acquiescence. Only Felix's interpretive views reveal Frank's full awareness of his failing control, of the uselessness of the rituals he is still determined to maintain. Only on the ride to the quarters in section ten do the two old men converse in honesty and mutual respect.

When Amalia speaks to Frank, she is moved not only by her fear of Copper's derangement and its results—Frank's final heart attack and the eviction of all blacks by his niece—but also by genuine concern for the old man. She has no fear of him and wants to honor the truth; so she is even bolder than Felix in addressing the danger to his heart, the fact of "us nephew" and his dependency: "Who you got beside me and Felix, Mr. Frank? Who?" "Nobody," he admits (184). Amalia and Felix, of course, have nobody but Frank between them and homelessness, and nobody but each other with whom to share information and fears. Together they analyze the motives of both men in this confrontation, something they cannot do in Frank's otherwise constant presence in the story.

Amalia quotes Copper; he is never heard speaking to her, the one person he might love. His exchange with Felix is short, blunt: "Mr. Frank want you. . . . Go back and tell [him]. . . . He told me come find you. . . . No one *comes* for the General" (167). So he wins that battle; Frank goes to him. Their final confrontation should also be read once without Felix's interpretations. Then it sounds like two generals exchanging rapid fire, until it is broken by Copper's long "chains and sticks" recitation of the historic barbarity to black men, and his level, then impassioned, rendition of his personal history. Frank's full-page speech is the dying general's assertion of his real motive for holding to the rules: "to do all I can to make up for what [Walter] did to these here in the quarters. I'm going to give them . . ." shelter, food, medicine, a church, and a burial plot (216). Patronizing, of course, *noblesse oblige*, but Frank does care. These monologues have been criticized as too long and strained, too heavily rhetorical for the action performed; they have also been praised for "the only real fury [Gaines] reveals in this collection."[16] The last word goes to Copper, but his "I shall return" is not a heroic promise; it is a threat. He will not give; he will "take," and he doesn't care if he has to "bathe this whole plantation in blood" to do it (217). A reader acknowledges his intelligence, awareness, and courage but shares his aunt's horror at the ruthlessness of her "own blood" (191).

Dialogue, sparse or flowing, reveals the camcorder technique. It must catch the speeches of Frank and Copper, which are too long for Felix to remember and repeat accurately. It records harangues, such as Munford's with content Proctor does not grasp: "I didn't know what he was talking about" (138). Or the dialogue may be detailed but rapid and agitated, like that of Felix, Amalia, and Frank, with notations of their facial expressions, volume shifts, and gestures. Verbal exchange may even be irrelevant to the main action; the exchange of Felix and Dee-Dee about giving Stateman "what he want" is incidental to Felix's call to the house (163). In each instance, not the narrator but the Gaines camcorder has recorded the talk so as to engage the reader as fully as any viewer of a film, to reveal the characters' views of each other and the mesh of relationships—black and white, owners and servants, men and women—in the plantation culture, a culture within which Proctor and Copper must find authentic manhood.

This outward dialogue is narrated in relation to the two men's inner thoughts. As the detailed acts and words occur, both narrators register instant impressions, interpretations, intuitions, and decisions. Proctor "hears" Munford's dislike of his uncle and interprets Hattie's looks, words, and gestures. He intuits T. J.'s and Paul's thoughts and motives: "I could tell Paul wasn't anything like T. J. . . . he just had to play mean. . . . [T. J.] thought I was a smart aleck . . . he wanted to hit me with his fist" (123). With each moment's impression, Proctor decides when to speak and when to be still, why and how not to cry or scream. His taciturnity is due not only to his self-defense against the brutality of lawmen and the image he sees in Hattie, it is even more related to the locus of his main and essential action: inside his mind. There he maintains a seemingly endless flow of dialogue: ". . . how come he didn't do it then? Don't tell me to do it. . . . I can make a phone call, can't I? But call who? . . . Maybe I ought. . . . But suppose . . . then what?" (144–5). Only in his mind can he talk, rage and blame, deny and admit, and finally come to a decision to "stand" and "take it"—if he can (152, 155). Felix's main service to Frank is to read his mind; but his service to himself is to decide how to act on the reading: "When he did that he forgot Copper was a Laurent. He thought Copper was going to answer him like I would 'a' answered him. . . . Since he had turned his head from Copper, he needed something to make him turn back. That was supposed to be my job . . . but I wasn't getting in it" (210). These narrative mental registrations are not thought out, not intended to be remembered and reported; they are noted internally by either man only long enough to produce the needed response—theirs and the readers'.

For both narrators, memories are crucial and mesh readily with considerations of the immediate situation. In Proctor, memory reveals his potential for a radical change of intent as he reviews his few good and many bad relationships and as he sees his future in memories of Jack, broken by the Cajun who bonded him out. Felix's memories come in many brief associations of past and present, in flashes of what he knows but does not elaborate, as if no one else is there who needs an explanation (for example, Walter Laurent's use of black women). The purpose of all his memories is less to reveal Walter than Copper, who is laboring with a notion of manhood almost as mistaken as his father's.

In Felix, emotionally unfettered, immediate considerations are registered simply in mental comparisons, and he does not deviate from the distancing of the past tense. But when Proctor is absorbed in heavy emotion and urgent decision making, deeply affected by all he remembers, he shifts into present tense, simply picking up the random sequences, repetitions, incremental phrases, and vulgar, unedited diction of his mind in its intense, immediate activity:

> Look how life can change on you—just look. Yesterday this time I was poon-tanging like a dog. Today—that black sonofabitch—behind these bars maybe for the rest of my life. And look at me, look at me. Strong. A man. A damn good man. A hard dick—a pile of muscles. But look at me—locked in here like a caged animal. . . . I wonder if Grinning Boy got in touch with Marie. I suppose this finish it. . . . I was treating her like a dog, anyhow. I'm sorry, baby; I'm sorry. No, I'm not sorry; I'd do the same thing tomorrow if I was out of here. Maybe I'm a' animal already. . . . I got to think, I got to think. (144–5)

And think he does, as his tormented mind vacillates between his options: plantation or pen. His choices refract through the lens of many bad memories: his father "somewhere up North" (145), Medlow or other white folks, Jack, Munford, his dead mother, his own loveless behavior. He sees only a life ruined.

That sequence of thoughts ends, however, with his first truly positive wish: "I wish I knowed somebody. I wish I knowed a good person. I would be good if I knowed a good person. I swear to God I would be good" (149). Enter the "good" teenage boy, beaten for stealing food when hungry, for whose sake Proctor is moved to tears, to "some kind of love" and to his own decision: "I knowed I was going to the pen now. I knowed I was going, I knowed I was going. . . . I was go'n do like Munford said. I was going there and I was go'n sweat it and I was go'n take it. . . . I wanted to stand. . . . they never let you stand if they got you out" (153, 152). It is the incremental style that marks these passages as the recording of a mind in action, and it is the intensity of that action that convinces Gaines's readers that this character almost certainly will "stand" in the proximate and long future, despite his own ambivalence at story's end.

Effective as this "camcorder" narration is in these two stories, it is not perfectly consistent. Both narrators interject comments and background information that seem more like explanations required by an audience than the workings of their own minds: Proctor's mention of the rituals expected in confronting white police, and Felix's history of Frank Laurent's heart attacks, troubles with overseers and his niece, and collapsing health, and of Walter Laurent's abusive behaviors and death. The last account is a reminiscence while Felix waits in the living room for Frank, yet it reads more like an oral narrative than the ruminations of his immediate consciousness, which, he says, "wasn't thinking about Walter . . . was thinking about that other one . . ." (193).

Most puzzling is the presentation of Proctor's nightmare (128–32). The lead-in does not clearly indicate sleep: "My eyes felt tired and my head started spinning, and I wasn't here any more, I was at the Seven Spots." That could be either the start of haunting memory in a fatigued, disturbed, and sleepless man, or a spin into nightmare. But the story is then rendered as a perfectly coherent, straightforward account. It has neither the restless fragmentation of wakeful torment nor the bizarre style of a nightmare, nor yet the style of an after-the-fact oral report.

The effectiveness of narration in any mode is judged, of course, in relation to a story's goals. Beyond the privileged insight that required Proctor and Felix as narrators, beyond consistency and technical wizardry, what else is the purpose of the immediacy and intensity of these stories? Like all the stories in *Bloodline*, these two are studies of manhood. Narration must make a reader understand and more or less sympathize with morally repellent young men as they move uncertainly toward that goal.[17] Given Proctor's gross crudity and Copper's questionable sanity, that purpose is not easily achieved.

17. Duncan, 92; Werner, 38; Beavers, 29–31, offer analyses of Proctor's character. For similar analyses of Copper Laurent, see Burke, 553–4; Shelton, 207–8; Robert M. Luscher, "The Pulse of *Bloodline*," in *CRF*, 76–7; and Gaines's own comments in *CEG*, 40–1, 49.

Proctor is amoral and self-protective rather than mean or violent. He does not carry a knife or intend to kill. He can distinguish among whites' attitudes and motives, is careful, even clever, and has feeling for certain people, like Jack and his own mother. But he defines manhood in terms of an ability to survive a fight and of genitalia and sexual activity. His first way of showing compassion for the jailed boy is to force him to smoke. To a man like Hattie, he can offer no compassion or understanding at all. His view of women is utterly crude; they have no identity except for the physical parts and pleasures that attract him. To resemble them in any emotional way is beneath contempt, makes him "sick a' the stomach" (149). The one exception is his mother; only through the memory of her can he begin to define love, assess his own deficiency in relation to Marie and other women he has used, and come to "some kind of love" for the boy.

To bring a reader to understanding and compassion for Proctor himself, Gaines needed to follow his every activity from within, in the heat of his stress, in all possible nuances. Only by a "camera" narration would we receive the symbols of his experience as he moves, however tentatively, from the phony toughness of vulgarity, sexual promiscuity, fighting, smoking, not crying, and never doing anything "like a woman," to the courage of self-assertion and endurance he needs in order to "stand." When his nightmare ends, it is indeed the coming of day for him; when he rinses out the boy's bloody shirt and his own "filthy" one, we sense his almost certain start on a life that is unbloody and clean.

Copper is not as easy to assess; because he, like his uncle, cannot change at all, he does not have a long story to tell and has no reliable perspective on it or on his own character. Felix alone has the perspective a reader needs: both objective and sympathetic, neither frightened by Copper nor appalled by his bravado, able to grasp his righteous indignation and the hopelessness of his intention. Felix is open to see and hear the data we need: Copper's valid assertion that the earth, stars, and sun are for everyone; his authentic sense of human rights and of the wrongs done to him, his mother, his aunt, and his people; his superiority to the half-men sent to force him in the back door; and his historical awareness of "what's in the air" (207). Felix's internal camera captures the hopeless contradiction that is Copper: a courage reflected in "eyes hard as marble" (167); a concern for his aunt that yet looks at her without seeing her and, she believes, would put even her in chains if she got in his way; a courtesy that compels even Frank's respect while he beats and humiliates the weak of his own people; and a determination to claim justice for them yet a willingness to slaughter them in the process. Copper is a conundrum; Copper recorded through Felix's immediate observations and thoughts is at least comprehensible. A reader wishes him well, better than Felix allows us to hope.

Proctor and Copper—changing and unchangeable; their stories accomplish a kind of inversion of character, foretelling perhaps an inversion in the course of their lives. Proctor begins with shedding blood, probably will go to prison for it, and may come out a saner, more peaceable man. Just before his decision, he realizes the weakness of his fellow convicts, like "roaches, like a bunch of mices," and has a tremendous desire to help them change, to "let all these people out. But would they follow me—would they?" (151). If he goes to the penitentiary and changes, they might. Copper has already been in prison; he has heard the weeping in the cells and scrubbed blood off the floor. But he has come out nearly insane, violent, intent to gather followers, and promising to shed blood. Will any follow him? Only if they are of the same violent mind. As the two protagonists move in opposite directions, they seem to converge thematically in their moments of dignity and empathy for fellow sufferers and the desire to liberate them. In that dignity, empathy, and desire is the contribution of these two stories toward a definition of manhood.

Sometimes a short story will spark in readers a sense of wonder that sets off a desire to know the source of its power. Such stories generate numerous rereadings and public readings, frequent anthologizing and classroom use. Such a story is "Just Like a Tree." Itself "like a tree planted by the water," it invites one to sit in patient contemplation, each reading as open to discovery as the first, until it offers glimpses of creativity and authorial skill that account, in part at least, for its fascination and reputation. Readers of this seemingly simple story intuit that its beauties are best detected not by digging but by watching and listening, by quiet attention to the topic and to details, until questions emerge like birds from branches.

Some such questions about "Just Like a Tree" include: If this story, like those preceding it, is about authentic manhood, why is the protagonist an old woman—if she really is the protagonist? Why are she and the young man so briefly seen and heard in the story and not among its numerous narrators? Why are there so many narrators? What becomes of short-story economy and focus when a new narrator appears every two or three pages? What does each reveal that another could not, and how? Is there a purposeful order in their appearances? What if that order were changed? And how does that spread of narrators relate to other techniques designed to establish or maintain focus and theme?

Certainly this tale seems, at first, to be about Aunt Fe, soon to be taken north by her niece before her house becomes another target of reprisal for civil rights demonstrations. She and her situation are seen through the various people of the quarters who have gathered to say good-bye. But well before this woman, deep-rooted as an ancient tree, evades being "jecked up" by quietly slipping into death, it has become apparent that the story's protagonist is really the community that has gathered around her, and the story is about her impact on its life and character.[18] Focus is on the community, as it has been, as it is now in face of a new kind of conflict, and as it may be in the future created by its young under the influence of its old. Perhaps the unit can survive when its old symbols die and it is, so to speak, deserted by its own or invaded by aliens—perhaps. But if it does, survival will be due to the bond of its Aunt Fes with its Emmanuels, old with young, wisdom with passion, one determination with another, deep womanhood with true manhood. Survival will be in unity of love and respect, and in the transmission of history. With that rooting, the people, in whatever manner or place they live, will be "just like a tree," immovable, purposeful.

A community, however unified, is made of individuals more or less imbued with its mores and values, experienced in its customs and history. The community of the quarters in "Just Like a Tree," like that in "Long Day in November," is composed primarily of fieldworkers, men and their wives, their children and elderly mothers. (Elderly fathers are barely mentioned, girl children not at all.) Unlike that first community, however, this one is responding to outside influences: Louise and Emmanuel, members who have been elsewhere and returned for this time; James, Louise's urban husband; and Anne-Marie Duvall, the plantation's owner. These four people are, in varying ways, "outsiders." Such a collection of characters is essential to display the diversity that is unified in spite of all threats of disintegration. Some techniques are essential to display all of them without disintegration of the story's focus and economy.

The blessings and hopes of this community, the force of its unity, and the threats to its survival are established in multiple contrasts, all carrying symbolic significance, all raising questions of relative values, questions provoking more reflections than rapid answers. Each of the three male fieldworkers has a different piece of equipment: a mule, a horse, and a "pretty red tractor" (226); clearly this is progress away from the need for men to work like mules. Yet when men have depended on their mules so long that they value them, almost love them, and insist on looking after them in old age, is the man who has a tractor better off?

18. Babb, *EG*, 37–43, discusses the elements of community identity: common quest, traditions, and history, all embodied in Aunt Fe.

With whom are readers to side—Mama, the protector of Mr. Bascom, or Emile, his frustrated driver, who intuits that not only Big Red but he himself is a "fellow mule just like yourself is," one who also wants to "come up" (224)? In what are Etienne and Chris more fortunate—in having horse and tractor, or in comprehending their people's culture and history and retaining friendship with Emile? Who is less comprehending of the real warmth in this community—the small boy Chuckkie or the "cool dude" James, who both note the cold of a "million cracks" in Aunt Fe's "beat up old house" (230, 234)? Who is more "kin" to Fe—Leola, who is "no kin" but has "washed . . . hoed . . . ironed . . . wrung a chicken neck" for her nearly every day of the year, or her niece Louise, who left her and now returns briefly to take her away because there is "nothing else but that" to do (227–8)? Who participates more in the wealth of the community—Anne-Marie Duvall, who owns the land and big house, whose husband will not drive her to Fe's, who brings the seventy-nine-cent gift, or the folk who work the land, drive or walk in the rain and mud to the party, and give the love and grieving that are crowded into that small house? Finally, in the long view of history, who will have benefited this community more—Aunt Fe, the taproot that cannot be moved from it; or Emmanuel, the lateral root, the young activist who cannot yet move the people but, himself nourished by Fe, will persevere in efforts to move a nation to justice? Questions about this community, its life and death, abound and may lead to ambiguous replies. But of its inherent value, Gaines leaves no question at all.

Lest multiplicity of persons induce a "melting" of his story, setting gives it a mold. Like "Three Men," the tale is confined almost entirely to one room. But the very similarities define the ultimate difference and meaning of these rooms. Each might be called a room in a location designed by white power to separate out impoverished blacks, confine them to their "place," and put them to work. Both rooms are small, crowded by even a few people, airless in summer heat, cold in winter. Both are symbols of discrimination by race and class; both offer the challenge to overcome by seeing the rooms as whites do not, as places to form salvific relationships. But in that challenge is found the difference of the stories. If Proctor Lewis overcomes, it is a success achieved contrary to his intent when he came to his cell against his will. To Aunt Fe's house, all come with free will, expressing a relationship that has already existed for years and years, against which rain and racism have no power. Ironically, it is the one totally uncomprehending alien in the house, James, who voices the meaning of the tight, crowded setting: "I mean, there's about ninety-nine of them in there. [All ages, sizes, colors]—you name them, brother, and they were there. And what for? Brother, I'll tell you what for. Just because me and Baby are taking this old chick out of these sticks" (231). Into this chilled, drafty room even Anne-Marie Duvall has to come for a truly warm personal relationship, however limited by her vision of class and race. In this one room is one community, with a few adjuncts.

James the urban alien also notes that "these country niggers . . . talk, talk, talk. Talk so much they make me buggy round here" (230). John Callahan noted how closely some of the interior monologues approach orality, as if the narrator were about to speak to someone else.[19] Actually, the sections are mostly "camcorder" representations of what the narrators are noticing, remembering, or thinking. The parts create a context of people conversing, but little is recorded. Most of the dialogue occurs in the first three sections, while Emile and his family are arriving and when his wife makes her fruitless appeal to Louise. These exchanges present the interaction of a solid family core in the community, the facts of living and relating there, especially to older women.

In Ben O's section, his exchanges about eggnog, shooting marbles, and not kissing Chuckkie are beside the point of the event; only children talk spontaneously at a time like this. Adults speak mostly to keep up a front against sorrow, the honored tradition of laughing to keep from crying, as Chris notes mentally. But Lionel's jokes are not given, not allowed to relieve the overall sadness of that section. Anne-Marie has two short, contrasting dialogues, with her loveless husband and with Aunt Fe; the latter breaks down into a moment of few words and genuine love, "Oh, Aunt Fe. . . . Oh, Aunt Fe" (243). Echoing Leola's mental iteration of the name, the "white lady" has her one moment of membership in the community. But then she flees from it. The power she exercises as owner obviates any power to experience a free and equal relationship in this house.

Two sections are entirely without dialogue: James's and Aunt Clo's. James considers all the folk there beneath him; he has nothing to say to them nor they to him. His "jived up" thoughts make very funny reading, hilarious listening; but the depth of alienation of this type of black man from his people is the saddest element of the story. In contrast, James's "old chick" is imaged in Clo's silent thoughts as the tree, the taproot that remains even if one succeeds in "jecking" and dragging away the trunk and branches. Fe—a part of the earth, of the elements—has nurtured the community for its survival.

What she has finally done to perpetuate its life, even when she is gone, is recorded in the mind of Etienne. His "why tale" of how slavery developed might be read as oral, as said to another guest, except that it is enmeshed in his

19. Callahan, African-American Grain, 193–4.

thoughts as he watches reactions to Emmanuel's entry, and it flows into the "now" of the young man's conversation with Aunt Fe. That dialogue is the central encounter of the story; as in the other tales, one prolonged speech is set amid shorter, terse remarks, to stand out from them and deliver an authorially approved theme. Technically, this dialogue is more a monologue; Emmanuel voices his reasons to continue the demonstrations, his long and loving relationship to Aunt Fe, and the personal history by which she motivated him and taught him nonviolence. She nods and nods; she speaks to him only her final benediction. Having given it, she can rest with Aunt Lou, where friendship is deepest and totally equal, and few, very few words are needed for a farewell.

If the community is to be known as a unit of diverse individuals all influenced by Aunt Fe, it follows that they must be not only seen and heard from without but also known from within. They, many of them, must be narrators.[20] A single narrator could observe much, could witness to Aunt Fe's and Emmanuel's importance for the at-home folk and the discordance of characters like James and Anne-Marie, and could interpret according to his or her experience and wisdom. Leola and Etienne are the best candidates for such a role. But Leola can find words only for her inner conviction that there should be "some other way" to safeguard Aunt Fe and that she "ain't go'n like that nigger [James]," that "Something 'bout him ain't right" (228). To understand his rootless, valueless character, his ignorant contempt of "the old girl" and "country niggers," and so to know what is wrong with sending Fe to his and Louise's house, we must go into his own mind. To see the sad mixture of Anne-Marie Duvall's ignorance and condescension with genuine affection and values, with pain and puzzlement, we must bounce with her down a road that she, the owner, has never improved, in a car she can take for granted even as she wonders if money for a car is the pitiful goal of the civil rights movement. We must walk with her through water and mud, guided through one puddle by lightning flashes but falling flat and "completely blinded" into another. And we must read her thought that the laughter in the house means "niggers can laugh and joke even if they see somebody beaten to death"—surely her most completely blind moment (241–2). Her jostling, the lightning flashed on her blindness, her progress by falling and rising, these are all metaphors for what must occur in members of both races if ever they are to meet in a community of genuine affection and simple human feeling for each other.

20. For other discussions of the multiple narrators, see John F. Callahan, "Hearing is Believing: The Landscape of Voice in Ernest Gaines's *Bloodline*," *Callaloo* 7 (Winter 1984): 107, 112; Luscher, in *CRF*, 83–4; Byerman, 90; Simpson, 238.

The outsiders are not the only characters who must be narrators to reveal their thoughts and personalities. To draw readers into the unified heart of the community, its members must reveal their perceptions of it. As was true in earlier stories, the viewpoint of children is the surest, least disguised way to present the facts of adult poverty and loss: exposure to wind, cold, and rain on old mule wagons, the shortage of chairs for a group gathering, and the waning authority of the old. The incomprehension of Chuckkie and Ben O, absorbed in warmth, marbles, and eggnog, highlights by contrast the seriousness of the pending event. The three men expose the male ways of dealing with poverty and degradation: get better equipment for easier work, swap "lies" to relieve sorrow, and engage in rebellion. Leola witnesses the woman's way of community: long-lasting relationships, loving service, comfort, hiding grief that would only add to another's sorrow—what it means to be "one o' the family" or "Same as one," what the Jameses can never know (228). Finally, to understand Fe's influence, we must know her through her peers, Clo and Lou, those who have been rooted in place with her, have felt what uprooting would mean to them, and have shared a quality of tenderness that even Lou's son and grandson cannot reveal.

Selection of narrators reveals the spirit of the quarters community. Arrangement, at first, seems just a series of natural connections, as paragraphs are artfully linked by words and images.[21] The child's view of mud and mules links to the father's; the father's entry into the house leads to what his wife sees there. Her intuitive dislike of James is followed by a validating inside view of him. Nonman James's stress on the importance of lacing eggnog leads to a real boy's wish to have some. Chris's knowing rumination on laughter as antidote to sadness is countered by Anne-Marie's ignorant thought about the laughter she hears, symbolically, from outside the house. She gets out of the house as fast as she can, and Emmanuel comes in. He leaves, and it is time for the people to leave. And so on.

Arrangement, however, is more than this simple chain. Narrators form three meaningful groups of three, followed by Aunt Lou's gentle coda. Chuckkie, Emile, and Leola (and Aunt Lou with them) are a smaller unit within the larger group; they represent the positive and negative experience and feeling that bind the community together yet threaten its disintegration. The most negative and positive forces are powerfully felt in James and Aunt Clo, with Ben O between them as a small, walking question mark about the future. Will he follow James in his devotion to "Mr. Harper," or ultimately listen to his Gran'mon (presum-

21. Washington, "Commentary," 39, and Luscher, 84–5, discuss the linear arrangement of the narrators from youngest to oldest.

ably Clo), even when she "be dead and gone"? What kind of men would these boys become without their parents, Gran'mons, and community? The third triad consists of two real men who comprehend and can interpret the mood of the community, its history and culture, and, between them, the white woman who can do neither.

To note the art of these groupings, one need only imagine reversing some sections; for example, Ben O's and Clo's. His possible future as a James-type character would be lost to the reader's sight, and the wisdom behind the great thematic image of the tree with the immovable taproot would suddenly descend to concern for marbles and eggnog. Or suppose Anne-Marie's section were placed before the pictures of the community were set; her inability to understand and participate would not be half as evident. If her section preceded Chris's and Etienne's, we would hardly note the contrast so sharply, that her loss is only personal, that she is devoid of real awareness of the community's loss and of comprehension of the history that has created Emmanuel and the movement. These two realities are highlighted by her position between the two men who voice them.

All these narrators—insiders, outsiders, young and old—are needed to reveal the community. We may ask, however, why Aunt Fe and Emmanuel, those most directly engaged in the event, cannot be narrators. Adhering to the premise that the focus of the story is the revelation of the community under the impact of Fe's departure, we see that neither her primary grief nor Emmanuel's motivations must preempt attention. If she were a narrator, she would quickly become the protagonist. Gaines noted that he wanted to convey the feelings of others about Fe, so did not develop the story of her life before the story takes place (CEG, 106). So she is seen in small but sharp cameos that reveal the "way of the folk": Leola sees her "trying to look joyful" (226) and remembers her trying to pay for services—poor women concerned for each other. Her response to Anne-Marie, even if shaped by old-servant deference, reveals a genuine affection far in excess of that which prompted "my lady" to give the inexpensive scarf; Fe and aunts like her are the best hope the white owners have to learn genuine love and attachment to the community on their land. Finally, Fe's silent listening to "the boy" affirms his stance of nonviolence, the best hope the community has for lasting change beyond the immediate damage of bombings and dislocations. If he is a defining example of genuine young manhood, she is the woman essential to his formation.[22]

---

22. Luscher, 77; Werner, 39. The strength of the elders and the daring of the young may be read in gender terms at this point in Gaines's writing, but later works would bring forth change through old men getting stronger, and through brave, insightful young women.

Emmanuel needs no special self-revelation by narration; he needs only Fe's attention in the presence of the community to assert his purpose, explain the necessity of his action despite the suffering it precipitates, and receive her affirmation. The rest of the folk then must understand him as a genuine man, not a dangerous boy, and must accept the future as the young like him will try to shape it. Fe can sing her "termination for Heaven" and slip away.

Further, their two names suggest why neither character could be an ordinary observing narrator. She is "Aunt Fe, Aunt Fe . . . Just like the name of God. Like the name of town—the city [Santa Fe—Holy Faith]" (227). Only Fe calls "the boy" by name, "Emmanuel," which means "God with us," and sends him out with the prayer, "God be with you" (247). Like Faith, like God, these two characters transcend the community even as they are and will be present in it, even in their absence. They are virtual icons in and of the community; they cannot be self-representing in the same commonplace way as the pained and puzzled but loving folk who see and represent them.

If Aunt Fe is the ancient faith of the past and present, faith not only in God but also in her people, still supporting and nourishing their strength and union, then Emmanuel is the tenacious hope for the future. She will cling to the soil she has lived on and be buried in it; he will cling to the stories and values she has taught him as he struggles elsewhere, until it is "his time to be turned over just like it's hers today" (245). They are the core of the community; some will stay in the quarters and grow old, others will grow up and move on. The camcorder has captured all of them in the now moment of this transition, has registered by their own inner voices the intensity of their immediate perceptions and emotions. Quiet and simple as this tale has seemed, its nuances validate the possibility of growth at all ages, the hope of a people for stability and movement, loyalty and progress, for both old and young, women and men.

Many of Gaines's critics have looked at *Bloodline* as a unified book, a sort of novel made from short stories. It has been called an "episodic novel," a "short story sequence," a "bildungsroman," and a "series of doors."[23] The sources of unity have been cited chiefly in the pattern of human development, specifically that of the black male in age, awareness, and the "bloodline" of painful experience; the regional portrait of the plantation and small town of the South; and the cycle of growth-decay-growth that is the South's historic progression from nearly unchallenged oppression to militancy, protest, and change. These broad themes

23. Simpson, 192; CEG, 106; Luscher, 62; Babb, EG, 15.

have been specified by the study of recurring others: shared suffering, the son without a father, the role of religion or alternative visions, and relationships between age and youth, white and black, individual and community.[24]

Some techniques have been noted as the essential configurations of these themes: the ordering of the stories for progression of age and wisdom, of relationships and hope of change; the "greater sophistication of vision" of the first four narrators leading to the "polyphony of voices" in the final story; the call-and-response, jazzlike repetitions and variations of themes and techniques; unity of setting in a single day in or near Bayonne; unity of style in authentic folk idiom; and consistent images from nature to symbolize and link characters by their changing, developing emotions and experiences.[25]

That the stories are related is evident on the face of it: similarities, progressions, and recurrences are obvious, and Gaines has testified to his intent to make them so. He defines that relationship in the same terms of progression and arrangement that his critics have used (CEG, 35–6, 46–9). Three of the stories had been published independently, and he thought them good enough to make a small book. As he was writing "Three Men" and "Bloodline," "suddenly I wanted them to fit in . . . once I realized that I was writing a group of stories that had some similarities, I wanted them to have some relationship with the other ones" (CEG, 46).

Gaines is also consistently clear that he had no intention from the start to write an episodic novel (CEG, 46, 245). Nor, in the end, *did* he—not if that term means anything like the definition Sheldon Sacks has given it: a single controlling "action" leading a single protagonist toward a resolution to which numerous minor characters contribute briefly and then disappear. Though Robert Luscher neatly describes a "composite protagonist" in *Bloodline*, a "young black male . . . in danger of being brutalized," he does not suggest that this is the protagonist of a novel, but rather a type variously incarnated in a "sequence" of five tales.[26]

We may note that none of these incarnations reappears in any other tale;

24. Luscher, 62–3, 67–74; Duncan, 86; Babb, EG, 21–2; Jack Hicks, "To Make These Bones Live: History and Community in Ernest Gaines's Fiction," *Black American Literature Forum* 11 (1977): 13–6; Hicks, *Singer's*, 15; W. Burke, 545–56; Ben Forkner, "Ernest J. Gaines," in *Critical Survey of Short Fiction*, ed. Frank N. Magill, vol. 4 (Englewood Cliffs, N.J.: Salem Press, 1981), 1430–2. The most thorough analysis from many angles is that of Luscher, 62–88.

25. Luscher, 64–9; Byerman, *Fingering*, 88; Babb, EG, 21–2.

26. Sheldon Sacks, *Fiction and the Shape of Belief* (Berkeley: University of California Press, 1966), 24–5; Luscher, 74.

James as teenager is not at Aunt Fe's to hear and learn from her or Emmanuel. Nor do any of the minor characters appear in more than one tale, as they might be expected to do if the protagonist were considered one man. Emmanuel in his protests has had no encounter with T. J.; yet in an environment as small as *Blood-line*'s, brief episodes could readily engage the same lawmen, laborers, aunts, and Cajuns. With repetitions and bonds of that sort, it would not be too hard or too inaccurate to label the collection an episodic novel; such elasticity of definition might not stretch the form beyond recognition. But no such bonds were created, and *Bloodline* is what its author envisioned and called it, a "series of stories," discrete though related.

Nevertheless, the very exploration of the notion of the episodic novel opens an avenue of thought about the techniques of *Bloodline*—the path of influence. Not the influence of other sequences on Gaines, or of his on other writers; rather, the influence of this collection on its own author.[27] When asked if there were not a great similarity between Aunt Fe and Miss Jane Pittman, if *Miss Jane Pittman* were not, in some sense, the story of Aunt Fe's prior life, Gaines retorted, "You're much too sharp!" (CEG, 49). He went on to elaborate on his early process of writing the novel and perceiving its similarities to the short story, especially in his early attempt to use multiple viewpoints. On many occasions, Gaines has explained his decision to recast the novel in Jane's voice alone; in doing so (as will be seen in chapter 6), he made her the single protagonist. And into her drama he cast almost innumerable, unnamable minor characters who come and go on her long journey. The story of Jane Pittman is a veritable series of stories, which are, assuredly, in a sequence. But they are not discrete; each is a tale of Jane, an episode in her forward progression. Whether purposefully or not this time, Gaines took all he had learned about connection of short tales and made a true episodic novel.

His experiments with viewpoint were to have the same sort of favorable influence. When he began *Miss Jane* with multiple narratives from the folk gathered at her funeral, their views must have been cast in the past tense, as of people looking back, remembering and telling tales. When they couldn't tell enough, he found the way to let her talk while she lived, let the people talk along with her, and then let an editor recast them all into her one voice—a masterful way

27. With more or less affirmation from Gaines's interviews, critics have said it was influenced by the similar collections of Turgenev, Anderson, Hemingway, Joyce, and Faulkner; is in the tradition of but not directly influenced by Toomer, Chesnutt, Wright, Hughes, and Baldwin; and is a precursor of collections by Walker and Naylor (Duncan, 85; Luscher, 65–6).

of creating a believable first-person narrator. In writing his short stories, he had also mastered the technique of the "camcorder" for immediacy and vivid emotion, whether of children or adults. His next experiment would be to try using it in a novel, at a suitable length, without losing other nuances of characterization, of time and sequence, or important elements of plot.

An examination of the novels published after *Bloodline* will show amazingly diverse yet coherent uses of viewpoint: multiple narrators living, in front of the camcorder, the distinct (but not discrete) segments of a plot line; within these larger segments, shorter tales told by old people remembering their immediate recorded experiences (*A Gathering of Old Men*); and one narrator recounting the essential, converting "travel" of his life while also gathering and reporting the small pieces of evidence from others most involved in its climactic event (*A Lesson Before Dying*). Small wonder that Gaines could say that "what we've done with the first person is as great in literature as anything else we have done . . ." (CEG, 235). With less modesty but equal truth, he could have said "I" as well as "we."

Short stories, with small but intensely focused episodes, purposefully crafted dialogue, symbolic settings, and a uniquely limited and focused narrative manner, plunge readers of *Bloodline* deeply into the experiences of a segment of the American South, its culture and history. By the very restrictions of this genre, which Gaines accepted and imposed on his art, he has recreated and brightly illuminated a land, a people, and a lifestyle that many would otherwise forget or never know. In collecting these stories, Gaines highlighted his themes by repetition and variation of his techniques and thus reinforced the impact of both. And he learned that for himself as artist, small is indeed beautiful. Small and connected scenes, viewed at the closest possible angle of narration, would make the best of his coming novels. Each episode, each short story, is "like planting a seed of grain that grows and spreads out a little more each time."[28]

28. Gaines, quoted in Simpson, 193.

4

The Trauma of Choice

Catherine Carmier

WHEN ERNEST GAINES turned the "little stream" of his adolescent efforts into "Catherine," named for Hemingway's heroine and a girl he himself had loved, he wrote an immense manuscript including all he knew of the culture and people of his boyhood. His editor insisted he cut that to the love story of Jackson Bradley and Catherine Carmier.[1] The finished novel, *Catherine Carmier*, however, is much more than a love story, as its critics have recognized. Their descriptions focus on relationships within the families of the plantation quarters; caste conflicts, past and present, within the Louisiana black community facing changes in old social and racial codes; the psychology of racial prejudice and racial identity; and the struggle for human relationships in this context.[2] The novel expands on all these issues. Taken as a whole, however, it is a story of the struggle for human maturation through choices—choices young people must make when early loves conflict with new loves, when commitments to family,

1. Babb, *EG*, 5–6; CEG, 32–3, 159, 264–5; *PT*, 129; Simpson, 143–4.
2. Rowell, "Quarters" 741–4; Grant, 171; Davis, 3–13; Hicks, *Singer's*, 106; Noel Schraufnagel, *From Apology to Protest: The Black American Novel* (Deland, Fla.: Everett/Edwards, 1973), 160; Winifred L. Stoelting, "Human Dignity and Pride in the Novels of Ernest Gaines," *College Language Association Journal* 14 (1971): 341.

race, culture, and religion collide with the need to move independently beyond the limits of those communities. As in the short stories, individual movement away from the quarters community is expected and reluctantly supported for young men; commitment to home folks and values is expected, and virtually required, of young women. The novel takes the boys of the stories into young adulthood, when manhood is still to be defined. It enlarges on "Mary Louise" by reintroducing the choices facing young women. It is a story of the question of whether, in their circumstances, young people can choose at all—freely choose any love at all.

The main interest of the novel is the situation itself, the dilemmas that faced young blacks in the 1960s, specifically in southern Louisiana, where all choices were still conditioned by inter- and intraracial codes and conflicts and by the long history in which these had already been played out. In that context young men and women faced different demands, options, and limitations. What constitutes freedom, promise, and progress for Jackson and Catherine, and, by extension, for other young black males and females—what can and will they choose? That is the broad question of the novel.

So broad a question seemed to justify, indeed necessitate, a novel with dual protagonists, male and female, and techniques to make them individuals as well as representatives of the situation. Commenting on the balance of interest between Jackson and Catherine, Gaines said, "I don't see it as Catherine's story more than Jackson's" (CEG, 159). Despite the final title (chosen in last-minute frustration, according to the author[3]), the novel attempts this balancing act. It seems to focus first on Jackson's dilemma: stay in the stultifying atmosphere of the plantation to teach, as his aunt desires and believes she has a right to demand, or drift back to California's less virulent racism for an undefined future. The story then shifts emphasis to Catherine's equally severe choice: stay as moral support to her possessive father and emotionally abused mother or leave them for the dubious freedom and future offered by Jackson's love. Neither young person seems meant to be subordinate in the other's story. The two are joined in a fierce dilemma, made poignant by the kind and number of obstacles to their union.

Carefully balanced obstacles are embedded in the situations of their lives: Catherine is a light-skinned Creole, Catholic, minimally educated, and untraveled beyond the local town; Jackson is black, Protestant or nothing, and returned

3. Gaines had decided on "Catherine." The editor required a longer name, so Gaines said to use her last name, anything "as long as I don't have to think up another title" (Simpson, 144). This, of course, overlooked the importance of titles.

from higher education in the West. An even larger barrier to their union appears almost at once. It is implied (if not obvious) that Jackson's growth need is to stay, at least long enough to draw from his roots an inner freedom, to stop roaming, to gain a purpose that includes the growth and freedom of others. Catherine's psychic need, on the other hand, is to go, to break her father's hold and follow her heart to freedom. As Thadious Davis puts it, Jackson sees Catherine as his life and thinks he must escape with her to save it; Catherine sees Louisiana as her life and is trapped by her own feelings for it.[4] Thus, if Jackson goes, it must be to act on a freely chosen purpose; if Catherine stays, it must be a choice made in the freedom of love. Each wants yet does not want both options: Jackson because he sees the plantation as a burial ground for the living yet knows California offers only a more subtle racism and no clear goal for work, Catherine because she knows she is a prisoner of her parents' needs yet is emotionally bound by custom and compassion. Jackson thinks he cannot change the cultural limitations imposed by the whites and internalized by his people; Catherine knows she cannot prevent the coming drive of Cajun tractors over her father's land and pride.

Despite all the parallels and seeming equality of the two main characters, this novel could not quite stay on the balance wire (if, in fact, any novel can). Catherine may be seen first and may often be more vivid and compelling in her pain than Jackson, but from the moment Jackson gets off the bus, he predominates. He absorbs far more of the novel's space and concern than does Catherine; his internal conflict is more fully represented; his choice becomes the focus, at least until the final chapters. Catherine, though far more than a minor character, is not a true protagonist. Rather, she is "the first figure *after* the protagonist, the one most closely associated with [his] happiness or misery. . . ."[5] As such she requires fuller presentation than any lesser characters, and some of the novel's finest sections are devoted to her. But their very fineness helps create the imbalance that shows up in the problem areas of the novel, especially in its structure and viewpoint.

Yet another issue of coherence in the novel is its overall tone. Almost from the beginning it seems certain that no happy resolution is possible. Both lovers seem fated, he to drift, she to be her father's keeper. Consequently, some discussions of the novel speak of its plot, and especially its heroine, as tragic. Gaines had read widely in Greek tragedy and felt he had approximated elements of it in

4. Davis, 10.

5. Mary Ellen Doyle, *The Sympathetic Response: George Eliot's Fictional Rhetoric* (Rutherford, N.J.: Fairleigh Dickinson University Press, 1981), 60.

this novel. But if we place the lovers up against the protagonists of classical trag-edy, their fates do not rouse any such pity and terror. Nor does their story seem to fit the wider Victorian understanding of tragedy as "an action culminating in a disaster of great finality, affecting a person of high potential and destroying his or her ultimate hope of happiness or success."[6] The height of potential in both lovers is arguable. The ending leaves Jackson with the hope given by Della that Catherine will come to him, but even if she does not, his life is not yet a disaster. This novel is not a tragedy. It does, however, fit Sheldon Sacks's definition of a "serious action," a story with characters we care about in unstable relationships whose shiftings can be resolved happily or unhappily. A "serious action" is not a failed tragedy; its effect depends not on the force of inevitability but on ambi-guity in the possible consequences of the characters' choices. The outcome need not be foreseeable or fixed until near the end.[7]

This "very young man's book" (CEG, 162) offers two questions for the criti-cal reader: What seems to be Gaines's unreached intention, and what, certainly, is his achievement? Either approach calls for analysis of his deployment of a se-ries of techniques: structure that parallels the two main characters and joins them in one struggle; controlled and measured interest in all the characters; se-lective use of viewpoint; a style spare enough to match their lean options, yet not dull, especially not in dialogue; and an outcome that is either clearly resolved or meaningfully ambiguous. Such analysis and evaluation helps explain the out-come of the author's "reach."

Gaines has reported in numerous interviews that form and structure were his main concern as he rewrote *Catherine Carmier*, with Turgenev's "simple, small book," *Fathers and Sons*, as his "Bible" and mentor (CEG, 60, 92). If the focus of interest is to be on the possibilities of choice for young black people, then narrative structure must offer quick insight into the problem of Jackson and Catherine, their outer circumstances and inner dilemmas. From then on it must balance them in the reader's consciousness and concern in proportion to their importance, must offer further insight into their characters and situations; it must offer a sense of probable, if not inexorable, denouement. Gaines accom-plishes this effectively yet imperfectly. One reader felt the lack of "quick in-sight": "I found the early chapters of the book slow going. I was not relating to or sympathetic to any of the characters, simply because I did not quite know what their problem was or . . . its source. I needed more information . . . than I

6. Ibid., 90, n. 3.
7. Sacks, 15, 20–3.

was getting."[8] The problem is one of making the situation paramount without obscuring the characters.

To solve it, Gaines employs structure, first by dividing the novel into three parts. Part 1 (five chapters) first sets up the situation and its psychosocial setting. At the store, where Jackson's return is discussed, racial prejudice is alive in storekeeper Claude's behavior: he ignores, delays, curses, and throws the mail at his black customer. For blacks, everything else is dying: the Cajuns are taking the land; farming for blacks is "all gone"; there is nothing for Jackson to come home to; and as an educated black, he will be feared as one of "Them things there. . . . Them demonstrate people."[9] In the next three chapters, Catherine is seen, barely heard, and then immediately merged back into her family's history, which illustrates the three kinds of racial conflict dominant in the novel: Creole versus landowning white (Robert Carmier versus Mack Grover), Creole versus black (the Carmiers versus their neighbors in the quarters), and Creole versus Cajun (the race to the derrick). This sight of Catherine before Jackson and the substantial account of her background establish her as a character of either equal or secondary importance to him. Chapter 5 then brings Jackson home to meet Catherine, with Brother and Lillian as background. The immediate attraction is obvious: Lillian's interest in promoting it is hinted clearly, and Brother states to his friend the potential conflict with Raoul. The central issue is identified as this chapter ends: "Nobody has taken her from him yet?" "And nobody go'n do it" (20).

The balancing of the two main characters is then forwarded by a four-chapter block on each of them. Chapters 6 through 9 set the trap for Jackson in his homecoming: his great-aunt believes that her prayers to have him back permanently have been answered, and she will never willingly let him go. These chapters end with Jackson's intent to leave. Chapters 10 through 13, on Lillian's homecoming, reveal the trap already clutching Catherine; Lillian's desire that Catherine leave with her is nullified by Catherine's compulsion to stay and her mother's willingness to sacrifice her, lest she now be "the one to hurt him" (59).

This precise balance of four-chapter blocks is tipped, however, by the nine chapters that complete part 1. They are solidly concerned with Jackson, his character and his questions, a focus required to establish him and his plight solidly in the reader's awareness. These chapters also have a pattern. Again, the setting

8. John Doyle to Mary Ellen Doyle, June 6, 1995. In Doyle's possession.

9. Gaines, *Catherine Carmier* (San Francisco: North Point Press, 1981), 5, 7. All citations are from this edition.

and situation are established first; before Jackson awakes, the people of the quarters come together and talk. The young men are thinking about leaving: "nothing but starving here." "But," object the older men, "where you go? What you do?" (61). These are exactly the questions Jackson must wrestle with. When he wakes and reluctantly joins the party in his honor, he is clearly "out of it," having no interest in the quarters' people, culture, or conversation; he is "as lost for words as they" (67). Only his old teacher, Madame Bayonne, can bring him out a little; she is now established as his mentor, his one source of full and accurate information and of realistic or moral outlook. After Madame Bayonne, Jackson converses directly with the two women who want to possess him, Mary Louise and Aunt Charlotte; to neither can he speak with satisfaction, for them or for himself. Into his nonconversation with Mary Louise is inserted his memory of racism in California, which, though painful, has disabled him for endurance of the worse variety in Louisiana. Finally, the conflict with his aunt is dramatized in their confrontation over his owning cards and disowning the church. Their previous loving relationship is then essentially at an end. Jackson sees himself as "dry, dead"; he is utterly alone, having effectively cut all possible relationships with blacks (102). He has no reason to stay in Louisiana—he thinks. As part 1 ends, two questions are left for the reader. Can Catherine be any part of Jackson's solution? And, structurally, will the next two parts create a balance of interest in Catherine by a similar in-depth exploration of her situation and dilemma?

Part 2 does not immediately switch the focus to Catherine; it remains for four more chapters on Jackson, with Catherine present only in Madame Bayonne's story. Much as she may be pining for Jackson in her paternally imposed seclusion, her situation cannot change until he begins to reach out to her, or someone else creates an occasion for them. The business of part 2 is to bring the lovers together to expose Catherine's conflicted feelings and create her dilemma, then to separate them long enough to create a demand—in them and in readers—for some essential solution. This pattern of movement and interaction is reflected in the pattern of chapters linked to elements of time.

Schematically, the chapters are arranged in blocks of twos and fives: In chapters 23 and 24, Jackson drifts alone, in tension with his aunt, while Mary Louise's futile love is rehearsed from within her own mind. This period leaves him ripe for a change, any change to relieve his loneliness and indecision and to give him a reason for further action. The love action is prepared in chapters 25 and 26 by Madame Bayonne's account to Jackson of Della Carmier's and Catherine's previous love affairs and the sons that resulted. We now have a similar insight into

Catherine's loneliness and vulnerability to any change that feels like genuine love.

Chapters 27 through 31 present the four nights of love—in walks on the road, at the club in Bayonne, and in the rooming house in Baton Rouge. Because Catherine has to make escapes from home, the narration has to follow her moves and decisions more than Jackson's; her dilemma becomes almost as clear and important as his has been so far. The rapid, night-after-night development of their passion accentuates the need—for them and for readers—to know if this has any genuine and lasting quality that can predict and produce lasting happiness for them. Nights of love are followed in chapters 32 through 36 by four nights and days of separation—from Catherine's frightened search for and tender encounter with her father in the field, through Jackson's pained night watches for her, their tortured encounters, and his crisis with Charlotte. The separation begins and ends with Catherine and Raoul together, a harbinger of the ultimate arrangement. Jackson is back where he was at the start of part 2, separated even more from his aunt—essentially alone.

In a final two-chapter block (chapters 37 and 38), Reverend Armstrong's ministry reconciles Charlotte to Jackson's decision to leave, and their relationship returns to the distant tension that precedes and follows each of their crises. Now his indecision is maintained not only by his uncertainty about where to go and what to do, but also by his desperate need to know if he can entice Catherine to go with him. Then comes the letter from Lillian. When Jackson chooses to go to the dance at her instigation, he has made his decision even if he has not fully articulated it to himself. He will try to meet Catherine, try to entice her again into love, into elopement, and will leave with her as fast as necessary to escape her father. The great unknown is whether Catherine can make such a break. Part 3 creates the balancing focus on Catherine that part 1 placed on Jackson. It, too, is patterned in chapter groups, three each before, during, and after the dance.

Before the dance, chapters 39 through 41 backtrack to show Catherine looking for Jackson for five days, as he has been seen looking for her. During the immediate preparations for the dance, Lillian asks Catherine to leave with her; this prepares both Catherine and the reader for the ultimate plea from Jackson before the night is out. Finally, the first view of Raoul from deep within somewhat explains the strength of Catherine's love for him in competition with her love for Jackson. Chapters 42 through 44, at the dance, call for crucial decisions from all three principals in this part: Jackson, Catherine, and Raoul. After the dance, in chapters 45 through 47, the attempted elopement is aborted by Raoul's arrival and the fight with Jackson. In the end, Jackson has chosen and acted, even if unwisely. He lacks a mature view of the long span of married life; still, he has chosen. Catherine, on the other hand, is mortally torn throughout—in thought, speech, and action. For this reason, Della's prediction cannot be verified nor carry more weight than the final action: Catherine's following her father into the house, Jackson waiting outside, alone. The ambiguity of the end, however, is an issue not of the novel's structure but of its theme.

It could be argued that the three-part structure, developing first Jackson's problem, then the joint problem of union and separation, and finally Catherine's dilemma, successfully balances knowledge of and concern for two protagonists. But not successfully enough. Part 3 is much shorter than part 1, fifty pages versus one hundred, nine chapters versus twenty-two. Of those twenty-two, only four are devoted to Catherine's home situation. The fierce intensity of her pain and struggle, combined with Raoul's psychotic desperation, does offset Jackson's "dry and dead" state, which seems to have consumed a disproportion of space. Yet if most readers were asked to title the book with the name of one character only, the one of most concern, the title would surely be *Jackson Bradley*.

The internal structuring of the three parts by blocks of related chapters has been noted. The design of those blocks, the relationship of their chapters, bears closer examination. The segment that deals with Jackson's homecoming, for instance, begins and ends with Charlotte and Mary Louise. In chapters 6 and 7, they await anxiously the sound of the bus horn and watch the arrival out on the road. Only half of chapters 7 and 8 are given to the actual encounter and strained conversation with this long-awaited and much-desired young man. In chapter 9, the two women discuss him and their wishes for his future. The chapters have flowed into each other with continuity and little or no time lapse in between. The effect is a foreboding awareness of the women's hopes and possessiveness; they want to enclose and possess Jackson. All time with him is too short. But he cannot respond and will seek every chance to evade their company and escape their claims. By contrast, the segment on the Carmiers that follows Lillian's arrival begins with Catherine and Lillian, the latter of whom challenges their father's illusions, and ends with Catherine and Della, the latter of whom admonishes her not to destroy those illusions. The chapters in between are divided by small time gaps for off-page activity or mere waiting. In this dismal family, time stretches out painfully, prolonging the distress of people at odds, physically together yet emotionally disconnected, with nothing to say to each other to unify them.

Throughout the novel, most of the chapters are divided according to natural switches in time, location, action, or actors: chapters 3 and 4, Raoul's background and marriage—the Carmier children; chapters 19 and 20, the end of the party—Jackson's walk home with Mary Louise. Some chapter breaks, however, occur where they might be least expected. The only significant conversation between Jackson and Mary Louise covers two chapters. The break emphasizes disappointed expectations: Charlotte's at the end of chapter 20, Mary Louise's at the start of chapter 21. Chapters 17 and 18 also divide a conversation, Jackson's with Madame Bayonne. She has been telling him of the changes wrought by the Cajuns' takeover of the land; in that context, "keeping your nose clean" is the price of peace, which she wants. "Don't we all?" asks Jackson. An enforced pause by chapter break invites the reader to reflect that peace by acquiescence may be acceptable for one too old to go elsewhere, but not for a twenty-two-year-old. The next chapter starts with an equally jarring question, emphasized by position, "Why did you come back, Jackson?" (78), which implies to both him and the reader, "And what will become of you here?" Yet another of their conversations, in which she tells him the history of Della's and Catherine's sons, is interrupted by the break between chapters 25 and 26. Granting that each chapter spotlights one woman's affair, the real cause for division is her pronouncement, "Catherine has been the only person in the world to mean anything to him [Raoul]. There's no one else. There can't ever be anyone else" (117). Its position at the chapter's end brings the sentence down like the final gavel in a courtroom scene. And finally, chapters 28 and 29 are one continuous evening episode; the chapter break between Jackson's declaration of love and Catherine's reentry into her house and family sharpens the terms of her choice and the parallelism of Jackson and Raoul.

Parallelism of characters is a pervasive substructure throughout the novel. Critics have noted it in relation to various themes or subplots: unfulfilled familial or erotic love; the inability to handle change and the search for refuge in nature, real or remembered; and characters as replacements for what others have lost or never had.[10] The parallelism extends into all sorts of functions and relationships, and it serves to reinforce the central parallelism of Jackson and Catherine as children whom a parent seeks to possess, who must resist these claimants if they are to find a purpose and freely choose to fulfill it. They fail in the end, ironically, because of another parallelism: Catherine is concerned for both her father and his aunt, and Jackson has shared her admiration for Raoul as a man who has "stood" and fought for his claims. He cannot fight her compassion or defeat her decision.

10. Rowell, "Territory," 5–6; Babb, *EG*, 50; Davis, 8.

The position of Jackson and Catherine as parallel (but still unequal) main characters is reinforced by parallels of subordinate characters. Most obvious is Raoul's and Charlotte's possessiveness of an adult child; no lover is allowed. That parallels Mary Louise with Charlotte, both desiring Jackson as a life companion; their yearning reveals the bleakness of plantation women's lives, without significance or pride except in the importance of a man whose devotion they can publicly claim. And it parallels Brother and Lillian, the one cautioning against any hope of romance, the other urging that caution be thrown to the wind.

Much more subtle is the parallelism of Jackson and Catherine with various minor characters. Catherine and Mary Louise both have their lives on hold, devoted to a parent figure while they wait and long for Jackson. Catherine and Della are women required to love and serve Raoul, women who each tried to love another man and bore his child, to her own lasting grief. Lillian is the daughter who was sent away and then goes of her own choice, Catherine the daughter who is held captive at home and cannot choose to go. And she is held not only by Raoul's need or threats, but also because she is like him in her pride, obsessive love, and inability to imagine any real life off their land. Jackson obviously is matched with Raoul as rival for Catherine and object of her compulsive and competitive passion. Finally, their competition creates parallels between Jackson and characters we never see. Like the Cajuns, Jackson threatens to take something Raoul most prizes, the source of his dignity and sense of meaning and relationship. Like Marky, Jackson is the black "son" Raoul will not accept or claim; the fight at the end is really between Marky and Raoul, as Della specifically states.

Jack Hicks states that the structural parallels show the "bleak helplessness" in the characters' lives, but that the parallels seem mechanical and the characters fairly lifeless.[11] While this judgment may stand about the most obvious parallels (Raoul and Jackson, Raoul and Charlotte), the wider web of comparison and contrast indicates well the thick mesh of relationships that ensnares both protagonists. And if the characters, especially Jackson, are somewhat impassive, that is not wholly due to a young writer's flawed efforts. Their lack of vitality is at least symbolically apt; there is no life for them on the "dry and dead" land.

Important as structure is for achieving and balancing interest in characters, direct depiction is more so. The two main characters must be made sufficiently sympathetic in themselves that readers can understand, feel, and respond to their divergent options, their difficulties, and their final choices—if any. The depic-

11. Hicks, *Singer's,* 107.

tion of other characters must also be vivid, to engage reader interest and response; purposeful, to reveal their personalities more clearly; and proportional,
to keep the focus on Jackson and Catherine. Every other relationship must serve
as a window into that of the lovers, shaping it, foreshadowing and justifying its
outcome. In all this, the novel is remarkably, though not wholly, successful.

Jackson Bradley at twenty-two, after ten years in California, has returned to
Louisiana with a college degree and awareness of his altered relationship to both
black and white, but with less imaginative sensitivity than he had as a boy, no
sense of adult purpose, and almost no voice. His story makes him a warning
within his own culture of the personal hazards of education and choice. Schooling has given him a sense of dignity that will not allow him to cooperate with the
indignities nor accept the limits that white society imposes. But he has almost no
communal bond left either, no zeal to be one of the "demonstrate people," to
integrate a "stupid grocery store" (7, 174–5).[12] He does not know where he is
going yet has an impatient contempt for those who are going nowhere. And
there is his real danger. Other blacks, Creoles, and Cajuns know that he knows
them, intuit his judgment of his own superiority; if he stays in Louisiana, the
blacks will leave him alone and the Cajuns will watch to see if he oversteps racial
bounds. Since he has no desire to share a lunch counter with any of them, the
danger for Jackson is not death but profound alienation. His education has
turned him not toward activism but completely inward to his own concern.
Should he try to relieve alienation by sexual passion alone, a woman may be in
danger from him.

In simple truth, Jackson Bradley is seldom depicted as a sympathetic or very
likable character. He has rarely written from California; he has come back to
Louisiana only to cut his ties; he seems able to love no one effectively or demon-
stratively any more. Because he has lost his sense of belonging in the quarters
community, he has also lost the courtesy that belongs to its culture: he either
sleeps through or deliberately stays away from most of his homecoming party and
then leaves it early. Nor does he show any interest or respectful love to those
once closest to him, his old friends and the older folk who have loved and supported him, especially his aunt. To Charlotte he is truly cruel. He is justified in
his resistance to her intruding, supervising, and correcting as if he were still a
child, and certainly he can be pitied for his dilemma about causing her pain by
his decision not to stay and teach. But he plans an elopement without any consideration for her, and he almost never speaks to her voluntarily. When she be-

12. Cf. Beavers, 134–6, on the risks in Jackson's education.

gins to express her long-held hopes, he does "not make the slightest gesture," is "as silent as he had been before" (98).

It is this lack of voice that makes Jackson both a too-distant and a barely sympathetic character, despite his near omnipresence in parts 1 and 2. He cannot or will not make an effort to communicate; he is hopelessly unable to engage in the simplest conversation or to tell anything about himself. He initiates the conversation with Mary Louise only because he needs her help; he neither shares himself nor takes her counsel. Even to Madame Bayonne, in all their thirteen-page conversation, he speaks only questions or short responses, only the briefest self-explanatory statements. All that he learns from her he could have learned earlier by initiating a conversation with Brother, the men, or his aunt. Later, he avoids responding to her history of the Carmiers and to her advice. With Catherine, he speaks first with pretended indifference, then brief invitations and passionate expressions, but never real dialogue. And when Jackson does finally respond to Charlotte, he offers her a rationalization for quitting the church, an accusation that his condition is her fault, and a bald assertion of disbelief in her religion, "that bourgeois farce" (99–100). This is "what he started not to say"; it is also the only time in the novel that he speaks to her as many as six consecutive sentences. Only after his crisis with Catherine (chapter 33), in anger, does he speak at length to Charlotte, and that speech is unrecorded except in its devastating effect on her (162). Had Gaines given Jackson more real dialogue, we might have known him better; it is not at all certain that we would have liked him better or approved of him.

Yet negative as much of Jackson Bradley's personality and behavior seem to be, it is unlikely that readers can completely lose interest in or sympathy for him. He is not presented as totally without sensitivity to others. He seems to wish he could respond to Charlotte and Brother as in the past; he is disturbed by what he hears and sees of the changes and losses of his people. He is badly frightened that Charlotte might be dead from the shock he gave her; he attempts to help her caregivers. These may be small interludes in his otherwise self-absorbed behavior, but they count. And there is just enough evidence of what he was before he went to California—warm playmate to Catherine, loved by her loving mother; inseparable friend of Brother; devoted and docile child to his aunt; and best, brightest student of Madame Bayonne—to make one ask, as Charlotte does, "What they did to you, Jackson? What they did to you up there?" (101). No reader at all familiar with either the racism in the South or the less blatant version of it in California can fail to resonate to his memories of what, in fact, life there has done to him. Jackson is an inversion of the westering myth, a walking critique of the American imagination of California. Westward movement has not provided him with an expansive sense of independence and opportunity, nor with any specific ideals, purpose, or hope of satisfying achievement. Readers who understand all this must pity him and hope for something—or someone—to help him find his way.

But the novel offers little hope that Catherine Carmier can be that someone. In his world, crossed with barriers of race, age, gender, geography, culture, and custom, Jackson cannot define a meaning or an ethic for life beyond a general wish not to hurt anyone he loves. In his last novel, Gaines will make that wish the impetus for rousing a "dead" man to real humanity. But here, without a more developed ethic, Jackson cannot really love maturely. Thadious Davis says he is seeking a romantic solution to real racism, a way both to retain the past through Catherine's love for Louisiana and to escape it by taking her away.[13] Even though a courtship circumscribed by Raoul's and Charlotte's unjust demands and norms must be conducted in such secretive and unhealthy ways, Jackson pushes it in a manner that further reveals his self-absorption. During the tryst in Baton Rouge, he is moved by passion ready to develop into genuine love. But as yet he is just using this woman to relieve his loneliness and burdened spirit. He speaks only of what she is giving to him, an undefined "life" and the "light" he needs to see over "the wall" of racism (148–9). He does not see that mutual giving is required for mutual happiness. If committed in love, he could "take it" or fight racism for her sake; he might also mature enough to be a father to her son. Without a commitment, Catherine is merely a powerful distraction from pain; her son is a nonentity, a factor not to be considered in a decision but merely brought along with the suitcases. Should she cease to be that distraction or become unhappy in their place of escape, his love for her could become even less than that he feels for his aunt.

In his self-concern, Jackson actually destroys any hope of Catherine's free choice by the speed and force he applies to her decision-making process. A walk one night, a beer in a night spot the second, and lovemaking in a rented room the third, when he asks her to be his "life": hardly the way to get to know her, to explore hopes and values, to loosen other lifelong ties, to form and tighten a new bond strong enough to last for life, not the vague "life" this "dry and dead" man wants to draw from her but a life of years and years of shared experience and love. When Catherine imposes their four-night separation, Jackson may well ask if all she wanted was "just once in bed," but he is brutal in his frenzy to get

13. Davis, 9.

her to take more (160). When he tries to elope with her, he really allows her no more freedom to think, feel, and choose than Raoul allows in trying to stop her. Every sort of psychological, emotional, and physical tugging is used to get her to "Come with me. . . . Come with me. . . . Come. . . . Come. . . . Come. . . . Come. . . . Come" (22–3). Not a fair way to win a fair and free lady. After the fight, his pleas are more reasoned, more respectful of her pain; but it is too late. Or, rather, it has all been too soon.

At the novel's end, Jackson has a clearer view of Catherine's need to be free than of his own goals and motives. Despite Della's hopeful admonition to wait, it is evident that any waiting by Jackson will be more from continued indecision than from love; nor is it at all evident whether or where he will wait. For him, as for any young black man in his time, a southern plantation could be a kind of "hole" or prison cell (à la Richard Wright and Ralph Ellison), where he could choose to wait, to do interior exploration, find self-knowledge, and come up into the freedom of purpose and choice. But for a young man of Gaines's creation, achievement of freedom requires loving acceptance of his connection to his people. Jack Hicks sees Jackson as finally unable to make a life anywhere or any way, disconnected as he is from his bloodline and racial history and so without hope of personal history.[14] We must pity him. Yet his "blame" for hurting himself and others leaves a thematic question: is blame a negative judgment on Jackson or a statement of the simple, inescapable human responsibility to make a choice?

Jackson, however, comes closer to free choice than does Catherine. Davis has noted that Gaines has taken the stereotypical figure of Louisiana literature, the tragic mulatto woman, and given her a realistic social setting and family history;[15] these both condition her choice and make it comprehensible. The critical question is whether he has also given her enough vivid and distinctive personality to make a real choice and to make readers understand or care what it is.

In all of part 1, Catherine is quite a shadowy figure, seen through others as adjunct to her parents or to Jackson. Even when she becomes the focus of narrative attention (chapters 11 through 13), she is seen from without and given almost no voice to reveal temperament or predict future action; Lillian expatiates, but Catherine responds as little as possible. One can read this part without noting much beyond generic sweetness, affection, and sadness for her family, conditioning by their demands and biases, and reserved friendliness to her black neighbors. She is making a life from her parents' need, from doing "what I think

14. Hicks, "Bones," 9–10.
15. Davis, 10–1.

is best" (45); there is little or no hint that she can or will ever choose to think otherwise—or act on what she thinks.

Parts 2 and 3 do reveal Catherine more sharply and, by putting her alone with both Jackson and her father, give an intensifying view of her conflicting desires and shredded emotions. She puts herself in Jackson's way and tries to take herself out; she knows she cannot leave so tries to convince herself he might stay. But she knows well that she can never marry and stay near her father, so she is really hoping to have more Baton Rouge nights and "not feel like a bitch afterward" (135). In hoping to keep this up, she is playing unfairly with Jackson; when she agrees to end the struggle by elopement, she cannot keep her promise. She is more a pitiful than a truly sympathetic character; that pity is compelling simply because no woman should have to endure what she does or make such painful choices, not because her portrayal is so vital and captivating.

Catherine cannot make a free, even if excruciating, choice, first because of her relationship to her father, which readers are asked to understand with compassion though obviously not to approve. Evidence is insufficient to say it is incestuous, and Gaines has averred that that was "the last thing that *I* had in mind" (*CEG*, 161). Nevertheless, her portrait indicates that this relationship is, if not physically, at least emotionally disordered. Raoul's possessiveness has created in Catherine a manner of substituting him for the masculine partner he will never allow her to have. Instead of his wife, it is Catherine who waits up for his return from town at night, makes his tea, and sits in the kitchen with him. The two have been together so long that "each could tell when the other was holding back something" (133–4). As a grown woman, she retains her habit of taking his hand "whenever she felt troubled or thought he was troubled" (145). Before the dance, she tells him he must take a bath "if you're going with me"—as one might speak to a date or a husband whose wish to please could be counted on (203). The night she searches for and finds him in the field, she is just "happy to be near him . . . loving him as much as she had ever loved Jackson" (153). Her cries of "Do you love me, Daddy? . . . I love you so much, Daddy" are like those she'd give Jackson or any other lover (154). They notify the reader that any abnormality in love is as much in her emotion as in her father's. Indeed, these cries are less questions or assurances to him than to her own captive heart, promises to herself that she will never leave him. A reader expects the promise to be kept.

Jackson's pressure, depriving Catherine of true freedom to choose, has been noted. However, she bears her own responsibility for neither effectively claiming her right to choose nor approaching a decision wisely. This, too, is a result of her lack of voice within her family, her community, within herself. No one is privy to her confidence; with no one does she take counsel. Granted, in Lillian she has a biased advisor; her aunts in Bayonne would advise by the Creole code, and there seems to be no one else. But Lillian would at least have served as a sounding board; and her aunt Elvira knows her unwholesome position with her father. At the very least, the lonely girl could have demanded time to think and resolve. Instead, she flounders amid silent, conflicting impulses and fleeting resolutions, surrenders in one word only, then recants. She cannot claim her own will because she has none. The ambiguity of the ending is an issue to be considered fully, but, if "not to choose is to choose," then Catherine may have made a more definite choice than Jackson. The thematic question of blame is also hers.

As the main characters must be flawed yet sympathetic if readers are to feel serious concern for their fates, so must their principal antagonists, Jackson's Aunt Charlotte and Catherine's father, Raoul. Both are possessive, resistant to any competing love or to marriage for their children. Yet neither is villainous; each has some legitimate claim to consideration. Their same selfishness has significant differences—and consequences.

Charlotte exemplifies the major temptation of those who rear their young at a high cost—to claim an equal sacrifice in return and so crush their freedom. Charlotte not only requires Jackson to "be somebody" (98); she has decided how and where he will be. The details of her preparation for his arrival indicate the depth of her emotion and expectations and therefore the potential for conflict if she is disappointed. Jackson's return, she asserts, is the work of God for her; so she claims its permanence in a location where she can "see him as much as she wanted to" (36). Her jealousy and fear of Mary Louise and Catherine, and her intrusions on Jackson's privacy and liberty, signal early conflict; when he rejects the God who sent him home, she in essence rejects him. He eats and sleeps in her house but has not really "returned home." She finally quits the effort to talk to him; he has never really made the effort for her. In a culture that is essentially vocal, Charlotte most harshly punishes Jackson for her disappointment by dead, cold silence.

But Charlotte can also emerge from resentment, can change. Chapter 37, seemingly disconnected from the flow of the novel, is needed to reveal this potential and contrast her with the protagonists. Unlike Catherine, she has in Reverend Armstrong an advisor of kindness and good counsel; unlike Jackson with Madame Bayonne, she will follow his wisdom.[16] She still can't say much to Jack-

---

16. Contrary to much criticism of Gaines, he did portray a sympathetic minister before his last novel.

son, but she will let him go. And that serves not only to redeem her selfishness in his regard, but also to spotlight his inability to reciprocate by even a simple gesture or thank-you. He cannot stop to consider what her gesture of forgiveness and release costs her; his consideration for her extends only to whether or not he should wait until she is well in order to "make it up to her some kind of way and then . . . get out of here" (185). His self-concern now makes Charlotte a more sympathetic character than her nephew.

Charlotte's letting go also serves to enforce her similarity yet contrast to Raoul. Alvin Aubert has described him as a kind of Faustian figure, the universal, tragic overreacher, victim of his own hubris who finally destroys his family and his own best chances for happiness.[17] Unlike Charlotte, he is a stronger personality than the child he seeks to control. He must, therefore, be seen just enough, and just unsympathetically enough, to create appropriate concern for Catherine, yet must have enough redeeming grace to allow sympathy for her choice. So, in part 1 we see that he, too, lacks voice, has none for his daughter Lillian, only "dry and abrupt" answers for Catherine, and false or insensitive put-downs for his wife. Yet through Della's grieving loyalty and continued love, we glimpse that Raoul may once have been something better; once he had the character to court her in opposition to his own family. Part 2 accentuates Raoul's selfish power through Madame Bayonne's blunt, insightful account of his marrying Della for "convenience," isolating her, and then punishing her "fall" by making her only a field hand. By implication, the story also explains his attitude toward Lillian, the failure of one last attempt to have a legitimate son, dismissed from home and ignored on her return. Raoul the monster, however, is humanized when seen through Catherine: she is proud of his stand against Cajun power; he is sensitive to her troubled demeanor; he does allow her some youthful pleasures. The field scene argues against a theory of incestuous love; she is his substitute for a son, not for a wife, and she knows it.[18]

Until part 3, the outline of Raoul's character has been filled in only gradually and only as others see him. Then a new and fuller portrait is painted, with lights and darks almost in balance to explain Catherine's coming torturous choice. He has brief regrets about Lillian. When his sister fights him, one has to pity Raoul—and still more when the Cajuns and two blacks manipulate and confuse

---

17. Aubert, "Mulatto," 69–71.

18. Cf. Joseph Griffin, "Creole and Singaleese: Disruptive Caste in *Catherine Carmier* and *A Gathering of Old Men*," in *CRF*, 34–7, for explication of the Carmiers' objection to Della, light-skinned but not Creole, and of Raoul's blind indifference to his living grandson, Nelson.

him so that he will murder and lose his land. His moment of pity for Catherine ("Of course she was lonely. A girl at that age . . .") is offset by his pulling his gun to reclaim her for himself (226–7). He remembers having loved Marky, yet he could not let him live. He does not want to kill again even as he is about to do so. He is tenacious in the fight with Jackson, gets to his feet when closest to defeat, the very quality that Jackson has admired in him. He acknowledges that Catherine has "been the prop long enough" (244) but cannot refuse her intent to continue to be. On his account, too, Della's final prediction is questionable. Raoul, beaten yet still powerful, seems less a fallen man to be lifted up than a rock crushing down the prop that supports him—and will still support him.

The minor characters are mostly in the background, commenting on or trying unsuccessfully to influence the action. If this were a tragedy, they might be called a chorus. Della is a most necessary explanation for Catherine's character, a warning of what trouble will come if she defies Raoul and what an isolated, miserable life she will live if she does not. A student once demanded, "How can Della bear all this punishment? She is a disgusting character. She has no self respect. She sacrifices both her daughters."[19] This harsh judgment may be rather widely shared. Certainly Della is what modern psychology has called a "woman who loves too much," who lives in denial of the truth about an unworthy man and sacrifices herself and her other relationships for him. At the end, she seems to have a wiser view of what should and may be. Readers may want to believe her but still see new life coming too late for Catherine and for her.

Certainly it is too late for Lillian, too late for her ever to be a happy, loving, and loved woman. "Too late" began for her in infancy, when she was taken away, taught to hate the "idle white rich" yet envy them, hate everything black, hate her mother "as an extra subject" and her father (without being taught) (39, 47). Somehow she has learned to love Catherine, but in trying to release her, she is as manipulative as any Cajun and almost as coercive as Jackson. He senses a motive in her, "something deep and evil"; Gaines identified that as "revenge for all three" of them, revenge on the family and the "whole system" (CEG, 161). Her motive is also, surely, justification for her own final act of leaving. Lillian's portrait is almost a moral and emotional negative of Catherine's. She never overpowers her sister in the reader's attention and sympathy, yet she is always hovering in the background, illuminating Catherine's character and choices. When she can do no more, she simply disappears, as if to wander like a restless and unredeemable spirit.

19. Diana Brooks to Mary Ellen Doyle, summer 1995. In author's possession.

Mary Louise serves in the novel as a pale counterpoint to make Catherine vivid and as witness to the limited life Jackson cannot choose. She darkens the outline of Charlotte's possessiveness and Jackson's nonresponse to all previous connections except one. When his and Catherine's love takes over the story, she simply drops out, except as Charlotte's companion. She might have been ex-pendable had she not existed in previous drafts and a short story.

Finally, there are Brother and Madame Bayonne. The former has the intu-itions, practicality, loyalty, and understanding bred by life in the quarters, not by formal education. He represents the intellectual limits Jackson has escaped and spotlights the moral, emotional limits into which he has fallen. The latter is the seer whose knowledge of the past and power to "look through" people in the present give her a virtual omniscience—and to her every word the weight of wisdom. Brother has very little voice, as befits his limitations; Madame Bay-onne's voice is large, as befits an oral historian. Neither is nor should be a self-revealing or affective character, but together they form a chorus of truth-telling and warning heard at every significant point of the developing drama.

The same necessity of revealing two main characters fully and other charac-ters only in relation to them controls the use of viewpoint. It serves as the ulti-mate control over our sympathy for them, over our evaluation of their decisions in light of the freedom and responsibility that belong to fully human persons. This technique is usually seen as *the* problem with the art of this novel; it has produced conflicting interpretations of characters, incidents, and authorial in-tent and objectivity. Certainly it has not produced the insights or the vibrancy of character that Gaines was to achieve later with first-person narrators. Gaines has spoken often of his difficulty with omniscient narration; he feels "trapped" in it, less in control, less able to create a voice distinct from his own (*CEG*, 235, 243; *PT*, 27). However, in attempting dual protagonists, he had no choice but to use the omniscient mode. We have to know the thoughts of both their hearts and, on occasion at least, the thoughts of others about them. Even had he fo-cused only on Jackson as the protagonist, the secondary importance of Catherine would have necessitated inside views of her, probably as many as we now have.

The problem is not with the omniscience of the narrator but with his vacilla-tion between intrusion and reticence. On occasion, the narrator presents infor-mation with explanation or comment that action alone would make clear: "Francois could tell that Paul did not care who Brother's friend was" (7); "That was all they could think of to say. . . . [Jackson] did not care about Lillian's read-ing, he wanted to break the silence" (123). The trouble with these explanations is that they are often tacked on to the end of a passage and weaken its power.

More often the problem is reticence; the narrator offers fewer interior views of the characters than is possible and usual in this mode and is nearly as uninformative as the characters themselves. The only notable exception is in chapters 2 through 4, where the Carmier history is revealed. In chapter 2, Antoine Richard is said to have brought the account of Robert Carmier into the quarters; this is a feature of the oral mode Gaines would later use to his best effect, but the omniscient mode has no need of a reporter-character.[20] Chapters 3 and 4 are dealt straight by the narrator without comment or even suggestive diction; he merely reports what Della and others said and did and the interpretations of folk in the quarters. These two chapters, however, are emotionally effective; the violence done to Robert Carmier, the suppression of Della's sweet nature, and the physical and moral destruction of Mark and Lillian are all more horrific for the understated, factual tone, for the absence of all that an omniscient narrator could say.

After that prelude, the viewpoint is more precisely described as objective-dramatic. The curtain goes up, the action begins, and the characters, like persons on a stage, act out their destinies, revealing themselves by their words, gestures, and actions. As on a stage, the characters supply information and interpret the meanings and motives of others. Jackson's childhood is narrated through Madame Bayonne's and Charlotte's spoken accounts and through the old folks' uninhibited displays of affection for the "skinny boy," the "great little Christian" they knew. Appropriately, either Jackson or Catherine is nearly always on stage. The only notable exceptions to this are in part 1, the opening chapters of the Carmier history, the dialogues of Mary Louise and Charlotte, and the homecoming party before Jackson joins it; in part 2, Mary Louise's internal reflections on her love life, Reverend Armstrong's talk with Charlotte, and the dialogue about Jackson by the people at the store; in part 3, Raoul at his sister's house and in pursuit of Catherine. Of these scenes, Mary Louise's self-reflections might be omitted, since they reveal nothing new about the lovers and serve to blur the focus on them. All the other scenes either explain Jackson or Catherine or prepare for their major appearances. Their almost constant presence enforces their roles as representatives of young people who must choose life or nonlife. Mary Louise, of course, is another young person, but she either has no choice or has never recognized that she has.

While much of the view of Jackson and Catherine—maybe too much—is external and objective, we are given necessary and significant entrées into their

---

20. Cf. the discussions of omniscient narration in Babb, *EG*, 59–60, and Hicks, *Singer's*, 107. Babb sees the style as closer to orality than I do.

thoughts and feelings. Sometimes the narrator exposes Jackson's thoughts: "Everything . . . seemed strange, and yet very familiar" (26); "Aunt Charlotte had really spread the news, hadn't she?" (65). Sometimes he gives words to Jackson's intuitive responses: his embarrassment at holding Charlotte's hand and inability to put his hand on Brother's shoulder. Jackson's memories of California are presented in a manner different from the way he would have recalled them consciously; the narration is far more ordered and coherent and includes a past conversation. The difference suggests that this background might well have been presented "straight," as the Carmier history was, even though Jackson is the only one who knows it. Certainly it is needed to offset the distaste we feel for his introverted, self-absorbed responses to his people. When the love affair begins, the narrator plunges often, deeply, and explicitly into Jackson's viewpoint, his thoughts of Catherine, his battle over being free or tied down, over staying away from her or going to her house or to the dance. When he denies to himself that he loves her and thinks he is "glad that it was over with" (167), we know that he does not know himself and that Catherine needs to shun him until he does.

Interior views of Catherine, by contrast, are scarce and come late in the novel; that is the main reason she is such an enigma for most of the book and seems to be a lesser protagonist than Jackson. In part 1, we see her only from the outside. Her dialogue (what there is of it) tells facts, suggests feelings, but never really lets us behind the wall of her intense privacy. Significant inside views do not begin until midway into part 2, after the walk with Jackson, when she begins to examine her feelings and motives, to struggle between loyalty and desire, and then to arrange contacts. She thinks, "Every time I look at a man, I feel like a bitch," but immediately begins brushing her lovely hair, ties a ribbon in it, then jerks the ribbon out and throws it on the floor (132). We see her feminine reality, sensuous and innocent, and her belief that she cannot be both. Only when she goes to Raoul in the field do we see her long and deeply from within; this prepares for her more tormented vacillations in part 3: "I will be happy. I will not be happy. . . . Our life does not belong to us. . . . No, our life belong to us. . . . I love them. No, I love him. . . . I love you so much, darling. I . . . Louisiana—my life" (231–2). As with her comparatively brief presence in the novel as a whole, the tardy presentation of Catherine's interior viewpoint is offset by its intensity, but it is still too little, too late.

Sometimes, however, the authorial wish to create characters who feel both intensity and confusion of emotion ends in unhelpful confusion of viewpoint. Sometimes it is not clear which mind we are reading, Jackson's or Catherine's or the narrator's: "He must have seen the car come out of the yard. . . . He must have understood why she did not stop. . . ." (138). *Did* Jackson see and so deliberately go to the gate? *Did* he understand and so accept Catherine's method to get him in the car, or did he merely seize an opportunity on impulse? Are these sentences views from his mind, or merely her hopes, or a knowing narrator's assertion? Either the lovers are true collaborators or Jackson is coercive in their meetings, so the questions are not unimportant. But the answers are not clear.

At other times, the lovers attempt to read each other's minds, and the narrator is reading both: "But from the look on her face, this was not half of what she had wanted to say. . . . Maybe she wanted to say. . . . Maybe what she really wanted was. . . . No, not maybe, this is what both of them wanted. . . . Then a little smile came on her mouth. It seemed to say. . . . Then the smile went away, and her eyes said . . . his eyes said . . . her eyes said. His eyes did not answer . . . her eyes said. But still he did not answer" (125). This passage is first Jackson's mind in the act of reading Catherine's; then it seems to be an interior view of her but is still really his reading of her face. And somewhere is an omniscient narrator reading both—but not so clearly or explicitly that readers know more than Jackson thinks he knows.

When the romance is the central focus, presentation of the main characters' viewpoints works more successfully. First the viewpoints alternate, Jackson's in chapters 27 and 28, Catherine's in chapters 29 and 30. He wrestles with the forces of his attraction and his need not to be "tied down"; she vacillates between competing loves. Then, in chapter 31, the night in Baton Rouge, we get a frantic alternation, his-hers-his-hers, and a return to the merged views: "she turned to him, pleading—but pleading what for? To be loved, kissed, to be taken? Or was she pleading for him to leave her . . . ?" (149). Both lovers ask themselves; both are frantic to know.

Because Jackson's and Catherine's inner views are so intense, biased, and often shortsighted or confused, some other characters' views about them are requisite as explanatory or corrective. Gaines said the novel was originally done from multiple viewpoints of people in the quarters. In the switch to omniscience, some of their voices and views were retained (*CEG*, 159–60). Brother notices Jackson's "thin smile" and concludes, "he just won't let go" (25–6). Mary Louise, Lillian, Della, Catherine, and others see the continuation and danger of Jackson's love for Catherine when he is telling himself it is over; his danger from others who love him is revealed in the occasional inner views of Mary Louise, and especially of Charlotte. The thoughts of Della, Lillian, and especially Raoul all serve to reveal and challenge the compulsion that Catherine calls loving duty.

With so little of the narrator's interpretive viewpoint and so much of the views of emotionally unreliable characters, the viewpoint of the author behind the narrator needs to be more easily discernable than it usually is. When Jackson cannot stare down the accusatory old woman, he thinks, "They were like trees, like rocks, like the ocean, these old people. Never understanding, never giving" (171). How much of that judgment is Jackson's and how much is the author's, implying a truth for which we should sympathize with the young protagonist? Gaines denied it was his view; in fact, he explicitly disagreed with it (CEG, 160). Nevertheless, the novel's style invites the question. A reviewer for the *Times Literary Supplement* said that the story is only occasionally and incidentally ironic in tone, that it is delivered so objectively as to "freeze" the characters; but Herman Beavers reads it as steeped in irony, since one must read "against" all the characters.[21] At this stage of his creative progress, Gaines was not able to achieve a consistent narrative tone that conveyed clearly his ultimate view of the situation—ironic, hopeful, hopeless, or simply confused. However, it may be that, instead of being coldly objective, he was, in fact, too empathetically identified with his protagonists, especially Jackson, and was trying to attain appropriate distance.[22]

Though Gaines had not yet found his most workable stance as author/narrator, he was developing notably his use of narrative style and symbolism. Like the story he tells, like his characters and their lives, the style is spare, even bleak, totally without exuberance. Though the narration actually is a composite of various sentence structures—simple, compound, complex, long and short—the overall effect is simple, as if each longer sentence were a series of short ones; this fits characters undergoing a series of short, chilled emotional experiences. Sentences may be genuinely short and abrupt: "Jackson walked away" (96)—the symbolic end to any past romantic relation with Mary Louise, to their short reunion, to her hopes and his attentions. Repetitions and parallel phrases serve a similar end: "stay at the house," "stopped by the house," "stopped by the house—before going to work," "came from work," "before going home—time for church," "after church—back to the house again" (108–9); the monotonous round of the

21. Review in *Times Literary Supplement* (February 10, 1966): 97; Beavers, 139.

22. The novel, however, is not autobiographical. Gaines did return to Louisiana after ten years in California, but his aunt had died five years earlier. There was no Catherine for him, and no one expected that he would stay (*PT*, 130–1). He assured the publishers that the characters were fictional (Simpson, 146–50).

same diction and phrases parallels the monotonous round of Mary Louise's life, the threat to his own life Jackson means to avoid.

By contrast to Gaines's later, highly oral style, this novel offers the barest minimum of dialogue. In early drafts, according to Gaines, minor characters had more conversation. In the final draft, however, these people have almost nothing to say to each other, not even those who love each other, not even when they are acting in love. Jackson is the most taciturn of protagonists. His dialogue with Madame Bayonne only seems fuller because she talks freely. Beavers notes that though Jackson presumably answers her questions about the civil rights movement, his opinions are not rendered in dialogue, thus stressing his egocentric nonparticipation.[23] His failure to converse with Charlotte has been noted. As she pleads with him and with God, he is "silent . . . silent . . . silent . . ." (101). He controls and conceals his feelings at all times until they erupt with Charlotte and Catherine. His character is either wounded to extreme defensiveness or cruelly indifferent.

Charlotte's own silences have another purpose besides character revelation; strong woman that she is, and not naturally taciturn, her portrayal could easily overpower Jackson's, not to mention Catherine's. In a narrative sense, she has to be denied center stage; in that sense, she says accurately that "nothing else 'round here don't seem to be no business o' mine" (110). When she recedes into her resentment and silences, absent from most of part 2 and all of part 3, she leaves the spotlight on the lovers, where it belongs.

What the characters (except Madame Bayonne) do say is generally in the most laconic, minimal dialogue:

> "How did it go?" he said to Lillian.
> "All right."
> "How've you been? Haven't seen you since the first day you came."
> "Can't complain," Lillian said. "And yourself?"
> "About the same." (122–3)

This quite obviously reflects the constraint felt by all three persons present as well as the narrowness and tedium of the lives they talk about. Such sparse conversation is often made more terse and unresponsive by breaking it up with bits of essentially unrelated narration. Charlotte asks Jackson, "How did you like the supper?" A substantial paragraph about her moving her rocking chair and fanning mosquitoes follows before he answers, "All right" (85). When Jackson asks

23. Gaines, cited in Simpson, 144; Beavers, 139.

Mary Louise if she expected his permanent return and starts to explain its impossibility, four pages of his memories of California are interjected before he abruptly forestalls conversation with "It's getting late" (91–5). The social "wall" in California, which she could not "possibly understand," nor he explain (he thinks), is now a wall between them, thick and impenetrable.

That this novel's consistently spare style, especially in the dialogue, is at least partially an imitation of Hemingway has not escaped critical notice, and Gaines himself has often acknowledged the influence, even overinfluence, of his reading and the tutelage of that author.[24] In this novel, however, the style has a purpose beyond bald imitation. It suits the bleak lives, the stifled feelings, and the limited choices of the speakers and the people of the area, Cajuns and Creoles as well as the blacks of the quarters. Nevertheless, this style makes it more difficult to reveal the characters in any depth, and it can get as tedious as the lives it reflects. One recalls the force and free flow of words, the rich metaphorical quality, the vigor and depth of feeling that Gaines was to achieve later with orality in the same restrictive setting. He rightly called dialogue "the meat of my writing" (CEG, 143).

What Gaines does begin to do very well in this early novel is to use symbolism in ways that compensate for the spare style without seeming obvious or contrived. What limited minds don't know or smothered emotions can't express is seen in characteristic action, a few material articles, and, above all, in the landscape. The excruciating, oppressive silences have been noted; words only accentuate the silence into which they break. When Charlotte wants to express reconciliation, she cannot "think of anything to say" except to tell Jackson to eat (184). His response to reconciliation is sometimes, but still seldom, to "say something to her" while he eats (186). Any communication between them is ultimately silence.

Objects can very subtly become symbols. Raoul's lantern is the light that Catherine follows and will not extinguish—though the shadows it casts are beginning to jerk in the opposite direction. His heirloom watch represents his family codes and hopes; his regret at having "no one to pass it to" (208) enforces his folly and shortsightedness, the irony of his misery: had he allowed Catherine to marry Bernard, he'd have had a son-in-law and a legitimate grandson; he could still hope for these through Jackson. The speedboats of the "idle white rich" (39), the Cajuns' tractors, and Jackson's book of Greek poetry are three very dif-

---

24. Jerry H. Bryant, "From Death to Life: The Fiction of Ernest J. Gaines," *Iowa Review* 3 (1972): 106.

ferent yet parallel symbols of the forces that are destroying the culture and liveli-hood of the quarters, forcing or enticing the young to leave.

As he uses his familiar landscape to mirror situations and feelings, Gaines cre-ates his best symbols. Bushes, trees, and houses have been barriers against the hostile outside world; now, in the midst of social erosion, trees and young people alike are disappearing. In the extreme heat of summer, customs and relation-ships, including love, dry up, become sterile, or die like the land itself.[25] The Carmier house would seem to be changeless, but its image is totally negative. As seen by Lillian, it is an old, paintless structure with a warped porch, in a yard full of dead leaves and trees hung with gray Spanish moss; it stands in perpetual semidarkness, like those who live there. Jackson stands in the road and on the highway, "not knowing which way to turn," the Spanish moss like "long, ugly curtains . . . hung over his heart" (172–3). At his aunt's house, the tree by the porch is "covered with dust from the roots up to the leaves" (34). Though her boy is home, Charlotte notes that "no birds sang . . . no dogs barked. . . . The grave is something like this" (36). The novel's only bird is the owl, the night bird that flies in the dark, stirred up without obvious reason except the need to search for sustenance; like Jackson, even "he must leave sometime" (82). Jackson has his moment of yearning for the old life-and-land symbols, such as the grass wet with dew. But mostly his walks show him all the old landmarks gone: houses, trees, places to gather pecans and blackberries; like his relationships, they are only uncertain memories. He cannot remember accurately where they were, what was—or might have been. On his final Saturday night, he walks "in the middle of the road," past the school, past the graves of his people, again in the dark, again in an "absolute silence," with shadows "all around him" (191)—a complete capsule of his position. Nothing is on the land for him except a piece of broken key chain: the broken links of his past, the lost key to meaning, all he can find yet must keep.

Or does the key chain represent Catherine, broken piece of a family chain that he must take away? When he has beaten Raoul on Sunday night, has he won Catherine? Della says yes; critics and students almost unanimously say no or cite ambiguity.[26] A few cheerful readings are offered: though noting the ambigu-ity, Keith Byerman suggests that Catherine will come to Jackson later, after she sorts out her relationships and he learns faith and endurance. Joseph Griffin sees

25. Babb, *EG*, 52–4, 58; Rowell, "Territory," 4–8; Hicks, *Singer's*, 104.
26. CEG, 31–3; Aubert, "Mulatto," 72; Beavers, 143; Grant, 171; Hicks, *Singer's*, 105; Jerry H. Bryant, "Politics and the Black Novel," *Nation* (April 5, 1971): 436.

the fight as preparing a way for both a "normal sexual relation" for Jackson and Catherine and a "reparation of the rift" in Raoul and Della's marriage. And Winifred Stoelting calls the ending "hopefully open, i.e., to be completed in the reader's mind."[27] Another thoughtful reader has offered the strongest case for a "happy ending" I have yet found: "Gaines' disposition of Raoul was as precise as surgery. Defeated, he loses his daughter . . . regains his wife. . . . Della and Raoul have much baggage to carry that will not permit them to enjoy run-away happiness. But whether he gets out of the field or not (he will), whether they move out of the South or not (they won't), the air has been cleared sufficiently well to allow them some peace and harmony."[28]

Whatever completion is possible in the reader's mind needs to be drawn from a close analysis of the diction, the action, and the interactions of the final scene. Raoul tells Catherine to "Go with him. . . . it's over with" (244); he speaks the words and shows the body language of defeat, but the one glimpse into his mind reveals a man who still cannot believe he can be beaten. Catherine insists, "It's not over with. . . . I'll stand beside you. . . . I won't ever let you down" (244–5). He has used exactly the right words to reclaim her pity and her adherence; her responses have a ring of final commitment. By contrast, her words to Jackson have a distinct back-and-forth quality: "I can't leave him now. . . . I love you with all my heart. . . . But I can't leave him now. . . . Have faith in me. . . . I will come. . . . Not now. But I will come. . . . Just have faith in me" (245). She throws her arms around Jackson for a passionate moment, but she deliberately arranges her arm and her father's so that she can help him up into the house. The scene makes it easy to believe that "she never did" come out, that night or ever; the emphatic final sentence is the final curtain.

But how then interpret the conversation of Jackson and Della? She explains the change that has presumably occurred in all the relationships that night, and she sounds enough like Madame Bayonne in her understanding of the past to win some credence for her analysis of the present and prediction for the future. "Tonight it was settled," and her version of the settlement—that Raoul will eventually send Catherine away and that Jackson, therefore, is to wait even twenty years—has a convincing ring of assurance. Still, the weight of the novel as a whole falls toward relationships stabilized in old sorrow; nothing has prepared us for a happy ending, and Della cannot make one. When she reenters the house, she will find Catherine bandaging Raoul's wounds, and nothing can really

27. Byerman, *Fingering*, 70, 85–6; Griffin, "Creole," in CRF, 42; Stoelting, 347.
28. John Doyle to Mary Ellen Doyle, June 6, 1995. In author's possession.

predict that his wife will become his "prop" or anything other than his field-worker and cook. Gaines said of her speech, "Della says Raoul needs her; he hasn't said that" (*CEG*, 162).

So where does that leave the reader? The novel itself should be sufficient evidence for a judgment, but it is not. One may look to what Gaines himself has said about both the fact and the meaning of his conclusion. In 1972 and 1976 interviews, he said that even if Catherine left, she would come back, that it was "almost impossible" she could exist outside the South, that she was "fated," like many other women he knew, to stay as essential support and "conscience" of her family (*CEG*, 31–3, 89–90). In 1983, he reiterated that similarity, yet allowed that Raoul "probably will make Catherine leave. . . . But all that's another story. When Catherine goes into the house, that's the end of the story. I suppose it is ambiguous" (*CEG*, 162).

The ending *is* ambiguous. And that ambiguity is not entirely meaningful. The two distinct "settlements" of the story create a wavering note of authorial ambivalence, of uncertainty about which way Gaines really wanted to take his story—toward pure misery of unfulfilled lives that cannot cross a "Little Stream" so deceptively deep and wide, or toward the eventual victory of love and pure humanity over barriers of ancient, senseless, cruel custom. Perhaps he was not yet sure what was possible for the youth of his own generation or how they would emerge from the reigning political confusion and conflict of the early 1960s. "It may be the writer just wasn't mature enough at that time to know how to end it," Gaines confessed in an honest self-assessment (*CEG*, 162). In 1990 it seems he knew; the mature author referred to his one-time title "Barren Summer" and wished he had kept it: "Nobody gets anything out of that summer" (*PT*, 117).

Perhaps the problem is that the ambiguity is created by Della, supposedly the wisest person of the older generation, whose word, from experience, can be trusted. Had she not reassured Jackson but merely left him wondering and waiting, pondering Catherine's self-contradictory pleas and promises, then the uncertainty would have rested totally and purposefully in the young lovers, representatives of their time and place who cannot make a choice and maybe do not even have one. Or we could affirm Stoelting's point that Gaines is concerned with *how* these characters make choices rather than the rightness of the choice, which may be predetermined.[29]

That idea bespeaks an ambiguity deeper than just the question of what Catherine and Jackson will do in the next twenty days or twenty years. The novel

29. Stoelting, 341.

implies the deeper issue of determinism versus responsibility. Jackson's and Catherine's fates are not fixed solely by their passions. They and their story are embedded in the soil from which they grew, their roots entangled in past relationships and customs. Predetermination by social factors suggests, among influences on the young author, the pessimism of classical, fatalistic Greek tragedy or of Ernest Hemingway's work. Yet the more consistent theme of Ernest Gaines as he matured was that humans are responsible for making something good out of their potential and possibilities. The "Old Man" (God) may seem indifferent; yet he has made humans free, and humans must make the situation. Can they, or can't they? *Catherine Carmier* does not answer, or, if it does, the reply proceeds too much from Hemingway, as many critics have complained.[30]

Let it be granted that this novel is heavily marked in tone, form, and style by early influences. Gaines himself called it "a college book in which you try to put everything your instructors have told you . . ." (CEG, 162). Nevertheless, he had learned much of value from his mentors; he had insisted on his own people as his topic and chosen his own issues; he was well on his way to the development of his own techniques. In speaking of Jackson's unsuccessful attempt to break with the past, Gaines said that others pick up and carry on such efforts, that in all his works, characters "make an attempt toward change, and some other character might continue where they left off . . . continue the effort to escape from darkness to light, or from past to present (CEG, 29, 31). In his own succession of short stories and novels, Ernest Gaines would more and more succeed in his effort to be his own authorial person, firm in his own knowledge of character and culture, his own thematic explorations and conclusions, his formal techniques, and his rich, oral style. Jackson Bradley may not have been able to resolve his issues, to learn what to do with his life or how to love well; but he would return in Grant Wiggins, in Gaines's latest novel, to try again.

30. Aubert, "Mulatto," 71–2; Babb, *EG*, 5; Bryant, "Death to Life," 111; Byerman, 86.

The big house at River Lake plantation in Oscar, Louisiana. It frequently appears in
Gaines's books. The lane to the quarters is at the left.
Courtesy Ernest J. Gaines

A former home in the plantation quarters, another repeated image in Gaines's work.
He was born in a house like the one pictured here.
Courtesy Ernest J. Gaines

The church at River Lake, which often figures in Gaines's writings. It was also his school for the first six years.
Courtesy Ernest J. Gaines

Ernest Gaines in high school, during which time he
moved to California and first attempted fiction writing.
Courtesy Ernest J. Gaines

The nightclub in Port Allen, Louisiana, used as a model in
"Three Men" and *Of Love and Dust*.
Courtesy Ernest J. Gaines

The live oak hung with Spanish moss used as a model for Miss Jane's oak tree in
The Autobiography of Miss Jane Pittman.
Courtesy Ernest J. Gaines

The sugar mill at Oscar, Louisiana, where many locals have labored. The sugarcane industry plays a role in several key scenes in a *A Gathering of Old Men*.
Courtesy Ernest J. Gaines

Ernest Gaines with the men at River Lake. His visits with them led to the writing of *A Gathering of Old Men.* Here Gaines (third from right) is wearing his trademark beret.
Courtesy Ernest J. Gaines

Ernest J. Gaines in 1996, at home in Florida.
Courtesy Dianne S. Gaines

5

——⬥——

Two Men in the System

Of Love and Dust

WHILE ERNEST GAINES acknowledges a certain fondness for his second novel (CEG, 126), a reader on first journey through it may experience a certain distaste. Both responses are understandable. After the years required to complete *Catherine Carmier*, *Of Love and Dust* was finished in a little over a year. Dial published it in 1967, a London firm in 1968, and Bantam Books in 1969; thus it was the first work that brought Gaines any income and enabled him to begin to earn a living by writing. The writing itself, by contrast to *Catherine Carmier*, was fairly easy, a result of the story's origins in reality and of his readily flowing imagination (CEG, 5–6, 248). And the plot, though admittedly melodramatic, enabled him to explore some themes of his overarching concern: How can a man live and be a man in a racist southern system?

A reader's distaste is equally explainable. It flows at first from that melodrama, a fairly standard southern plot of two triangles of black-white passion, each involving adulterous biracial sex motivated by lust or revenge but developing into a love frustrated by the very system that allowed its beginnings. Gaines admitted that in plotting the novel, he was partly motivated by his literal hunger and general economic need; he planned a story he knew would sell. The dust jacket advertised to the market for melodrama, with its crude, simplistic description: "Magnificent scathing novel of forbidden desire on a Louisiana plantation in the heat of summer" (*CEG*, 5, 127). The situations are distasteful in themselves, and the characters enmeshed in them can hardly be less so. Not even the best of them can change enough to be fully sympathetic, let alone appealing or admirable. They can neither escape to joy nor rise in moral stature to tragedy.

But distaste is the point. This novel is Gaines's picture of hell, which he asserted could be artistic if the writer gave it form (*PT*, 16–7). Its plot is worked out in seven weeks of the blistering heat and stifling dust of a Louisiana summer in 1948, by blacks and whites seemingly condemned to live forever in the restrictions, the boring idleness or punishing labor, of a plantation, without hope of relief, escape, or meaning in what they endure. The system of this hell is the triangle of southern codes of employment, criminal justice, and sex; the novel goes well beyond melodrama to explore *that* triangle, especially its sexual side. While the work bears marks of the young writer's learning process, its explorations and techniques raise it to genuine significance.

A clue to the novel's significance is found in its origins, which Gaines described in several interviews.[1] Imagination took hold of memories: a Lightnin' Hopkins blues song about an overseer, with the line "Mr. Tim Moore's man never stand and grin . . ."; a bar fight he had witnessed in 1958; and incidents of two men imprisoned for the murder of a fellow black, one of whom chose to go to the penitentiary, the other to be bonded out. "Three Men" had already been written, though not yet published; it offered its author the question What if his young convict chose to be bonded out? How would he react in the face of intolerable years of field labor and an overseer's abuse? "So what am I going to do with these two people? . . . Let me see now. Let me see. My young killer . . . Yes, yes, he will need a woman" (*CEG*, 5, 6). In other words, the *situation* seized Gaines's imagination and generated questions, and as imagination answered them, Marcus Payne emerged as the character at the center of the plot. He would be a citified, drinking, gambling, lover-boy, rebel type, unrepentant for killing and determined to get away from the plantation. Conflict with "Mr. Tim Moore's Man" would be inevitable; so would his arrogant attempt to get the most attractive woman on the plantation and, failing that, the most forbidden. Conflict would be complicated by obstacles to his getting both woman and freedom.

Yet for all his centrality in Gaines's early thoughts and planning, Marcus Payne does not seem to occupy a protagonist's unique position as focus of all the

1. CEG, 3–4, 27, 100, 107–8, 182, 319. Simpson, 172–9, quotes an undated speech giving a full account of the development of the plot.

novel's interest and meaning. This is not due to a young writer's lack of success in characterization; Marcus's personality and actions are as fully portrayed as they need to be for the novel's purpose. But Jim Kelly, the narrator, seizes interest on the first page as a contrasting character, and his experiences, his longings and frustrations, his strengths and weaknesses of character, are portrayed beyond requirement—if his primary function is indeed to observe and report on Marcus. Even the liaison of Bonbon, the overseer, with the black Pauline is portrayed, in its origins and emotional ramifications, beyond what would be needed if it were only the occasion and motivation for Marcus's revenge. Whether Marcus will soften and learn to adapt to his status as laborer, will succeed in escaping with or without a woman at his side, or will die in the attempt—none of this seems to be the central issue of the novel. Marcus's action is at the core of that issue, but the novel is not primarily about Marcus.

Some additional light on purpose and significance is shed by looking at crucial decisions Gaines had to make about tone and direction as he developed his plot. His editor returned the first version with the comment that he liked both the first and last parts of the novel but that they had nothing to do with each other. After an opening suggestive of inevitable doom, Gaines had begun to have "all kinds of fun" with Marcus, who plays tricks on the plantation folk to get money and successfully escapes with Louise. Though the editor did refer to lack of "poetic justice" for the killer, his concern was less the ethics than the form of the novel, its two incompatible halves (CEG, 214–5). Gaines does not explain his choice to unify the work by rejecting the lighthearted escape and leaving Marcus dead in the dust; presumably he saw in this outcome both greater probability and stronger significance. Plenty of comedy remains in the story, as Marcus attempts to take control of his life on the plantation and prove his prowess, but it is ironic, not joyous, humor. The trickster will be tricked, and who knows who will pay, and how much, for his rush to disaster?[2]

If the tone of the novel is not comic, neither is it strictly tragic. "Playboy Marcus," as Jim calls him, displays not just a single flaw in an otherwise grand character; nor has he the heroic stature of a "tragic revolutionary" in battle with a deterministic social environment.[3] He is pervasively selfish and hard. Even when he softens in response to Louise, he is not concerned with making a change for his people, only for himself and her. The endangerment of his people

2. Cf. Estes, "Gaines's Humor," 231–40, in CRF, on the comic aspects of this novel.
3. On the novel as tragedy, cf. Jerry Bryant, "Ernest J. Gaines: Change, Growth, and History," *Southern Review* 10 (1974): 854–5; Babb, *EG*, 61–2; Grant, 172; CEG, 34–5.

does not concern him. Hubris he has, enough to think he can get away unharmed with what he wants—revenge, freedom, and even love. Maybe his daring has moved one man to think of possible change in the social order, but Marcus is not a martyr hero or martyr revolutionary or figure of Greek-style tragedy. No catastrophic loss has been sustained by his people when he dies, nor will they form a chorus on any local stage to lament him. The very fact that Gaines could conceive of a comic ending suggests that he knew he had not begun to draw a tragic hero. In fact, *Of Love and Dust*, like *Catherine Carmier*, is a "serious action" leading to an uncertain outcome. A reader senses that the denouement will probably be disastrous; that is clearer and more predictable in this novel by virtue of Jim's and Aunt Margaret's voices. But Marcus's disaster destroys only one other person: ironically, the one for whom he finally does care. He is the land mine in Louise's field.

The purpose of the novel as a whole, then, is not to reveal a memorable character about whose fate we are to be concerned; rather, it is to reveal a *situation*, the crying need for, but seeming impossibility of, change; change for the good of many about whom we *are* genuinely concerned. Moreover, the purpose is the exploration of whether and how man can live with any dignity, any true humanity, within this situation—or if he can challenge it effectively. This exploration requires not one but two men as its main figures: Marcus, the "bad nigger" rebel, to test the system by defiance; and Jim, the "good nigger" worker, to test himself by living within the system with what moral character and dignity he may. These two characters are two versions of one notion—manhood. They present two views of plantation culture, two ways of meeting it. The question of identifying a protagonist, therefore, is moot. It takes two sides to make one coin, two men to make one contrast.

In portraying the three sides of the novel's (and the plantation's) "system of hell," the novel stresses first what directly affects everyone—employment. Jim and Marcus are both fieldworkers, Jim by capitulation to the only form of employment for which he has skill, Marcus by minimal capitulation to a temporary degradation preferred to that of the penitentiary. Around them are the other laborers: the homosexuals, John and Freddie, and the "men" nicknamed Jobbo, Jocko, Snuke, Burl, Jack, Sun Brown, Black Ned, and Tram, oldest of "the Aguillard brothers," who have no other first names given because they must run as a clan to be men at all. All these characters represent the system of plantation labor by workers deliberately kept uneducated and underpaid for brutal physical toil that leads nowhere beyond the plantation and to no greater advancement on it than driving a tractor under a sunscreen umbrella. For this labor, the strong white sun, the intense heat without a breeze, and the very cornstalks, hot and indifferent to those who must pick them, are all apt symbols.

Even more than the scenes in the fields, the Saturday afternoon with prostitutes in Bayonne and the Saturday night "house fair" in the quarters depict the results of this system, which so encourages degrading and enervating dissipation as to make labor seem more dignified, almost preferable. The brawl at the fair serves as a comic interlude to offset the deadly serious business to come. "Honor munks gent'mans,"[4] however, is comic and ironic only because none of the black men will really injure each other or hold anger for this release of their daily frustration and submission to indignity. The rough male crudity and short, meaningless dialogue with which these men address each other and women reflect the lifelong, systemic demeaning of men, young or old, from whom courtesy, fidelity, and respect for women or for each other are neither expected nor even desired. Their degradation as men is the necessary basis for keeping them as degraded laborers. Even the better, decent, sensitive, caring, and careful men, like James Kelly (called "Geam" only by the overseer), are caught in this system and demeaned by it. It will take the open rebellion of a Marcus (who never has a nickname) to make Jim act to free himself.

Such a system cannot exist, obviously, without also degrading the white men who manage it. These types are represented first by Sidney Bonbon, the overseer, from the despised poor-Cajun class, who can assert himself only by brute male power over black men and women. His power is symbolized in his riding a stallion over and behind the fieldworkers and in his traveling everywhere with a gun. The scorned middleman, he must be subservient to the fields' owner; his only "dignity" comes from profiteering from him by theft and blackmail. The owner, Marshall Hebert, has the "dignity" of having nothing to do but pay the blacks on Saturday, try to control his overseer and pretend he has not failed, and maintain the social code or manipulate it to his own advantage. It is significant that in his narration Jim refers to the overseer by his last name without "Mr.," and to his employer always and only by his first name; "Hebert" simply doesn't deserve so much respect.

A system that universally degrades men in their daily work cannot but interlock with equal injustice in the penal system. Let one man kill another. If the killer is white, he may go to the penitentiary for a white victim—unless he is rich enough to bribe someone else to pull the trigger for him. But even the poor-

---

4. Ernest J. Gaines, *Of Love and Dust* (New York: Norton, 1979), 105. All citations are from this edition.

est white will have only a "hearing" to determine his "justifiable homicide" of a black (277). When a black man has deprived a fellow black of life, he has a choice of slaveries: segregated, abusive labor in the penitentiary or bonding out to a plantation, with no pay, loans at the store to add on to his time, close control by the overseer, and no Saturdays in town. For rebellion, for any act that would dishonor a white man, above all for the death of a white man, he can expect an immediate lynching, which could endanger everyone in the quarters. The whole quarters, therefore, is supposed to help control him. This system of "justice" underlies the actions of Bonbon and Marshall Hebert, of Marcus as he tries to manipulate them for his revenge and freedom, and of Jim, Aunt Margaret, and other folk as they try to control Marcus for everyone's safety.

It is the third side of the triangle that makes the other two so oppressive and deadly in this novel, as in the actual life of the South. The normal expectations of white power over employment and criminal justice are poisoned beyond any antidote of humanity when they become mixed with sexual relations and power over black life.[5] White men are expected to use black women sexually according to their own impulses. Bonbon originally took Pauline in the field like any other woman; that he eventually settled into a steady liaison in her house and fathered her children is no disgrace to either of them as long as he does not neglect his wife and only her child openly calls him father. He may, though he should not, grow to love "his black woman"; he may give his mulatto sons clothes and toys as long as he gives them no name, no paternal authority or control, no recognition or acknowledged love. An electrified fence as a means to control the children is against the law, but the lust that created them is not. Only a marriage of their parents is strictly illegal. All the other women in the field, all the neighbor folk around the house, are expected to accommodate this reality for their own protection, "like nothing in the world had happened" (62). If the favored woman chooses to "make the best of it" by improving her work situation yet stays kind and respectful to other folk, she is sufficiently "virtuous." When Bonbon wants to take Pauline to the big city for pleasure, a black man is expected to go along without protest as cover until they reach a place where one can "bring your own girl and get the room" (149). The act need have no moral meaning. But any black male intruder into the relationship could and would be killed by her white "owner," with absolutely no hesitation and no recrimination or penalty. Denial and pretense thus create dysfunction in individual psyches and in the whole society.

5. Cf. Fabre, 115; and Schraufnagel, 163, on the components of the South's sexual myths and fears.

A white wife also is expected to know and simply endure these facts without shock or resentment, at least without enough to make her retaliate in kind. Louise is one of the most used and abused of poor Cajun women, married as a child to a man too poor to be choosy, intended as a breeder and worker just as much as any black woman. Her husband has no love or patience, no skill or sensitivity to understand her past suffering or help her grow into a woman. Between them has been no love, only minimal sex to produce Tite. But let a black man look at or touch a white woman, no matter how unattractive, unloved, or ridiculed that woman may be among white men, and the lynchers must ride. So Bonbon can safely neglect his wife, leave her, with no expectation of trouble, while Marcus rakes his yard and Jim and Margaret desperately attempt to control the young man, expecting nothing but trouble. The sexual code explains Marshall's willingness to help Marcus escape in return for the death of Bonbon as long as he doesn't yet know Louise is involved. It also explains his betrayal, after Marcus has been fool enough to tell him about Louise, by bringing Bonbon back in time for a confrontation that must end in Marcus's death, one way or another, and Bonbon's removal from the plantation, one way or another. By that betrayal, Marshall escapes the social stigma of having colluded in the elopement of a black man with a white man's wife.

In this steamy sexual system, black men who do not marry and settle for life in the quarters can react two ways: they can use black women in much the same casual way white men do, as town prostitutes or as "easy-going" girls in the quarters, like Tick-Tock, whose nickname suggests she has no respected identity of her own, is merely "wound up" for a time then set aside. Her giving Jim sex is equivalent to his buying her a beer; both are "friendly" things to do. Or the black man can rebel against the law of sexual limitations and try to get a black woman "owned" by a white man or even, if he is daring enough, a white woman. Marcus Payne is daring enough to try both. The plot question of the novel is what his efforts will cause to happen, how they will affect blacks—especially himself and Jim—and their futures as men. The thematic question is what their actions and the outcome will tell about manhood within the southern system. All the novel's techniques—characterization, narration, structure, and style—are designed to answer those questions.

Reviews of *Of Love and Dust* were mixed, chiefly on the basis of reactions to characterization, which was seen as either rigid or realistic, stereotypical or original.[6] In a novel focused on situation, especially a situation fraught with melo-

6. Cf. Simpson, 188–91, for quoted reviews.

drama, those characters who most embody it are always potential stereotypes. To reach the status of art, the novel must show them capable of variant emotions and reflections, of change and unforeseen decisions. Marcus and Jim are less complex than characters in Gaines's later work, but they are much more than a flat photograph and its negative. On all sides of the plantation triangle, they are revealed in their contrasted yet shifting relations. The other, minor characters must and do exist to influence or reveal the two men; they constitute the backdrop of the action, like a huge curtain across stage rear, depicting all the scenes and personae of a plantation. Bonbon and Louise are somewhat more than their type; she especially can change, grow, and assert herself, though not enough to stay sane in the debacle. All the other characters are necessarily and appropriately flat; they will not, cannot, change.

Marcus begins as the personality type called "arrogant-vindictive"; his "solution" to the oppressive system of his world is to "move against" everyone and everything in it.[7] He is Number One and Only, recognizes no limits, physical or legal, that he will not try, and expect, to break. When he appears in a cloud of dust, Jim cannot "tell if he was white or colored" (3)—the crucial distinction Marcus will never acknowledge as a concern. Toward his own black family, his godmother Miss Julie, her son and daughter-in-law, who gave him a home for her sake, he is merely indifferent, contemptuous, or exploitative. That he has desperately worried Miss Julie, that she and Jim wait up for him while he gratifies himself with a prostitute, counts for nothing. He demands the use of George's car; for that—for Miss Julie's affection and hard-won five dollars, for Jim's food, tools, and clothing—he has no thanks. Not to Miss Julie, not to George, not to Jim, not to anyone will he listen for any counsel that might ease his work or even save his life; rather he returns an insult for it. This form of self-assertion is, of course, ridiculous; if he is "used to silk," it has been at someone else's expense. A reader wishes, as Jim says, "to feel sorry for Marcus, but God knows he didn't help you" (31).

Toward whites, Marcus is as resistant, rebellious, and cocky as he can be and still live. Jim is told to tell Marshall Hebert (with suggested vulgarity) that his convict will run away at first opportunity. That Pauline is "Bonbon's woman. . . . don't cut no ice . . . not with this kid" (55). He speaks like the adolescent he acts like while boasting of the man he *thinks* he is. Marcus is the folkloric "bad

---

7. Bernard J. Paris, *Imagined Human Beings: A Psychological Approach to Character and Conflict in Literature* (New York: New York University Press, 1997), 22–4. Karen Horney's psychological typology, elucidated in several books by Paris, is especially useful for this novel.

Nigger" who inverts and defies all the rules of his oppressors and their definition of "bad."[8] There may be a touch of the heroic about this resistance, but he is perforce in a system of subjection, symbolized by his position in the truck between a fellow black who would advise and restrain him and an overseer who suddenly slams on the brakes just to let him know who's boss. Rejecting any restraint, having no concern for any other human, Marcus is essentially self-destructive and dangerous.

Jim, by contrasting psychological typology, would be called "compliant".[9] He acknowledges what he knows to be true—the goodness, even if weakness, of most of his own people, and the brutal exploitation of the white-dominated system in which he and most of them must live. His solution is to "move toward" others, black or white, to meet their wishes or demands as far as he can without being a "whitemouth." Far from being a rebel, Jim is considered, and is, a good worker and a "very nice person" (10). He is not unassertive, especially when someone like Marcus has roused his anger; he can even refuse to pimp directly for Bonbon and Pauline. But he values goodness, compassion, generosity, and love too much to resist the pressure of an elder like Miss Julie or leave her godson to his self-destructive devices. He is therefore in a bind of "to care and not to care" and cannot "sit still"; he assumes a semiparental or grudging host role toward Marcus, trying to protect him, hoping he will learn. Jim knows his own weakness, that he lets people use him, that he, not the "Old Man" (God), has done this to him. At thirty-three, he has let his life slide into a pattern of inertia. The work required of him he does with skill; repair of an old outdoor toilet in his own yard has been waiting "a couple of years now" (22). The possibility of change in his own life or the system controlling it seems never to occur to him; like the God he describes, he sees all but is unmoved to change it, even in small ways. Like his God, who plays solitaire and chess alone, he plays his guitar and mostly gives up on humanity. "One of these days," he tells himself, he will boycott the "nigger room" at the store, but thirst and fatigue are always sufficient excuses not to (42–3). The one change Jim, needy for love, seems to consider possible and to sigh for is the return of his woman, Billie Jean; in that slim hope, he came to Hebert's plantation, and he stays.[10]

As antidotes to their restricted lives, both men turn to women. Marcus has

8. H. Nigel Thomas, "The Bad Nigger Figure in Selected Works of Richard Wright, William Melvin Kelley, and Ernest Gaines," *College Language Association Journal* 39 (1995): 143–6, 157.

9. Paris, 19–21.

10. Cf. Beavers, 73–5, and John Wideman, "*Of Love and Dust*: A Reconsideration," *Callaloo* 1 (May 1978): 76–7, on Jim's character.

long exploited them; his hangouts are places where there are "women everywhere—women, women, and more women." Whichever one he wants he goes
after, "he didn't care what it cost him" (52). One has finally cost him a fatal
fight. This episode is fittingly depicted as crudely as possible: he has been gambling in the toilet with the "nigger" who "owned the woman he was trying to
get"; a brutal fight with fists and knives is the appropriate end of such an attitude
and effort. One might think so close a brush with his own death would make him
cautious around the forbidden, "owned" women on the plantation. Not with the
arrogance of his nature. Assuming he is irresistible, Marcus actually becomes a
victim of the stereotype that black men are more sexual than white men; believing that, he believes no white man can compete with him as lover and no black
woman could really love a white man. Thwarted first by the man he killed, he is
now thwarted by Pauline in a violent altercation, which activates the vindictive-
ness that goes with his arrogance. Every woman should be at his disposal; if she
is not, she deserves abuse. The man for whom she has rejected him deserves even
more. Such a man as Marcus is unlikely to change—or to live long.

In telling the story of Marcus's liaison with Bonbon's wife, Jim makes it perfectly clear that Marcus did not know at first that Louise had been "looking at
him" (116). Had he known, he would have left her alone; for his revenge on
Bonbon to be complete, the conquest must be his. Having revenge, he would be
fearless of the consequences, would laugh at his lynchers. So far, he fits the pattern of the folkloric "bad nigger" who humiliates both woman and husband either by having sex with her or by winning and then refusing her. What Marcus
cannot foresee is his coming deviation from the pattern; before he dies, he will
come to love Louise genuinely, commit to her, and put himself at risk for her
sake.[11] Many pages and no small skill are required to make this change credible.

At the start, speaking of the man he killed, Marcus declares that "any man's
a fool to die over a woman" (78). At this point, the remark displays his brash
immaturity in assuming that he can have Pauline without dying for her, and it
foreshadows his dying for Louise. The beginning of his change occurs with his
thought that Louise looks like a girl who had long been lost in the woods and
wonders if he is one of the "things back there" (126) or a real human; the question, by implication, is in his own mind, too. At their first meeting and touch,
he digs his fingernail into her hand, then tries to ease the hurt, while all around
them are living, sounding creatures: crickets, frogs, lightning bugs, and birds. By
contrast, the yard behind her is thick with the dead leaves of many years.

11. Cf. Thomas, 161–3.

As he rakes those leaves on the fatal Saturday, Marcus acts like an adult, almost a father figure to Tite, even as he uses her to get to her mother. Louise, however, is more a child than Tite, barely conscious. Both begin the sexual relation like irresponsible children, neither having the least concern for Tite's awareness or Aunt Margaret's grave danger. Marcus would not be expected to care, since his people mean nothing to him, but Louise owes to Margaret any love and care she has ever had. Margaret's memory and understanding present Louise's past and her woman's motives for revenge, along with her careless disregard for the fate of whatever black man she succeeds in using. At this point, if Margaret's "probably" is to be believed, Louise is as casual about black life as any racist lyncher (165). She is indeed trying, symbolically, to "kill a rat" of a husband as well as "make up for all the playing she never had" (176). Her persistent nonresponse to Margaret's questions and pleas to think of her child indicates her intent not to be held accountable in any way. A change in her is requisite to any change in Marcus.

Their initial transformation is to become "innocent" children rather than avengers. Margaret intuits this as she reflects that the thrill of Louise's first real sex has changed her mind about using Marcus for revenge—at least if the thrill does not wear off or her pain with her husband is not stronger than her pleasure in Marcus. The pleasure of both at this point is chiefly in their game of catch-and-toss with the furniture and their own bodies; despite the danger, their slapstick sexuality is ludicrous. The presence of Tite, however, the actual vulnerable child, reminds the reader of their irresponsibility; it is improbable that she would not see them playing in the yard "like two children who didn't have a thing in the world to hide" (183), nor say something to her father of the racket she has been hearing indoors. Tite is symbolic of the child inevitably victimized by the sexual system. Sickly, pale, and unnatural-looking, she receives no real parenting. Her father loves her in a deep but pathetic way; she is his reminder that he cannot demonstrate love for his other children. To Louise, she is an object of vague affection, also a reminder of her own neglect and suffering. So mother will jeopardize child in carrying out her own intent to run away.

But just when the "children" show most disregard for the danger to others, a swift change in mood occurs. The talking and sex play suddenly go quiet, the room is put back in order; Marcus enters and leaves the house through the door rather than the window. Louise asks Margaret whether "a white girl could love a nigger. . . . I mean a nig-ro" (184); both her question and concern for terminology suggest her first notion of a black man outside the stereotype and her first real notion of love. Marcus, in turn, admits to Jim that real feeling is developing between them; these are the first times in the novel that any man and woman have talked openly about real feelings (though Jim has remembered his for Billie Jean, and it has been implied that Bonbon and Pauline may have so spoken to each other).

As long as Marcus's and Louise's affair remains a matter of chasing, jumping in and out of windows, slamming furniture, and thrashing on the bed, it elicits either laughter, or a contempt like Aunt Margaret's. Readers' attitudes change somewhat when Louise's adolescent fantasizing and Marcus's exploitation change to real passion and then to love, to the willingness of each to live and die for the other. This change does not erase remembrance that the affair is adulterous and dangerous, but judgment is softened by the behavior of Bonbon to Louise, by her own self-assertion and condemnation of the double standard, and by Marcus's ability to understand her at last, as Bonbon never does.

Ironically, as Marcus increasingly usurps Bonbon's rightful place—in his house, in his bed, at his table—he also gives to Louise more and more of what her husband has denied her: love, conversation, sensitivity to what she has suffered, appreciation of the love she has given him, and a desire to protect her and set her free. All this he asserts to Jim, for whom he now has developed some appreciation and friendship. Marcus has now reached the maximum of humanity of which he is capable. He is, as Jim recognizes, "the same Marcus" (261) and will continue to be arrogant and selfish, yet greatly toned down by recognition of his own measure of "heart."

In the matter of women, Jim Kelly would seem to be a sharp contrast to Marcus. He is as kind, passive, and forgiving as Marcus is brutal, aggressive, and vengeful. Jim has already had one intense experience of love and sexual fulfillment, to which he would have committed. An interviewer referred to Billie Jean as Jim's "wife," and Gaines repeated the term (CEG, 35); but Jim never calls her that. She is remembered as his "little chicken" and "baby," whose preferred toys were "fur coats, perfume, silk dresses and silk drawers" (21). When "Daddy" could not provide them, he lost her. Yet he does not blame her, apparently never challenged her desertion, and now regrets her as a father does a wandering child. As lover, he seems to have lived with her for hot baths, dancing, and lovemaking, without the shared decisions, responsibilities, or fertility of a mature relationship. Without her, he is sad, lonely, and longing, but just as inert to go get her or to find another worthy relationship as he is to fix his sagging fence. He makes casual, uncommitted use of other available women as substitutes for her.

Jim's use of women differs from Marcus's only in style; he takes only from the willing and makes no effort to "win" or overpower them. He distinguishes his feeling for Billie Jean from the "piece" of pleasure and relief he gets from Tick-Tock, who accepts gumbo or a beer in exchange for sex. No beer could be more flat than Jim's Saturday session with a prostitute, each pretending the other is the "best ever"(85). He likes Pauline, knows she considers him a "loser" yet treats her with courtesy. His own loss of Billie Jean has sensitized him to the frustration and loneliness of others, even including that of Bonbon and Louise. But unlike Marcus, he will go on singing the blues and doing nothing to change his or anyone else's situation. A reader's sense of his manhood in the end depends on what he finally learns from Marcus, what he sees of himself, and what action he finally takes on behalf of others or of his own dignity.

Since Marcus's life and death are to be revelations of the plantation system, any sympathy he garners as lover of the pathetic Louise must be enmeshed with his roles as laborer and convict. For that sympathy, he is placed up against the two white men on whom his labor and his chance for freedom depend. Jim, too, if he is to be seen as a black man of any strength and independence of character, must reconsider and adjust his labor relations with those same white men.

At first, Bonbon is seen as simply the lord of the field, the power figure on the stallion, following after Marcus, making his work harder, letting him know that he rides with a gun and is expert at using it. The overseer creates the little drama of the hawk's attempted escape and death; Marcus's continuing intent to disregard its message is at least daring, though foolish. As long as Marcus makes his own trouble, sympathy is limited to his position as underdog to such an overseer. Sympathy increases when he is assigned exhausting extra labor on Saturday. He and Bonbon and Jim all know this punishment is "not for the boy" he killed but to break him. He is left in the dust "white as snow, hot as fire" (82), symbol of the dry, lifeless existence he must endure on the plantation and of the white lyncher, the white power Marcus as "boy" can't really fight. Paradoxically, if he is to become a man, he must first begin to break under the pressure, to experience feelings he cannot hold in, the human capacity to cry "deeply and fully" (80). Only that release of feeling will free him for genuine feeling for Louise in her confinement on this loveless farm.

But to leave it, he needs, or thinks he needs, to trust Marshall Hebert, the owner, the man with power to "get him off" both the murder charge and the plantation. Once Marcus has become Marshall's pawn, the latter's unscrupulous character and use of power win sympathy for Marcus, who at least is unwilling to murder again at his behest. The very fact that Marcus guesses the wrong motive (homosexuality) for Marshall's getting him into his yard and talking to him underscores how much worse his real motive is and how vulnerable the young man is to anything this white man wants. When Marcus reveals his real intent to Marshall and offers him a deal short of outright murder, is this a spasm of morality, a determination not to risk another killing, or merely that ultimate piece of arrogance that makes him so sure of success and in fact costs him his life? Either way, he draws both Jim's and the reader's sympathy, since both know that when Marshall has gotten all he wants from him, he will toss him away like the piece of moss torn from a tree, will spit him out like his bit of candy.

Jim's role is to reflect the truths about both the white men, which Marcus cannot or will not see. Viewed only through Marcus's eyes, Bonbon is brutal and hateful, the usurping "owner" of a black woman, from whom his white wife and daughter can justifiably be stolen. It is Jim who sees that Bonbon has ceased to look at Marcus with brutal intent and has merely become puzzled by him, Jim who tells us that Bonbon does love his white child. Resentful as he is of being used as cover and procurer for the tryst in Baton Rouge, Jim recognizes that Bonbon really is "Crazy 'bout that black woman" (149) and for her sake has cut himself off from other disapproving whites. He knows he is the only person Bonbon trusts, the only one to whom he talks about his impoverished background, present feelings about Louise's people, and, indirectly, about his little sons. Seen in his relationship with Jim, Bonbon earns a modicum of sympathy for his loneliness, his status as one of the "little people" manipulated by the big; he then seems, as he is, a better man than his employer—however little that says for either of them.

Jim has no direct relationship with Marshall; he tries, rather, to monitor and modify that which Marcus sets up. Every warning to Marcus not to trust the Big Man, to just stay and work or to get away while he has the chance, serves to show Marcus's arrogant folly and Jim's practical wisdom. But when Marcus is dead at the hands of Bonbon, killer and killed both manipulated and betrayed by the "innocent" landowner, Jim at last comes into the greater manhood of which he is capable. He feels no pity for Bonbon as Marshall's second victim; after all, he can now escape with Pauline. If the relation and intent of Marcus and Louise were wrong, then Bonbon's long adultery with Pauline must be at least as reprehensible and not be rewarded with the fulfillment denied the other two. He accuses Marshall in the only way he can, by refusing to accept a recommendation as his "good worker" (278); to Aunt Margaret, he pronounces judgment on him as a murderer. Seen in relation to Bonbon and Marshall, Jim is known not only as one they have used, but as one who can judge men fairly in their variant levels of guilt.

Has Jim, however, been able at the last to judge Marcus accurately, and are

readers meant to accept his judgment? He has done everything he could to persuade Marcus to live by the law or, failing that, to get away without attempting
to take Louise. Though touched by Marcus's declaration of love and loyalty to
her, Jim notes that "whatever happened, he was still going to be the same Marcus" (261), boastful and cocksure. Out in the field, however, he comes to the
conclusion that "it's not Marcus, it's them. Marcus was just the tool" (269). And
he moves from blaming him for killing and endangering his people to admiring
him for being the "bravest man I had ever met," for "starting something that
others would hear about, and understand, and would follow" (270). This is a long
leap from his previous, ironic "We were waiting for you to lead us" in "chunking"
on Bonbon's house at night (56). He even thinks, "I worship you."

Critics have variously assessed Jim's assessment. They note that Marcus has
shown contempt for the black community in telling them of his plans to elope,
knowing they will never have the courage to get involved to stop him; that he is
a rebel with a cause who at least fights for some personal dignity, understandable
if not excusable; that he is a needed figure of resistance in the black community,
the therapy as well as disruption that could end the system if the people were not
too fearful to follow him; that he is redeemed by his act of waiting to take Louise
along when he could have fled safely alone; and that he himself becomes a re-
deemer figure for blacks and whites alike.[12] All these views have at least partial
accuracy.

In addition, Marcus could have run from Bonbon at the last moment, leaving
Louise to her husband's mercy. It is in his staying to try to defend himself and
her and complete their escape that Gaines most fully grants Marcus his manhood
(CEG, 34). Certainly "nothing in his life became him like the leaving of it." Yet
the real test of his moral shift would have occurred past a different end of the
novel. If he had escaped with Louise and her sickly child, would he have been
loving and loyal through the work of supporting them, through the experience
of the North's prejudice, through the time and trials of Louise's real maturation?
Would he not have run then? But that, as Gaines said of Jim's and Bonbon's future, is another story.

This novel, like its predecessor, ends in ambivalent evaluation of its outcome
and main character. Jerry Bryant notes that a reader is primed for an ambivalent
view of Marcus; then Jim articulates a very positive judgment, which seems to

12. Thomas, 160; Babb, *EG*, 73; Beavers, 76–80; Hoyt N. Fuller, review in *Negro Digest*, November 1967: 85; Joseph Griffin, "Ernest J. Gaines's Good News: Sacrifice and Redemption in *Of Love
and Dust*," *Modern Language Studies* 18: 3 (1988): 81–3.

come from Gaines himself.[13] Since the intended action of the lovers here is of more moral consequence than that of Jackson Bradley and Catherine Carmier, any "waffling" by the author is more puzzling and unsatisfying. And since Jim has repeatedly made the point that Marcus is brashly doing wrong and putting all sorts of other people at risk, it is really not possible to validate his judgment of him as a hero—only as a better human being than he was in the first three chapters. Perhaps one must rest with Jim's final pronouncement to Aunt Margaret: "At the last" Marcus was likable and possessed of a "lot of courage" (280). The call to worship is not compelling.

Finally, in assessing Jim as a man and human, one must gauge the depth of his inner shift and the accuracy of his self-assessment. His creator asserts that he has changed, and all critics agree. Gaines said Jim's is *the* change of the novel, achieved through the impact of Marcus's death (CEG, 34). Describing it, critics say that the change is Jim's awareness of his own fears and resistance and a judgment of the black community for theirs; that he ceases to be "self-pitying and self-protective" and learns to take risks; that he understands the balance of opposition between Marcus and Margaret and affirms Marcus by his own choice of independence and challenge to the system; that he sees the potential for change in rebellion and recovers integrity and freedom in regard to Billie Jean; and that by changing, he gets beyond inertia, reconciles himself with the past, and moves on.[14] All these views have greater or lesser accuracy when tested by the text.

All critics cite Jim's refusal of Marshall's letter of recommendation as his great act of courage, revealing his change. However, his new courage is first and best discovered in his return to see Marcus and Louise leave. If caught there, he would share Marcus's fate. When he arrives and sees that Marcus is dead, obviously at the hands of Bonbon, he still goes into the yard and kneels by the body in obvious mourning. Were Bonbon feeling and acting according to code, that too could mean death for Jim, as he knows. His demonstrated involvement contrasts sharply with Sun Brown's reaction as witness to the killing; he wants Marcus to run, and he himself runs all the way home and hides for a week.

Gaines suggested that Jim might change even more after more time to think about Marcus, but that is "after the fact" (CEG, 34). Within the novel, he has the guts to naysay Marshall to his face, then to insist on the truth of Marshall's murderous guilt in the face of Aunt Margaret's denial. Yet seeing himself between

13. Bryant, "Death to Life," 108.

14. Wideman, 78; Byerman, *Fingering*, 87; Simpson, 181; Beavers, 82; Hicks, *Singer's*, 107, 112–3.

Margaret and Marcus, he admits that one day he'll be like her. That means that unless he changes further, unless he goes beyond the "wisdom" of the old aunts who counsel caution and security in the status quo, he will not be even as much a man as Marcus became. As he walks away, the question is how far he can go, either literally or metaphorically. The old "go back home" and make no advance against the system; the young and brash are killed by it. The middling in age and wisdom, like Jim, seem more able to advance in awareness and moral maturity, but not enough for effective action. There is a saddening implication that Jim may drift to the next job without necessarily changing very much his lifestyle or his values.

The question of any major thematic change in Jim's character hinges inevitably on his role as narrator of the story. With Jim, Gaines returned to first-person narration, with the freedom, the options, and the problems this mode gave him. Michel Fabre describes Gaines's characters as thinkers who "meditate, ruminate," and try to understand events so as to foresee and prevent them.[15] Certainly this applies to James Kelly. Once the brutal events have occurred, the story as he tells it has all the characteristics of a long, mulled-over experience.

Critics have also tried to decide to whom, when, why, and how Jim is telling the story. Herman Beavers explicitly assigns a time frame for narration, within a year after Jim has left the plantation. Having had a "conversion" from "complicity to voice," he now sings his blues again, giving words to his memories, resisting the silence that hangs over the plantation he has left and the counsel to "forget it." Marcus, as an outsider, never communicated with plantation folk and needs Jim to tell his story; Jim needs to tell it because of the impact Marcus has had on him, and he can do so because the folk trust him as good and knowledgeable. By this reading, Jim is Marcus's Horatio, drawing his breath in pain to tell his story. Valerie Babb agrees that Jim's popularity gives him an acceptable voice for the community's thoughts and judgments; she views him as telling the story orally.[16]

Both these analyses view the novel, in some fictive sense, as Jim's production and its narration as more than a device. True, Jim would almost certainly have to unburden himself of his memory and sense of accountability for Marcus. And with Jim, we do not face the same questions of realistic and possible narration as was true with the short stories; he has an eighth-grade education and is fluent enough in speech. His style supports John Callahan's idea that Gaines's early

15. Fabre, 113–4.
16. Beavers, 70–2, 80–5; Babb, *EG*, 61–3.

narrators talk to themselves in an "interior voice," remembering before they talk to others.[17] However, the novel requires no debate asking, "Could Jim write it?" or "Is its style truly oral? Truly reminiscent?" We really need not "explain" Jim's narration all that precisely; it need not be more than a novelist's way of creating a character and getting inside his mind, saying what he must remember and think, what he would say if . . .

Assuming, however, that Jim is telling his and Marcus's story (not Marcus's alone), and that he has reflected for some sufficient time after Marcus's death, then we see his own character in what he includes. When he left the plantation, all his sympathy may have been for Marcus and Louise, but it has not stayed so limited. It is not true, for instance, that "all the human understanding" between himself and Bonbon is "over with now"; even before he leaves, in his final conversation with Margaret, he says that Marshall killed Marcus, "Bonbon didn't" (278–9). Their dialogue indicates that he would not deny to Bonbon and Pauline their escape to the North but implies that Marcus and Louise should have had the same chance to achieve love and permanence beyond racial barriers. And everything Jim says about Bonbon in his account indicates a balanced understanding of both the overseer's meanness and his pathetic entrapment in the code system that used him just as it would any black. It is by no means certain, or even likely, that the Jim who tells the story will be a second Marcus, one to defy all barriers. But the Jim who initiated his account by saying that when he saw dust coming, he went inside until it settled, ends it by defying the one who truly roused the dust of death. He walks away to a future made less secure by his defiance. Gaines, as the "voice" behind Jim's, seems to imply both the narrator's limits and progress from the story's start to its last page.

As author, Gaines of course had to regard Jim as a necessary and appropriate device for his own written storytelling. He needed a narrator who would be believable and acceptable, likable to both readers and other characters, able to communicate with the latter so that they could plausibly tell him what he could not otherwise know, yet without revealing a label, "Big, thick trick" (CEG, 230–2, 107). Jim's numerous "covers" have been called cumbersome and needless; as a sort of Greek chorus, he could read minds, report extended, even imagined, conversations, and be believed without explanation.[18] But Jim is a Louisiana storyteller, not a Greek; on a plantation, events are always known and told by a chain of folk. (The real doom-saying choral figure is Aunt Margaret;

17. Callahan, *African-American Grain*, 192–3.
18. Wideman, 78.

her pronouncements on Louise's and Marcus's views of the North and of escape there ring so true that the reader must expect fulfillment.) In the context of the novel, the chain of Aunt Ca'line, Jack Claiborn, Sun Brown, Marcus, Bishop, and Aunt Margaret is none too long or complicated.

The narrative chain is a bit strained at times. Bishop, for instance, has not only to report events to Jim, but also to have heard open references to the planned escape and to Bonbon that Marshall would probably not make in his presence. Indirect narration of Marcus's death is awkward in that Sun Brown's presence is accidental, and he is hiding out of sight in pure terror yet can give all the details. Jim's main source of information is Aunt Margaret. Her rendering of the details of Marcus's and Louise's movements and dialogue is as complete as if relayed through omniscient narration, or at least third-person limited, as events occur. Yet in fact all this is Jim's narration of his recollection of Margaret's narration of her recollection after the event. Even granted her hypersensitivity to a situation so fraught with danger, it seems unlikely she'd recall every detail of movement, dialogue, and her own thoughts. What we tend to think—and accept—is that Jim, as storyteller, has done a fairly free reconstruction, in his mind or on his tongue, from both their memories.

As narrator, Jim also has the privileges of an interpreter and commentator. He can read minds, as when he constructs Marcus's thoughts on Pauline and Bonbon, or what Louise "probably thought" about "How? How? How?" to get Marcus into her house (132–3), or Aunt Margaret's thoughts about Louise's motives, or the meaning of Marshall's and Marcus's looks at each other, or Bonbon's views on stealing from Marshall. Though Jim says he can't read minds, he clearly intends his listening to "eyes talk" to be a credible source (230). Even when no clear indication is given that characters have shared their thoughts with him, Jim implies that he knows them well enough to infer readily, to interpret, and to imply an appropriate response: "Her sad gray eyes were the only thing about her that made you feel Louise wasn't a child. They had seen too much sorrow, they had seen it much too long" (119).

When Gaines was asked where he, the author, was in relation to his narrators, he replied, "not there at all"; he gets reality of content, by research if necessary, then gives it to his character to tell in his own way, as in ordinary porch talk (CEG, 233–4). John Wideman noted, however, that Jim's style is not entirely oral nor entirely consistent, in that he uses a composite of down-home southern black speech, informal but perfectly literate standard English, and a variety of dialects of other characters, black and Cajun.[19] This is not so much in-

19. Ibid., 82–3.

consistency as the flexibility of a storyteller who has lived long and listened well in so mixed a setting. Jim can adopt Aunt Margaret's diction and phrasing when he recounts her report of the action at Bonbon's: "[She] said she stood there looking at that convict trying to drown that child, and that woman, the child's own mon, just laying there with that skirt pulled halfway up her thighs, not saying a word" (154). A typical paragraph of his own observations is composed mostly of simple or compound sentences with easily placed phrases and subject-predicate order of syntax—the style of one with an eighth-grade education.

In fact, Jim's semi-oral style is Gaines's written style. Gaines himself noted that he was influenced by listening to radio stories in the '50s, hearing narrated description and sound effects without visuals. Aunt Margaret *hears* the bedroom scene and tells Jim; he listens to her, observes her face and gestures, interprets what she says she heard and also what she wouldn't say. Then his creator has him tell it. Yet Gaines says he is not an audience-conscious storyteller; he writes as to a diary, not a live audience, tells a tale with letters, not voice and gesture (CEG, 231–5). That combination of listeners and diary explains his narrative combination of lively, accurate orality with literate, "composed" phrasing. Jim Kelly, creation of Ernest Gaines, shares his listening ear, his memory of sound and syntax, his senstivity to the feelings under words, looks, and gestures. Jim's sympathies and judgments, then, come to us very like his creator's. They are close in their understanding and interpretation of a difficult and dangerous situation and of the people in it.

If Gaines is behind Jim as voice and judge, he is even more necessarily there as designer of those elements of form on which depend his artistry and the power of his theme. Unless we are to suppose Jim to be truly writing this novel, it is his creator—editor—who has also carefully structured the parts and chapters and has set a pace appropriate to the feel and meaning of each event or dialogue, to the danger, disgust and fear, or expectation and suspense building up as action unfolds.

Each of the three parts depicts one of the three interlocking facets of the southern system, whose exposure is the novel's purpose. Part 1 centers on the systematic "breaking" of Marcus to hard field labor amid those already broken in, and his rebellious efforts to prevent such reduction. Sex in this part, like food, gambling, and fighting, is simply black-on-black relief from the stress of labor—except in the white overseer's use of Pauline; he has put her out of bounds for blacks and so made her more desirable for the rebel. Part 2 focuses in on the deep evils in the system of sexual liaisons, allowed as lust but forbidden as love, or forbidden altogether. The parallels of Bonbon to Pauline and Louise to Marcus raise the insistent question of why one adultery is accepted while the other is wrong. Slowly, horror at the recklessness of Marcus and Louise changes not to approval but to understanding of the pains and desires of each. The moral dilemmas of Jim and Margaret emphasize the deep systemic evil. Part 3, activating Marshall, focuses the story on the interlocked legal and economic powers that sustain the whole rotten system. Marcus's story of his past is the underside of the main story; the black men who are "whites' men," agents to demean other blacks and profit from their labor, are the dark shadows of Marshall. The demeaned, used men are the shadows against which Marcus is trying to assert his reality.

Gaines's arrangement of these parts and the chapters within them make the story's action seem interminably slow and suspenseful. Yet it actually occurs in only seven weeks (unless the time between Marcus's death and Jim's departure is an eighth week). Thus, the sequence of events is very rapid, a mere interlude in a hot summer. Though parts and chapters are divided by climactic action, not chronology, examination of those seven weeks reveals a remarkable pacing within the overall structure that gives significance and intensity to the action.

Part 1 is one slow week, almost dragging itself through twenty-two chapters. Three are required to introduce Marcus and get him to the plantation. The next six chapters (4 through 9) move the men through one interminable workday; the text is as slow-paced as the work itself. No real plot action occurs in all those pages except the slowly building conflict of Bonbon's will to power and Marcus's will to resist. An evening interlude (chapter 10) functions as a brief notation on Louise and Margaret and on Jim's sad love; by setting up the situation into which Marcus will intrude, it constitutes a thread running into the next section. Seven short chapters (11 through 17) render Marcus's short, repeated attempts to intrude into the now solid relationship of Bonbon and Pauline. Finally, Saturday afternoon takes up five chapters' worth of Marcus's extended labor, Jim's unsatisfying "recreation," and a fair that ends in a general knock-out brawl. In the plantation system, the time off is almost as slow, as prolonged and painful as the workday.

By contrast, parts 2 and 3 are shorter yet cover more time, three weeks each. Part 2 parallels the two adulterous Bonbon liaisons. In the first week, four-chapter segments present Marcus's approach to Louise (chapters 23 through 26), Bonbon's and Pauline's tryst under Jim's screen (27 through 30), and Marcus's and Louise's simultaneous coupling despite Aunt Margaret's vigilance (31 through 34). The question reverberates: Why is one worse than the other? After that, events move rapidly, two more weeks in only five chapters. Signs of genuine love have appeared amid the thickening "dust." Part 2 ends with Aunt Margaret and Jim in intense moral dilemmas as "collaborators," and Marcus at the mercy of an unhappy, jilted woman if he doesn't return to her, or an unscrupulous, manipulative landowner if he does.

The three weeks of Part 3 seem to move with excruciating slowness, though in fact, events are moving with deadly, reckless speed. The pace seems so slow to readers because it does to the principals, who are either impatient to escape or expecting disaster, and who are all in excruciating suspense. For five chapters (40 through 44), Jim, Margaret, and Bishop watch Marcus plot and place himself boldly into the jaws of Marshall. For five more (45 through 49), they see him dangle there as Marshall comes daily to the field to observe him. Only then, late in the book, is the story of Marcus's past revealed, how he was used by other nonmen, dehumanized blacks named Big Red, Cadillac, Horse Trader, and Boxcar—until he determined to rebel and look out only for his own interests. The irony is evident and painful: the black folk whose safety he should care for and look out for will survive him; he, having put himself at the mercy of a white "Big Man" and "trader" in humans, will not.

But no day is so slow as the fatal Monday of week seven. Its five chapters are as long and detailed as is the day for all the folk who now know the plan and await Armageddon; the tone, like "the whole evening," is "just too quiet" (263). Love comes to an end in the dust raised by Marshall's cars. Once that day ends in death and insanity, however, only one short chapter is needed to convey its aftermath, its sense of anticlimax for everyone else. Margaret goes back home in the quarters; Jim walks out into the unknown, at some time and place to tell this story.

And when that telling is done, when all the passions of fear, hate, and love are exhausted in bloody action, when all the violation and violence of the plantation system have been exposed, what does it all signify? What is the answer to the novel's central question: How shall a man live with human decency and dignity in such a situation? *Can* he live, or is a man socially determined, so that if he rebels, he is inevitably destroyed? Gaines acknowledged the motif of determinism in his work, but also stated that the death of the lovers in this novel was required to make others see the possibility of change (CEG, 34–5). He has often noted that his main characters make some change by small personal choices and actions, which some other persons or generations may advance to the next, greater changes.

In this novel, Gaines has put the focus on black men because they are more apt to be in direct conflict with whites in the white-male-dominated system, more apt to take it out on each other and to use women as motives or means; as Marcia Gaudet noted, his violence rarely pits men against women (CEG, 227–

34). What he wants his protagonists (all male up to this point) to do is attempt "to live with courage and dignity under deprivation."[20] The change, then, for these men, for all their people, for society, comes when "man" is seen to mean "human." Immediately after Marcus's most utterly, crudely selfish statement, that the whole world can burn "long as I ain't caught in the flame," Jim says to him, "I want you to be a human being, Marcus" (225). Marcus, at this moment, at this late date, is still in the same category as Marshall and Bonbon—indeed, worse than the latter. But when he comes to realize that he does love another, that he wants "bo' of us to get 'way from here," wants actively to return Louise's love for him and assure her freedom even at his own risk, he has moved to a new level of humanity. We may still feel he is loving the wrong woman and wrongly endangering too many others, but he has come to approximate the level of humanity that is Jim's all along—care for the good of others.

When Jim, on the other hand, loses his excessive caution and passive acceptance of the system; when he goes to Marcus's body and mourns with Louise, fearless of Bonbon's instant revenge; when he asserts himself by rejection of Marshall's power to "help," he takes on some of Marcus's courage. It is too much to say that either man has a fully developed humanity in the end, but together they have shown an outline of it. To be a human being requires the decency and kindness, the care for others, of Jim, integrated with and energized by the courage and boldness of Marcus. Each has, by the end, taken on some of the other's characteristics. When the best of both is found in enough individuals, Gaines seems to say, social change may be truly possible. Dust may turn to love.

20. Aubert, "Gaines," 483.

6

⟶•◆•⟵

Tales Within Tales

The Autobiography of Miss Jane Pittman

ONE WOMAN, FOUR men, dozens of minor characters, a plot that stretches over a hundred years and dozens of episodes—what kind of novel is this? Is it going anywhere, from any definable complication to any resolution? Or is it, with generic validity, just "moving on" with its very elderly narrator? Miss Jane remains undoubtedly Gaines's most beloved character, and even with his later successes, her story is still widely acclaimed as his masterpiece. But the critics who praise it are not of one voice in saying precisely what form of the genre it takes, only that it is no ordinary novel.

The question of "kind" is not irrelevant to other questions of meaning and art; most critics relate the novel's thematic values to the definition they assign to its form. Gaines's experiments with narration, his sampling of titles, and his later comments on his process all indicate that he, too, saw the importance of form to what he wished to accomplish in the novel. Though the finished product can, I believe, yield its own identity, it is helpful to look at the novel's place in Gaines's sequence of publication, as well as his method and what he has said about it.

When he began to conceive of *The Autobiography of Miss Jane Pittman*, Gaines had just collected and published the stories of *Bloodline*, in 1968, only one year after *Of Love and Dust* was published. That novel had explored plantation life at its worst within a short, specific time, 1948; now Gaines wanted to go back, back even to the time of slavery, to explore the plantation scene in ways more reflective of both struggle and dignity, setbacks and successes, and in a much wider time frame (CEG, 150–1, 189). Some negative elements of the novel had been resolved in the short stories. Marcus, the young rebel, had died in the dust, and the otherwise admirable Aunt Margaret had met rebellion first by trying to prevent it and then by denying its truth when it failed. In the stories, however, as Jerry Bryant has noted, Gaines achieved a reconciliation of past and present, a love for the old aunts and affirmation of young male rebels for the strength and courage that lead to change. In *Miss Jane* he gives that strength and influence to the woman who is the vehicle of change for her men.[1] Aunt Fe becomes Miss Jane. The men in *Of Love and Dust* had advanced halfway to personal inner freedom but could do little to advance their people toward social or civic liberty. The men in the short stories had moved toward positive influence and action. Those in *Miss Jane* advance the people of each era by action and example of manhood. Emmanuel becomes Ned, Joe, and Jimmy.

In addition, the short stories had provided Gaines experience in composing a series of intense, short but related episodes. And the success of *Bloodline* had justified his preference for the short form. The variety of episodes required for a novel of a century's duration released that penchant again. Later Gaines would say that though he had not read Toomer's *Cane* when he wrote *Miss Jane*, he loved it for doing what he wanted to do—create a novel out of "little short chapters" (CEG, 222).

Creation of *Miss Jane* might be said to have begun in a certain primordial chaos of authorial imagination and experience. "In the beginning," he intended to write "just a series of conversations" on a "wide range of many subjects" around a "central life." Jane would be "just part of it" for the sake of order. He had read Booker T. Washington's autobiography and was aware of three desires of ex-slaves: name change, movement, and learning to read; he would begin with a young girl moving from a plantation, but he had no particular people or episodes in mind beyond that. As he wrote, he got flashes, and his own mind "would begin to move, move, move" (CEG, 61, 70). During the writing, Gaines was reading and "hearing" the WPA narratives of ex-slaves; he was listening to Mussorgsky's "Pictures at an Exhibition" and was learning how different kinds of pictures could be linked by a common motif. And he was thinking of "sketches of

---

1. Bryant, "Death to Life," 113–4.

a plantation . . . sketches, sketches, sketches." The first working title was *Sketches of a Plantation* (CEG, 103, 209, 213). Today, no reader can be unaware that the final novel is still loaded with sketches—self-contained "pictures" in which a few characters in a small setting engage in brief dialogue or action. Yet the whole is far more than a simple collection of sketches, and Miss Jane is far more than a simple thread of connection.

How that change occurred has been told in many Gaines interviews and speeches (CEG, passim). Jane's character began to fill out when Gaines conceived the idea of making her the focus of the "series of conversations"; they would take place on the porch after her funeral, a custom familiar from his boyhood. At that point, the title became *A Short Biography of Miss Jane Pittman*. The conversations, however, would range over "a hundred years of history, superstitions, religion, philosophy, folk tales, lies." After one draft, he discovered that "it was untrue" (CEG, 101). In addition, Jane herself was captivating him; he wanted her intimate thoughts, but could not get at them through the biographical form. His editor at Dial Press was telling him to use Jane's voice; after a year of experimentation, he was convinced. She had taken over his mind and interest; with his help as "her editor. Never her advisor," she would take over the narration.[2] To make that feat possible and plausible, he invented his fictional editor, the young history teacher with the tape recorder. And *The Autobiography of Miss Jane Pittman* was born.

It grew to be a novel whose final form, its gathering of sketches, relates glove-to-hand to its purpose and meaning. Gaines calls it a "folk autobiography"—"folk" in that Jane narrates from memory alone all that she has experienced or has heard others say year after year. What information to give her or create for her memory had to be, of course, the product of his enormous research in Louisiana libraries and his talk with the folk. He and Alvin Aubert noted and discussed twelve events of statewide or national importance that an ancient woman like Jane might have noted and remembered (*PT*, 10–1; CEG, 94–5). Inevitably, she would recount her memories in small segments, tales, in her author's preferred "sketches, sketches, sketches." And Jane, one of Gaines's beloved people, would be their spokesperson, implying, consciously or more often not, the significance of the life they had all lived together.

Other critics have assigned the novel other generic designations, nearly all likening it to some form of personal or communal history. Bede Ssensalo names the book "pseudo-autobiography," with characteristics specific to black autobi-

2. Ernest Gaines, "Miss Jane and I," *Callaloo* 1 (May 1978): 37.

ography, modeled originally on slave narratives. Like Gaines, Albert Wertheim calls it a folk autobiography; he, Valerie Babb, and Herman Beavers all label it an epic in that it is the history of a people: an oral history suited for the combined history of generations of blacks; or history seen through the black female; or random, chaotic history structured by an editor to show movement from disconnection to community, with Jane as "articulate witness" to the issues involved. For Mark Charney, the work is a folk narrative, for Keith Byerman a "serious," as distinct from "popular," historical novel, in that it shows the complexity and reality of ideas and conflicts through the life of common people rather than through clear heroes and villains and the glorification of American ideals. Jack Hicks sees it as "less a novel than a racial repository," original in its use of all sorts of folk material in a manner less structured than that of the traditional novel.[3]

All readers and critics seem aware that a paradoxical combination of episodic, seemingly random storytelling with clearly structured, purposeful form makes the power and glory of the novel. Interviewer John O'Brien noted that the fictional editor's objections to stories going in "ridiculous directions" would make him miss "the most important and subtle things," the "how" of history. Gaines replied that since Jane had not read the "books on what a narrative should be," she would tell history "the way she saw it" and, in so doing, capture the "true history of blacks . . . the story of the average black" (CEG, 38). The novel's "how," therefore, must be life's "how," which, in the popular phrase, is "just one d—— thing after another"—a series of episodes, some brief, some lengthy, some "peaks," followed by "slopes and valleys" (CEG, 96–7). Yet a novel must add up to something meaningful, go in a "definite direction." Jane relays the episodes; her fictional editor (the author) gives them direction. In another essay, I explored how the editor's prerogatives of selection, ordering, reconstruction of language, and implied evaluation all give form and credibility to Jane's narration; I labeled the book a "fictional edited autobiography."[4] Here, I focus on the multi-

3. Bede M. Ssensalo, "The Black Pseudo-Autobiographical Novel: *Miss Jane Pittman* and *Houseboy*," in *Insiders and Outsiders*, vol. 14 of *African Literature Today*, ed. Eldred Durosimi Jones (London: Heinemann, 1984), 95–100, 107–9; Albert Wertheim, "Journey to Freedom: Ernest Gaines's *The Autobiography of Miss Jane Pittman*," in *The Afro-American Novel Since 1960*, ed. Peter Bruck and Wolfgang Karrer (Amsterdam: Gruner, 1982), 220; Babb, *EG*, 76–7; Beavers, 145–9; Charney, in *CRF*, 131; Keith Byerman, "A 'Slow to Anger' People: *The Autobiography of Miss Jane Pittman* as Historical Fiction," in *CRF*, 107–8; Hicks, "Bones," 16–9; Hicks, *Singer's*, 125–31.

4. Mary Ellen Doyle, "*The Autobiography of Miss Jane Pittman* as a Fictional Edited Autobiography," in *CRF*, 89–106. For other studies of narration, cf. Callahan, *African-American Grain*, 189–216;

plicity and meaning of the tales themselves and, taking the useful definition of Sheldon Sacks, call it an "episodic novel."

In his important study, Sacks distinguishes two kinds of fictions: "continuous" plotted actions, which stay on the high road from complication to resolution (e.g., *Tom Jones*) and "episodic" actions, which *seem* to ramble through many byways before the protagonist reaches the goal of the action (e.g., *Joseph Andrews*). The distinction is chiefly in the way minor characters contribute to the controlling action. In the episodic novel, characters "are introduced, perform their roles, and disappear . . . within a single episode or so. . . ." But if they hinder or advance a resolution ever so slightly or even create a stronger desire for a particular resolution, their roles are relevant; the episodes in which they appear are not digressions. Later, Sacks notes a third variation of fiction, one that is not a true episodic action but a series of episodes unified and made coherent only by the constant presence of the same main character, whose life has no clear resolution but could go on much the same way beyond the end of the book (e.g., *Moll Flanders*).[5] Translating all this for the Gaines canon, his first two novels are certainly continuous actions; *Miss Jane* combines both forms of episodic fiction.

It is certainly a novel, not a simple series of tales or sketches; as a whole, it is an action that "goes somewhere." Jane is a unifying protagonist, and her life moves, from start to end, toward the goal of freedom; all the episodes are selected to define it or show her progression toward it. In this she represents her people as a whole. Yet the people's goal of freedom is not yet fully achieved, so the novel ends with Jane and them still walking toward it. Age says she can't walk in many more demonstrations; the editor's introduction reveals that she is dead before his publication. But except for that information, we could assume she was still on the march, assume "more of the same." Her episodes are not as random as Moll Flanders's are; though her goal is not achieved definitively, as Joseph Andrews's is, she has one. *The Autobiography of Miss Jane Pittman* is an episodic novel. And one may again quote Sacks: "*Joseph Andrews* . . . is not only one of the best but may also be regarded as the crystallization of a type of fiction whose special effects were not again so fully exploited" until *Huckleberry Finn* and *Ulysses*[6]—or *The Autobiography of Miss Jane Pittman*.

Though love for "my little character" and a sense of form caused Gaines to

---

Marcia Gaudet, "Miss Jane and Personal Experience Narrative: Ernest Gaines's *The Autobiography of Miss Jane Pittman*," *Western Folklore* 51 (January 1992): 23–32; and Gayle Jones, *Liberating Voices: Oral Tradition in African American Literature* (Cambridge: Harvard University Press, 1991), 161–9.

5. Sacks, 24–5, 267–70.

6. Ibid., 25.

make Jane the one continuously present character and the sole narrator of the novel, he was later to have second thoughts about her role as protagonist. Five years after Jane took on fictional life, he noted that she "becomes almost a recorder. . . . She's gone from action in the first part to just sitting down and observing things in the latter part of the book" (CEG, 102). Twenty years after publication, in 1991, he declared that he "just came to the conclusion" that the novel was not about Miss Jane but about four men in her life, Ned, Joe, Tee Bob (white but "really very important"), and Jimmy; each of these four represents one era in the panorama of the novel. "Twenty years later I realize what I've done" (CEG, 248–9). Three years later yet, he still held to the idea that the book was "structured around four men . . . about those four men, really as much as it is about Miss Jane. . . . And each one is a different kind of story." These kinds he describes as: an adventure story, Jane and Ned being paralleled to Huck Finn and Jim in their wanderings and observings; a story of settled-down peasant life; a romantic southern tragedy; and a sort of diary recorded by Jane as she observed Jimmy and talked with him. Again Gaines asserted that Jane was less and less actively involved as the stories progressed (CEG, 303–4).

Awkward though it is to argue with an author about his own book, one may validate Gaines's insights of twenty-plus years and yet challenge two of his observations. First, Jane may be chiefly an observer of Tee Bob Samson's tragedy, but Jules Raynard is not wrong in saying that she, too, is "in there"; and Jimmy's bringing out the people as demonstrators is the direct consequence of Jane's quiet, determined walk through the quarters, leading the way. Secondly, a strong case must be made for Jane's claim to be sole protagonist, first to last. Granted that the four men are not "minors" in Jane's life or in the structure of her story, granted that their tales could be lifted out as separate novellas or substantial short stories, still they cannot be protagonists in the novel as it stands. If their stories were lifted out and clearly focused on them, then substantial segments of each of the four books would have to be excised—such as Jane's encounters with Molly and with Albert Cluveau after Ned's death, many episodes of life at Samson unrelated to Tee Bob's love and death, and her philosophizing on people, trees, and rivers. Present throughout the novel, these episodes indicate that the focus of the men's stories is still on Jane—not on Ned and Joe, Tee Bob and Jimmy, as seen by Jane, but on Jane as developed by her relationship with them. The four books focus on her at four different ages in differing environments, within which the men, all real or possible leaders, exist briefly and die, leaving her each time more mature, more wise, and in that measure, more free. Jane is individual and also representative of her people; they all progress by raising up and then learning to support leaders. Tale by tale, they "walk" toward greater freedom.

Thus is the novel structured. And so what? What is gained by this episodic form? Simply put, the centrality of Jane and the accumulation of meaningful events together make the emotional and thematic power of the novel. Since a circumstantial history of a person or a people runs not in a plot line but in episodes, the craft and art of such a history is in the selection and depiction of those episodes, which, each in its way, illuminate and validate the significance of the whole life story. Structure and significance—these are the elements to observe and judge, book by book, episode by episode, tale within larger tale.

Book 1, "The War Years," concerns Jane's early maturation from childhood to young womanhood in her first experience of freedom in the South. Wertheim reads the whole of book 1 as "sassy" Jane's lesson in survival by silence and obscurity.[7] This lesson is a true part but cannot explain the whole of book 1, which also includes the necessity for Jane to reveal herself and speak up for what she and Ned need. Book 1 as a whole presents her early grasp of definitions and nondefinitions of freedom. Her defining process requires many varied experiences, or episodes. Many characters are required to represent the South; hence, again, episodes. Jane, with the South as her antagonist, requires for maturation and freedom a self-affirmed identity, a goal for living, techniques for survival, and a location where she can work and mature.

Book 1 as a whole divides in plot and theme into two main sections, each composed of several chapters, their episodes and briefly required characters. The first portion, including the first four chapters, through the massacre, might be titled "The Coming of Freedom." In plot, the slave girl meets her first kindness and respect from a white, a Yankee who gives her a "free" name; she adheres to that new identity at the cost of a beating. Having heard of emancipation from suddenly "kind" owners, and with the sense Brown has given her of freedom as "movement," she insists on starting out for Ohio.[8] She experiences danger from and with her own black people; she observes true power, dignity, and leadership in a black woman, Big Laura, who saves her from rape and takes control of the whole group of ex-slaves. By following Laura's direction swiftly and intelligently, she survives the massacre and saves Ned. Thus Jane learns initially the nature

7. Wertheim, 223.

8. Cf. Bryant, "Death to Life," 114–6; and Wertheim, 221, for negative views of the results of Brown's well-meant kindness.

and cost of freedom: it involves a new identity, new self-reliance and self-defense, ability to be who you are and say who you are, to "move" but not "break hearts" in the process, to relate to and manage various people in their various moods and impulses, to pick your battles wisely and distinguish your friends and real enemies. Freedom involves both canny silence and self-assertion without aggression or rudeness, care for others while fighting for yourself, emotional and tactical powers to survive, and wisdom from experience—your own and others'. Finally, freedom is the ability to cope with and move on from disaster. Suppose these first four chapters were "lifted" as a separate tale that ended with, "I looked at it this way, we had to keep going. We couldn't let what happened yesterday stop us today."[9] One would feel the tale was "done." There would be no need to know if this Jane made it to Ohio. Her basic character would be revealed; assurance would have been given that somewhere she would achieve some measure of genuine freedom by the force of her inner nature and her ability to survive any pain and mature.

From "Heading South" to the end of book 1, we have a "Journey Toward Freedom." Traveling toward mythic Ohio, Jane has to learn her limits, learn the variety of people to be met on this sort of journey, the ways to cope, survive, and relate to both the helpful and the dangerous. She must keep her goal and keep going yet learn to listen to people, to recognize and accept reality. The text of her lesson is multiple encounters with "All Kinds of People": the woman with slaves going back home, who would take Jane back into a gentle servitude; the rough southern ferryman and the Yankee investigator from the Freedom Bureau, who get her over a river; the people at the home for colored children, whom she views as new masters and restricters of freedom; black Union soldiers who mock her, and their white colonel, who does not; the "poor white trash" woman, who gives her water and curses; the hunter, who gives good food and unheeded good advice; the man with the map, who gives a comic lesson in geography and a fantasized yet severe one in reality; poor white Job with the crazed wife, who gives a night's shelter; and Bone, who gives her her first work for pay. Encounters and more encounters, brief episodes in rapid succession—these give meaning to her educative journey. No one character is more vital to her progress than another; each needs to be a sharp etching, to be, like Jane, a real individual yet one of a type. Together they are the people of the South among whom she must learn to live.

9. Ernest J. Gaines, *The Autobiography of Miss Jane Pittman* (New York: Bantam, 1972), 24. All citations are from this edition.

In book 1, Jane is clearly the protagonist, the only developed character. Ned is simply "there," a silent feature of Jane's story, her motivation for "walking the walk" to freedom, quite undeveloped in personality except for tenacity in holding onto his flint and iron. In caring for him and by finally listening to others, Jane becomes a woman early. When the "sketches, sketches, sketches," of book 1 come to an end, she has matured by changing from "sass" to respectful boldness, by keeping her determination but changing to the realistic goal of getting what she can: a full wage and improved living quarters. She has learned that freedom consists in letting people help you but not stop, misdirect, or intimidate you, and that help and hindrance may come from both black and white. Like the rivers, all kinds of people can be barriers or movers or sustainers for a freedom seeker. Most important to her growth in wisdom, she has learned the paradox of freedom: it is a continuous journey but it is found where you are.

Like book 1, book 2 is titled by its historic time frame, "Reconstruction." In book 1, the time and immediate after-time of "The War Years," the issues for black and white alike were conflict over slavery and the challenge of new black freedom. In that context Jane learned her first definitions of freedom. Here the question is whether the South can reconstruct a social structure, one changed enough to allow blacks to settle, learn and earn, and participate politically with dignity and safety or, if not with safety, then at bearable, worthwhile risk. The plantation under Bone and then Dye, its school and Ned's, the political rallies, the riding of the Klan, the exodus of black people, the conditions at Clyde's farm and in Kansas, all these are the context in which Jane must face those questions, not only for herself but for others as they relate to her.

Book 2 might also be titled "Son and Husband." Once settled, Jane cannot continue to be the only developed personality, either in a significant life or in the structure of her story. Just as she learned individual freedom by brief interactions with many people, now she must learn the interpersonal nature of freedom by lasting, in-depth relationships. Ned and Joe Pittman each represent a new aspect of freedom; through them, Jane must extend her definition of freedom to include freedom for others, specifically for men, and learn its cost for them and for the women who love them.

The story of Ned Brown/Douglass might be read as a novella in two parts; student readers have tested its "independence" that way. Part 1 (pages 65–76 and 78–80) would constitute Ned's education to freedom, part 2 (pages 98–116), his effort unto death to educate others. As his story, the text would require some modest revisions. Initial details make clear that the setting is a postwar plantation with a school for blacks, and that the narrator is Ned's foster-mother; she needs only a name and a few details to clarify the location and context. The first two chapters would be condensed to provide only enough preparation for Ned's later activity—something on his education in Bone's school and his introduction to politics as an observant youngster. The real Ned story begins with "Ned Leaves Home," which by itself could be a complete though very short story, one of Gaines's excellent little dramas of "place and dialogue" (CEG, 224). In it, Ned sets his conviction that "people move when they're slaves" against Jane's realistic question, "What's up there?" (75). His story will be one of learning that true freedom may bring you back from "there." Ned's news from Kansas (pages 78–80) prepares for part 2, linking his leaving and his coming home. Part 2 of Ned's tale, which also could be a distinct short story, would consist of the chapters "Professor Douglass" and "Assassination." The intervening "Albert Cluveau" would be greatly condensed; the assassin would be known only enough to set up his moral contrast to Ned. Perhaps a few later pages (124–5) might be retained as a brief symbolic contrast of their deaths. Ned's story would essentially end with his death, with the image of his indelible blood on the road, symbol of his permanent influence on the journey to freedom.[10]

The very possibility of such an independent reading of Ned's story, with the revisions it would require for its own coherence, indicate why it is not, as it stands in the novel, a tale of which Ned is the center. It is a story about Jane as she is affected and educated by him. His education and sense of obligation to educate others parallel hers. In book 1, she learned freedom from experience; now she sees that he has his chance to learn it from books. The first two chapters of book 2, "Flicker of Light" and "Exodus," are expansive. They detail Jane's experience of Reconstruction's brief hope: the comic brawl at a political rally and the gross cruelty of the Klan, the pride and security of being on Bone's place and the sense of betrayal by the Yankees when he loses it. Bone's announcement is an inversion of Master Bryant's in book 1; the return of "slavery" calls for a new decision and a new discovery of freedom's definition. Leaving or staying is discussed in the group, just as in book 1. Jane's decision looks both backward and forward by way of contrast. Back in book 1, she was hot for leaving; now she stays. Then she had faith in moving but no realism; now she has realism but "no more faith in heading North" (70). In a few years, however she will urge Ned to

10. On the character of Ned and the symbolic values of his story, cf. Bryant, "Politics," 438; Beavers, 150; Alvin Ramsey, "Through a Glass Whitely: The Televised Rape of *Miss Jane Pittman*," *Black World* (August 1974): 34–5.

leave to escape danger. Much later, she will have to learn that such a decision, legitimate as it is, can be only temporary; freedom requires those who have it to take risks to extend it. As Ned later returns to teach the young and to preach at the river, so Jane in her later years teaches Jimmy what she has learned of freedom and how to "bring out" the people. And, in going past Robert Samson, she takes the risk for others' freedom that she has learned from Ned.

Another clue that the story of Ned's return and death is essentially part of Jane's story is the enlarged emphasis on his assassin. The chapter "Albert Cluveau" expands on his paradoxical relation to Jane, on her ability to see him both as a human being with whom she can fish and converse and also as a fool who cannot see the moral horror of his indifference to human life. These pages reveal Cluveau's moral contrast not only to Ned but also to Jane. She is developing a philosophy of independence through self-employment, through the provision of her own food by fishing and the care of her own health by "plain steady work," plain food, water, and exercise (102). Cluveau, however, is morally dependent on his Cajun gang, even for his own life. When he has killed Ned, the story does not end there but shifts focus to the grief of Jane, Vivian, and the people, the injustice of the sheriff, and the decline of education for freedom. Yet Jane's growth into moral freedom takes a forward leap when she dares to pursue and confront Cluveau, to pronounce judgment and "sentence" upon him; she achieves a peak when she also moves beyond hatred and the desire to "hear him scream" at his death and even begins to "feel sorry for [him]—'specially Adeline there," his daughter and also his victim (124). The chapters on Cluveau's madness and death are all Jane's experience, the finish of her story of her relationship to Ned's life and death. From the boy she saved, she has learned an ethic of valor and compassion, of justice and love; these components of inner freedom she will carry and will teach on the rest of her journey.

The story of Ned, with its two component parts, is interrupted by the life and relationship of Jane with Joe Pittman. The interjection of one story into the other is necessitated first by the fact that Ned has to be away long enough to come back educated and experienced. However, the interlocking of the stories relates the two men not only to Jane but, thematically, to each other. Joe Pittman's tale, like Ned's, is in two parts, first a going away to achieve greater freedom, then a standing fast, at risk of death, for an ideal of free manhood. Ned represents freedom achieved by both tactical withdrawal and frontal rebellion against injustice at the cost of certain death; he is the "warrior" out front, training and leading the troops to defy the system. Joe Pittman is daring rather than overtly defiant. He achieves freedom by maneuvering Colonel Dye and the system for liberty to do "the best thing I can do in this world" (89), which is to ride and break horses and not have to take orders from any white who would prevent him. Unlike Ned, he is not a speechmaker. He is given almost no dialogue; most of what he does say Jane reports indirectly (another clue that his story is mainly hers). His one notable speech is key to his personality: independent of spirit and motivated by an inner goal, proud to be "Chief" in a dangerous profession, fearless of death and even of displacement by younger and abler men, but not courting death or seeing himself as a leader by anything else than his philosophy and practice of "doing it as good as you can" (89). When that doing requires risk with a fierce black stallion, Joe will take it.

What Jane needs to learn is to let him. One purpose of the Joe Pittman tale is to make Jane understand the true needs of men, especially black men, the value of their proving themselves by acts that are independent, even if not entirely prudent. Madame Gautier as a hoo-doo is presented with Jane's own ambivalence about her power, but narrative tone affirms the woman's wisdom about "man's way." She judges that "he must prove he is a man. Poor fool. . . . And he's always proving how foolish he is" (93); yet she echoes Joe's own philosophy of life and death: "man is put here to die. From the day he is born him and death take off for that red string. But he never wins. . . . The next best thing, do what you can with the little time the Lord spares you" (95). Jane's folly is in trying to evade that truth on Joe's behalf. Her fatal error in trying to prevent his riding the stallion prepares her to respond to Ned on his return, to let him take the risks he believes he must, and eventually to help Jimmy and the people have the courage to do the same.

But it is much more than Joe's daring with wild horses that teaches Jane what a "real man" is and the freedom a real man and a real woman give each other. With Joe, she first experiences adult commitment as freedom. On his first proposals, fear overcomes her inner freedom to follow her own heart and say yes; when she finally tells him of her barrenness, he says only, "Ain't we all been hurt by slavery?" (77), and so frees both of them for a new future. Their relationship cannot be called anything but marriage. Joe has asked her "to be his wife" (77); their rejection of broomstick and church ceremonies and their lack of a civil option cannot negate the force of their commitment. With Joe, Jane first experiences joint decision making and joint risks in implementation. She agrees to leave Dye's plantation but not until she has heard from Ned; Joe agrees to that. In the face of Dye's injustice, as Joe's true partner, she helps think "what *we* ought to do next"; "*we* both said . . . *we* needed . . . . So here *we* go, up and down the quarters selling . . . *we* traveled. . . . *We* ate anything *we* could get" (81–3, emphasis added). The partnership is not quite equal. She lets Joe choose the new place and lead her there much as she had formerly led Ned; Joe requires her to continue working at Clyde's house. She cannot order or persuade him to leave Clyde's and stop breaking horses nor to avoid the black stallion. Had he been willing to negotiate his form of employment or had she allowed him to carry out his self-fulfilling skill unhindered, he might have lived. Each has a share in the folly and the wisdom; perhaps in that is man and woman's ultimate equality. And that is part of Jane's learning about freedom.

Another sign that Joe's tale is part of Jane's is the chapter called "Molly." This little story likens Jane to Joe by giving Jane work analogous to his: like Joe with the stallion, Jane has to "break" Molly to prove herself. She has to manage the old cook's wild resistance, keep getting up and going back into her arena when thrown down or out, and not quit. In the process, Jane learns "woman's way," not only her own strength, but also the vulnerability of other black women. Molly is a house servant with primary devotion to her white folks, who do love her but can never see her as other than their servant; she has only limited relationships among her own black folk in the quarters and no sense of a possible happy old age among them. In relation to Miss Clare Clyde, Molly is like an aging mother who feels useless and therefore believes she is unwanted and un-loved; this is the other side of being "one of the family" of her white folks. The lesson of this short episode, this one character in Jane's life, is not lost on her, though she does not make an explicit connection in her narration. When she goes to the Samsons' plantation, even when she becomes their cook, she main-tains the freedom of one who stays close to the black folk of the quarters. Her old age down there among them is a striking contrast to Molly's stubborn and pathetic decline alone in town.

If the stories of Ned Douglass and Joe Pittman are not mainly about them but about their impact on Jane, still less is book 3 mainly about Tee Bob Samson. The title of the book is the clue to its purpose: "The Plantation" implies the whole place, all and anything that occurs there. Jane has lived on plantations before, but the focus of the story then was not on plantation life itself or what it taught her. At Samson, she is first a fieldworker, then the big-house cook—two key positions from which to observe all aspects of intra- and interracial life on a plantation, to mull over the meaning of each for herself, for her people. Samson Plantation is the context in which Jane observes, participates, evaluates, and learns, not now as a child or a young woman, but as a woman matured and able to convert all she experiences into wisdom.

"All aspects" implies multiplicity of episodes. Plantation life for black folk means field and house labor, minimal education, and the search for relief or strength through communal bonding, through conversations and stories, amusements, and religion. It means tenuous relationships with the owning family over several generations of black and white, as both races learn, enforce, or rebel against the "rules" that govern them. And it means the miscegenation—practiced, known about, and denied—that is the plantation system's principal abuse of freedom. Before the tragedy of Tee Bob's fatal love begins, five chapters quite unrelated to it and two that prepare it are presented. All are in some way typical of how things are on a plantation. All of them Miss Jane, now over sixty, must turn into lessons about freedom.

Since most of plantation life is one episode after another, one day after another, most things about the same, most of this book is done in representative sketches, nearly as much as book 1. Field labor and breaks in labor, competitions among the laborers, conflicts with the overseer, problems of children and schoolteachers and parents, religious conversions and church meetings—all these are represented by sketches that will relate Jane to the people of the plantation as book 1 related her to the people of the South. The difference now is that she is neither a detached observer nor a cautious seeker of survival; she is genuinely integrated into her people. What she tells of them in these chapters she is telling of herself. She is out in the field getting water three times a day and her dime bucket is on the cart at noon. Even when she is required to leave fieldwork and become the Samsons' cook, she arranges to ride back to the field and keep contact with the workers.

Jane is, however, in her maturation in book 3, learning a new and deeper aspect of freedom. She is again "moving," psychologically and spiritually, from a stance as one of the many innocent black people victimized by whites, from a simplistic "we" predicated on a "them," to the moral awareness of a responsible participant in the plantation system. "*We* was all for it. I got to say it now, *we* was all for it. . . . Work, work, you had to do something to make the day go. . . . *We* thought the race would be fun," she says of the contest that pitted Katie Nelson against Black Harriet and ended in violence, insanity, and the dismissal of a worker with a family—the "worse thing happened in the field while I was out there" (131, emphasis added). Though the overseer, Tom Joe, beats Harriet and rouses Bessie to threaten him, Jane implies that he was not solely responsible. "Now, why a Katie Nelson? What good is one?" she asks. But neither is Katie all to blame. The fieldworkers wanted the competition, egged Katie on against a very vulnerable member of the people, and failed to stop Harriet and take her hoe before the white man acted. Old Jane has clearly mulled over this episode and is at pains to evaluate it. As she ages, book 3 shows her gradually changing from a seeker-learner to a sharer-teacher of the lessons of true freedom, responsibility being one of the foremost.

The theme of responsibility makes Harriet's story a ready structural preparation for "The Travels of Miss Jane Pittman." "Not too long after" that grievous event, Jane "gets religion" and joins the church (133). This new episode urges a series of thematic issues: "what good" her experience of conversion has done her, the significance of her "travels," and the question of whether religion is only the way a "White Man" God (136) keeps her carrying a load, or is rather a way of helping her to deal responsibly with burdens that are truly hers so she may find relief and wisdom.[11] Certainly the text suggests mild authorial skepticism about the reality and value of such conversion experiences. They may be real to the person's mind (Jane's) or invented for the occasion (Lobo's). Their value may be release of feelings in the exhausted body at the end of the workday, or strength to maintain control before an overseer, or full "belonging" in the community that validates the reported "travels." Tales of "travels" may be merely entertainment in a locale with little other, or a means and symbolic expression of faith and valuable self-awareness. Ambivalence clings to this chapter and to Jane's symbols. Yet she is presented, as always, with respect, and she believes in her own change. Now, as in her girlhood, she has crossed a river to get to freedom.

At her faith level, the symbols of her travels present demonic opposition in the guise of good people and human loves which entice a person to go back to an old life instead of forward through trials and cleansing waters to forgiveness, relief of guilt, and a new, internally free spiritual life. At the level of her moral and psychological maturation, Jane is learning a fresh definition of freedom. The men she loved in her past, however they helped before, cannot carry the load now. They cannot relieve her of her responsibility to move to her own freedom, nor the responsibility for others that freedom brings. And no form of evil, however personified, need overpower her or stop her progress. This episode of Jane's spiritual travels looks back on the very recent episode of Black Harriet, and forward to Tee Bob, Jimmy, and the final march past Robert Samson.

Tee Bob's story begins in the next chapter, "Two Brothers of the South." If

---

11. This chapter has been fair game for analysis of religious experience and of Jane as a church mother. Cf. Wertheim, 228–9; Babb, EG, 90–3; Beavers, 152; Arthenia Bates Millican, review of *The Autobiography of Miss Jane Pittman*, *College Language Association Journal* 15 (1971): 95; Lee Papa, " 'His feet on your neck': The New Religion in the Works of Ernest J. Gaines," *African-American Review* 27 (1993): 187–92. Not all these views are Jane's; probably not all are Gaines's.

we are to feel it as Jane does, to evaluate all involved in it and learn whatever she learns, then we must know Tee Bob as she does, from his childhood. We must see him through Jane long before he sees Mary Agnes LeFabre. Jane's bond with Tee Bob begins in his boyhood, when he rides out to the field and moves her full sack or sends her to warm herself at the fire. His fondness and his wish cause her transfer up to the house as cook. But the volatile combination of black and white personified in Timmy begins and predicts Tee Bob's undoing. Timmy, son of an arrogant white father, can endanger Jane and get away with it, but he cannot insult the overseer. When he is sent away, Jane makes one futile attempt to explain to Tee Bob the "rules" by which he lost his loved half brother. The final sentences foretell his tragedy and imply the question of whether Jane will have or exercise a measure of care and responsibility for his well-being when he is grown and heading again for black-white trouble.

Structurally, Tee Bob's life cycle must be split as Ned's was, to give him time to grow up under Jane's observation. Meanwhile, she has been observing many things around Samson and hearing much of the world beyond the plantation. Her learning has begun to encompass the events of nature, such as the 1927 flood, and events of local, state, and national history, such as the assassination of Governor Huey Long. From long reflection, she has found her own interpretations of these events—variants, to be sure, on those of engineers and historians, but full of the folk wisdom and sense of social justice that experience and moral sense give to the uneducated. The two chapters of her reflections are not episodes in the same way previous chapters have been, but they do represent what she has been learning about freedom. Rivers, like the Indians who preceded the white people, must run free; so, it is implied, must the restricted black people. It is a law of nature. Huey Long, like Ned and any man who tries to help and teach the poor, must die for it. That is the law of political power and savagery. But Jane, who like her oak tree has "been here all these years and knows" (148), can tell how life and learning have flowed on.

Learning, however, has flowed into the quarters only in trickles and in spite of great obstacles. Two more chapters tell of the first three teachers on the plantation, Miss Lilly, Joe Hardy, and Mary Agnes LeFabre. They might all be put under one label, "outsiders." The point of the first two short episodes is to show how hard it was to get a good teacher for plantation children, one able to understand their poverty and cultural limits, to become one with them even while leading them forward, one truly and unselfishly dedicated, who would not exploit their labor or their girls. "The LeFabre Family" contrasts Mary Agnes to the other teachers and provides background for the coming tragedy by illustrating the "rules" as they apply to her from her own Creole Place and its culture. The seriocomic tale of Sappho and Claudee, another small marvel of "place and dialogue," is told to "show how these people looked at things" (159). What Mary Agnes knows of her own people, her resistance to them in order to teach yet her acceptance of their color caste system, will induce her resistance to Tee Bob as much as the rules of his people. According to Blyden Jackson, that acceptance will make her an accomplice in the tragedy—his and hers, everyone's.[12]

Since Tee Bob's disruption of the sexual rules will create a major disruption in the life of the whole plantation, as well as a story to be repeated and discussed in every cabin, it necessarily occupies a substantial segment of book 3, with character development enough to enlarge and enforce the lesson to be learned—by Jane and reader alike. The story must be the book's longest and most emotionally charged for several reasons: it is the biggest event of Jane's working years at Samson; interracial sex is the biggest issue in black-white relations on that or any plantation; the "rules" must be seen as the destruction of a "decent" white man just as they have been of two black men; and the event faces Jane with the question of her being "in there" among those responsible for the tragedy. This question and its implied answer are an emphatic turning point in her life, her interactions with blacks and whites, and her learning about freedom. The story then must be in the emphatic, final position of the book.

The four-chapter tale is set up like a history of responsibilities. It begins as it ends, with a death. It opens with Robert Samson denying and his son declaring the truth of black-white relationships. Robert demands that blacks come to a wake and keep the quarters quiet as if in genuine mourning. Tee Bob objects, saying the children had nothing but fear and hatred for his uncle; he is thus established at once as a person of truth amid pervasive falsity and denial. And we know that is the beginning of his end.

The question of Jane's responsibility in his fate is also raised at once; she is the first to note Tee Bob's attraction to Mary Agnes. To tell Robert Senior she knows is useless, and she assumes the same of telling his wife. But Amma Dean isn't Robert; she has a moral sense he totally lacks and might have speedily intervened with a son she can talk to. In addition, because of Tee Bob's long affection for Jane, he would almost surely have allowed her to speak to him and might have listened, might have made some honorable, even if not daring, decision. But

---

12. Blyden Jackson, "Jane Pittman through the Years: A People's Tale," in *American Letters and the Historical Consciousness: Essays in Honor of Lewis P. Simpson*, ed. J. Gerald Kennedy and Daniel Mark Fogel (Baton Rouge: Louisiana State University Press, 1987), 268–73.

"who was Jane Pittman to tell Robert Samson Junior what he ought to do . . . when anytime he wanted to he could tell me to shut up my black mouth?" (164). By immediately describing her own rationalization, Jane is admitting she did not try to intervene, did not do the *something* that was possible. In this first chapter, she chooses to be an observer.

When Jane does speak up to Miss Amma Dean, it is already too late. Tee Bob is coming home every day; everyone on or around the plantation assumes he wants to "sow wild oats" before marriage. His father doesn't care if he hurts a Creole woman; his mother does care but shares the general denial that he could ever love her honorably. Jane's feeble attempt to divert him, "Judy at that house," is a lie; her forthright attempt to warn Mary Agnes is offset by her reiterated "it ain't none of my business" and by Mary Agnes's overconfidence that she "can handle Robert" (168–9). It needs only Jimmy Caya's crude insistence on the old rules to set Tee Bob at the edge of self-destruction. The chapter "Confession" might be called "Culpabilities"; Robert, Amma Dean, Caya, Jane, Mary Agnes—all in some way inculcate or assume the rules, teach nothing or teach wrong, blind themselves to reality, and do nothing or too little to avoid disaster.

The titles of the following two chapters suggest the two aspects of the disaster. First, it falls on "Robert and Mary." Mary has assumed that Robert is "decent," is "more human being than . . . white man" (169). True, he is, but an impulsive and weak human being who can neither restrain himself to live decently within his race's code nor challenge it openly by carefully planned and daring action. Unrealistic and unprepared for the loss of his name and home, he cannot handle his choices. When the first one collapses, he despairs. Mary Agnes has strength he lacks, might have had courage to challenge the code as she challenged her family, but she cannot imagine doing so. She talks to him like a child and does not qualify her admission that "Jimmy is right" about her socially defined identity and limits (176). She cannot offer any alternative to her rejection and his despair but continues her assumption that he could not "do her anything" and would not do anything to himself.

"Samson House" extends the disaster from the pair to the family and way of life that are responsible for the death of Tee Bob. The ax taken to the door of the library, the shaking of all the portraits of the ancestors, the shattered mirror, and the death inflicted with the letter opener Tee Bob's grandfather used in the legislature—all these are obvious symbols of the destruction of a code and of a "house" that insisted on following it. Robert, Amma Dean, Jimmy Caya, Sheriff Guidry (who cannot fathom a reason for the suicide if Tee Bob were not feeling guilty or avoiding blame for rape)—all these have accepted or approved the code.

Only Jules Raynard has made a serious effort to reason with Tee Bob; he could see the unreason of the rules but, like Mary Agnes and Jane, has surrendered to them, expecting no possible change.

Raynard now can and will tell the truth; that all who accept or surrender to injustice, even "for just a second," are responsible to some degree for its destructive consequence. "All us. Me, you, the girl—all us." Raynard goes on to reconstruct the scene between Mary Agnes and Tee Bob; he assures Jane it is not "specalatin" but "gospel truth" because he is talking with her, white with black (193–5). Presumably, two whites would have been in denial or seeking to assign blame elsewhere; he and she together can be as honest and wise as possible. Various readers, however, dispute Raynard's version and believe Jane also resists it. The objectionable phrase is "she *invited* him" (194, emphasis added), which smacks of the assumption that black women somehow ask for their rape. The key word, however, and any accompanying look, can mean either "allow, even want" or "is helpless to prevent." Given Mary Agnes's character in conflict with her Creole background ("grandma . . . Verda") and her position on the floor, Raynard's "invited" may fairly be read by his other words, "helpless" and "waiting" (195). On that basis, even granting his "specalatin," we are inclined to take his word. Jane may well be doubtful or ambivalent about his version of the story; however, her recounting this conversation years later indicates that whether or not she has ever accepted it, ever figured out "Where I fit in," she has remembered and reflected on the question, has not forgotten its import. And her editor, presumably cued by her emotion in the telling, has placed Raynard's "Poor us" (196) at the emphatic end.[13]

Five years after the death of Tee Bob, Jane moves to "The Quarters," the scene and focus of book 4. Retired among her people for the last twenty years of her life, Jane lives in her half of a house, sits under her oak tree or on Lena's gallery or at her firehalf. She goes to church when able and not absorbed in baseball. From these posts, in the manner of the very old, she observes all the changes affecting life in the quarters, all the remaining people and children, especially Jimmy. She seems not to move anymore, to have anymore to learn or any reason to be active. That seeming is too simple.

Book 4 gives an immediate and initially puzzling sense of difference in con-

13. The issue of "asking for rape" was raised in conversation by Mary Helen Washington. Callahan, *African-American Grain*, 204–5; and Hicks, *Singer's*, 132, discuss Raynard's version and Jane's response.

tent and style from the other three. Books 1 and 2 report almost exclusively the experiences of the young Jane. Though she was presumably narrating them into the teacher's tape recorder and might be presumed to have stopped her story to comment on it, no such lessons of the "wise old woman" are given. What Jane learned from experience is implied by what others say to her (Unc Isom, Joe Pittman, Madame Gautier, and Ned, especially in his sermon) or by her reported new awareness at the time of an event ("All of a sudden it came to me how wrong I had been for not listening to people" (48). The only pearls of wisdom from the old woman narrator are her brief reflections on the benefits of fish and greens and hard work and on the importance of Ned's grave site to remind the children that "a black man . . . shed his precious blood for them" (113). In book 3 Jane begins to tell and also explain her experiences with matured perception of others' motivations (Tom Joe's for beating Timmy, Mary Agnes's for teaching black children); and she adds her own long-seasoned reflections on "Men and Rivers" and on the administration and murder of Huey Long. In all three of these books, the strong focus is on Jane the protagonist of her own experiences in distinct periods of her life, and only slightly on the old woman reminiscing and commenting on their meaning.

Book 4, however, opens with a general comment about the people's search for "the One" in all eras, from slavery to the present. After that, a sense of history pervades everything Jane narrates. Events in her twenty-four years of retirement are relatively few and, to her sense of importance, all about Jimmy—his birth, his services to the people, chastisements for attempted sex, gain and loss of religion, departure and return to ask the people to demonstrate. In these events, Jane is more an observer than an actor, as Gaines rightly noted. But she is also a profuse and persistent commentator, connecting each event to distant past events, teaching the deeper meanings to be found, and especially interpreting each episode in relation to the essential qualities of "the One," what the folk look for in him, what they do to and for him, what they owe him. The difference of book 4 may be described as Jane the protagonist merging with Jane the narrator.

The abundance of folk history and spoken wisdom accounts for the rambling quality of narration in book 4. So does Jane's age, which is now allowed to affect her style with much less editorial control. In the manner of the very old, she wanders from topic to topic—Joe Louis, her denial of Robert Samson's authority to say where she will live, Jimmy's service as reader and writer for the people and listener to their stories, Joe Louis again, Jackie Robinson, Coon's boy as reader/writer, the giving of the land to the Cajuns—and so on. Yet the rambling is not uncontrolled by significance. Everything is really linked to Jimmy, in her mind and assuredly in her editor's. Like Joe Louis and Jackie, Jimmy is "One sent" for the comfort of the people; like Ned, he will mature into serious purpose, go away to learn, and return to give a sermon, to call and challenge and die. Jane's preoccupation with Jimmy in book 4 explains why it is not divided into chapters, only marked by spatial pauses between her "rambles."

Jane's abundance of commentary in book 4 is a function not only of her age, but also of another integration in her person; Jane the learner with Jane the teacher. Marcia Gaudet notes that Jane is an older aunt figure in the community, with the authority of her intelligence, verbal skills, and independence, yet is never called "Aunt" but always "Miss Jane." This she attributes to the fact that most of the people at Samson were adults when Jane came there.[14] It may be even more a result of her independence of character and of the fact that she is no one's surrogate mother, yet everyone's teacher of life.

What unifies and focuses this book, what it is mainly about, is Jane's influence on the quarters people, especially Jimmy, what she teaches them by her conversations and ultimately by her example. Jimmy is "the One" she most teaches, prepares, and calls to leadership. All the stories she and others tell in his hearing, all the advice and commands, all the nickels and pralines—all are intended to infuse him with her sense of her people. His commitment to religion, so urgently sought (not to say imprudently pressured), is one form of needful unification with the people. When he returns from school in New Orleans without religion, her distress is not doctrinal; she deplores the loss of "that fire," that empathy with the folk, that has rendered him unable to speak with them effectively and left him sitting among them, yet "all by himself" (217–8). Education has only partially prepared him for a role in the civil rights movement; he must understand the fears of the people who have heard Robert Samson's ultimatum and seen Yoko and her family expelled. He must come back to Jane as a mentor who can explain that fear and call him to the patience of the poor, who have nothing but time.

When Jimmy in turn calls her to participate in the demonstration, Jane the learner undertakes her last great lesson in freedom. It is essentially a review of what she learned beside Tee Bob Samson's body and in Jules Raynard's car: that not to protest is to accept. Her "speech" to Jimmy on the last Sunday is in her mind, but that mind is made up to go with him. In admitting to herself that "the

---

14. Marcia Gaudet, "Black Women: Race, Gender, and Culture in Gaines's Fiction," in *CRF*, 143–4; cf. also Bryant, "Gaines," 857.

black curtain hang over my window . . . the veil cover my face" (237), she again unites with her people; in determining to push the curtain and veil back, she completes her lesson in responsibility. One must do what one can, and a woman of 108 years can still teach by inspiring action. To Lena, she explains the significance of all they had done in Jimmy's boyhood and affirms, "He is a teacher" (240).

Her final lesson learned, Jane can teach again. By readiness to risk all she has and to be moved away, she undertakes the culminating experience of her long life. She becomes Big Laura, moving ahead, leading the people. By moving into the road, she affirms the lasting value of Ned's and Jimmy's blood on the road and Joe Pittman's "doing it good as you can." By staring down years of white power in the person of Robert Samson, she overcomes at least some of the rules that killed his son. Jane the protagonist's story ends at that point.

But a reversion to the introduction of the novel reminds readers that Jane the narrator had one more course to teach. Jimmy was followed by the young history teacher; through him, his tape recorder, and his edition of the tapes, she would also teach his students. John Callahan suggests that Jane may have been talking on the tapes even before Jimmy was killed, and may have taken courage to join the demonstration from the mastery of her experience that storytelling gave her. This attractive idea is not easily reconciled with her repeated word to Jimmy that she is "a hundred and eight or a hundred and nine" (229), and to the listening teacher that she is "more than a hundred and ten" (211). The gap is not covered by "eight or nine months" (vii) of taping—unless the gap is in her memory of her own age. Callahan's alternative suggestion is more plausible: that Jane may have agreed at last to tell her story because Jimmy's death had occurred shortly before and motivated her. In any case, he is surely correct that this last event, so terrible and wonderful, confirms her awareness that "any story of her life would be the urgent story of her people, from Ned Douglass to Jimmy, to all those gathered around her in the living moment of her storytelling."[15] So she teaches once more, and from the few episodes of a young life cut off and the many episodes of a long life recorded, from the many stories in which oral history is collected, total memory and meaning are preserved.

Ultimately, through the fiction of tapes turned into edited text, Jane the narrator is teacher to all readers of the novel. Her instructional, wise-old-woman tone draws them onto the gallery with the teacher, Mary, and the folk. There she teaches "what happened to whom and why, what it meant to them and means to

15. Callahan, *African-American Grain*, 194, 202, 209.

you"—the essence of a novel's way of instruction. Callahan has noted that in book 4 Jane increasingly speaks to "you." Her "you" may be a counterpoint to "I" or "they" or a complement to "we"; its reference shifts from local people to the porch listeners to all readers, black and white.[16] To expand on his observations, we may note that whereas in book 3 Jane used a "we" that affirmed her sense of inclusion with the plantation people, here she uses a "you" that expands to a kind of multiple yet unified reference. She asks, "Do you know Bayonne at all? You done drank from that fountain . . . used that bathroom in there?" That "you" has to be the history teacher, or anyone with him who is not from the local area; it is also any white reader who has been in any town of the segregated South but never thought about its conditions, any black reader who has benefited from the changes that followed heroism like Jimmy's, anyone born too late to have seen what she describes, or anyone who has just never heard of it. "You think a store would let you use the bathroom when they wouldn't even let you try on clothes there?" Here the first "you" is the auditors just described; the next two are specific to blacks of her time. The learning act is clearly called for: all of you, think; imagine the experience, what it felt like to undergo this degradation. "Lord, have mercy, the poor nigger done gone through plenty, you hear me there?" (230–1). And the porch listeners there, all "we" readers here, have caught the purpose and essence of Jane's talking and teaching, the theme of Gaines's novel—what it feels like to be a human being in such circumstances. Her "you" has taken a generic value, inclusive of all who will ever "hear" those tapes.

One woman, four men, and dozens of minor characters—if the novel is essentially the story of one woman—protagonist and narrator, learner and teacher of freedom, woman who ever moves on even when she stays in place—we may conclude with asking where she and the others with her have arrived. Nearly all Gaines's previous protagonists, except for Catherine Carmier, were men, and he was frankly searching for the definition and practice of manhood in a racially conditioned world. In the four men of this novel, he continued that search and projected some conclusions about responsibility, courage, dignity, care for one's own and others' freedom, realism about limits and courage to challenge them, willingness to "stand up" at a moment of crisis, to die early or to live long and fully, and, above all, moral power to live with love for one's own people and without hatred for others. In varying degrees and expressions, these qualities

16. Ibid., 207–8.

make up the achieved manhood of Ned Douglass, Joe Pittman, and Jimmy Aaron; they mark the innocence and the fatal weaknesses of Tee Bob Samson. They are equally the qualities of Jane Pittman, especially of the matured, wise Miss Jane.

Gaines did not finish his exploration of manhood in this novel; he was to continue it in several more novels in which men seek their own definition partially through relationships with women. But his "little character" was teaching him. He would come to recognize and say that what he most respected and required in men was also found in Miss Jane Pittman, that such qualities were a matter of humanity (CEG, 242). And that is Miss Jane's final lesson to all her listeners, to all who walk with her to freedom and find it where they are.

7

The Man or the Message

In My Father's House

THE LONG INTERVAL between *The Autobiography Miss Jane Pittman* (1971) and *In My Father's House* (1978) was, by his own account, one of the most difficult in Gaines's writing career (CEG, 85). He was again trying various subjects. After *Miss Jane Pittman*'s success, he thought of going back in history again to explore the conflicts of slavery, and he published "Chapter One of *The House and the Field*, A Novel" in the *Iowa Review*. It was to have been about a house servant who escaped (or planned to escape) by "passing" for white. The work never came to fruition; Gaines must have realized it had distinct signs of "old plantation stereotype" and could go nowhere. But above all, he was engaged in the long struggle to deal with his most compelling concern, the absent black father and his son. In this period, he published in periodicals two stories that were trial opening chapters of *In My Father's House*, which did appear after the seven-year struggle. But neither of the two possible chapters found their place in the finished book.

Every author may be allowed one subject that obsesses him until he writes it out. Whether or not the obsession is a spur toward artistic achievement becomes the critical question. Certainly critics have debated the quality of this novel that Gaines "had to write," that gave him in its seven-year process "more hell than anything I've ever written" (*CEG*, 85). Gaines himself has acknowledged both the extent of his inner compulsion to write and his partial dissatisfaction with the result: "I had to get rid of it. I had to . . . exorcise it before I was free to do other things. . . . I'm not terribly, terribly happy with it." He described it as "a good book" with "a good dramatic situation," but perhaps not "a successfully readable book, one you can go back to and go back to." He never uses it for public readings, saying the whole cannot readily be sectioned for that purpose; interviews suggest that he also has emotional resistance to such reading (*PT*, 57–63; *CEG*, 184–5).

Critical judgments have reflected his ambivalence; they range from Virginia Burke's scathing early review to William Parrill's preference for the novel as Gaines's best. Where Burke sees a "pastiche" of stereotypical characters, transparent plot, and mostly flat, redundant writing,[1] Parrill sees the "stark inevitability of Greek tragedy . . . totally honest and almost foreordained" with "nothing wasted" (*CEG*, 184). Other critics have more moderately praised or blamed the novel's thematic coherence, structure, and characterization. They have explored issues of central conflict(s), history, determinism, and pessimism in the novel and made comparisons with other Gaines novels. Yet nearly all have expressed an uneasy sense of "something askew" in this novel. A close reading of what was attempted, needed, and accomplished will reveal the validity of critiques both pro and con.

When asked why the novel took so long to write and gave so much difficulty, Gaines has cited the multiple approaches and endings he tried and his fatigue by the end of it. In one telling sentence, he put his finger on the problem: "I just didn't know how—it was a combination of theme and character development" (*CEG*, 142, 248). These are the two areas of the novel's real potential and achievement and also of its weakness. The importance and force of what he wanted to say was surging within him; to say it he required at least one, preferably two, powerfully developed, credible, and moving characters. All other techniques could be negotiable and evaluated by their contribution to theme and character. But he had to decide which of these two elements was to dominate.

---

1. Virginia Burke, review of *In My Father's House*, *Library Journal* (June 1, 1978): 1195. Other general critiques of the novel include Alvin Aubert, "Self-Reintegration through Self-Confrontation," *Callaloo* 1 (May 1978): 132–5; Karla F. C. Holloway, "Image, Act, and Identity in *In My Father's House*," in *CRF*, 180–94; John McCluskey, "A Brooding Novel, Important Questions," *Obsidian* 6 (1980): 239–43; Frank W. Shelton, "*In My Father's House*: Ernest Gaines after *Jane Pittman*," *Southern Review* 17 (1981): 340–5; and Mel Watkins, review of *In My Father's House*, *New York Times* (July 20, 1978): C19.

Was he writing a moral apologue in which realistic characterization and plot events are subordinated to a "formulable statement" of theme, or was he writing a meaningful "represented action" about a man in "unstable relationships," about whose fate we are to care?[2] The two "kinds" of fiction are notably different in their purposes and technical requirements.

Gaines is clear that the story was meant to reflect his constant concern about the separation of black fathers from their sons and the resultant damage, moral or physical, to both. No black man can be fully a man if he cannot be, or simply is not, responsible for his children. But, Gaines asks, if he has not been in the past, can he hope to retrieve his error, attain his full manhood, and lead others to their responsibilities and rights? Since this pattern is obviously cyclical—absence in one generation leads to the expectation and then the repetition of absence in the next—the theme carries historical nuances. As the black community acts to demand and attain its freedom in society, will that change the pattern of deserting fathers and fatherless sons? These questions frame the haunting central issue of *In My Father's House.*

Gaines has certainly striven to focus the issue and articulate at least tentative answers to these thematic questions. The novel says clearly enough that a father's failure of acknowledgement of his paternity and its responsibility is gravely destructive to his sons above all, also to all his other relationships: marital, parental, civic, and spiritual. So far, so good. But efforts to state his theme and subthemes indicate much greater complexity of meaning, raise a spate of questions. Whose fault are the failures, past and present, that are embodied in Phillip Martin? Are they due to the old culture of slavery? To a defect in the civil rights movement, which attempted to solve the wider social issue without addressing this grave problem at the core of black life? To a defect in the Christian culture and tradition of conversion? To personal character and choice? To all of the above? And is Phillip's failure solely responsible for all the failures of his first family? Beyond the questions of responsibility are others. Are Martin's character and uncertain future at the end of the novel an evasion or a statement of theme? In its theme, is the novel guardedly hopeful or frankly pessimistic? If all these questions that lace the novel get only partial answers or none, is that a defect in the novel or Gaines's truth to the complexity of human problems?

Beyond all question, the issues that beset the life of Phillip Martin are complex, too complex to allow the novel to be organized as a moral apologue with theme as the dominant element. The title, with its allusion to "many rooms"

2. Sacks, 8, 15, 55–6.

and the promised "return to take you to myself" (John 14: 2–3), suggests the multiplicity of Phillip's character traits and desires, the conflicting, contradictory obligations and choices of his past and present, and the problem of either the son or the father being able to return, ever again to be with the other. The scriptural source of the title further imparts a moral value to the issues, their resolution, and their meaning. Jack Hicks calls the novel a "secular meditation" on the passage in John, on Christ's delivery of the Father's message and reassurance that the children are not orphans.[3] That interpretation reinforces the title's irony; Phillip returns to his house intending but too late to reassure his son; Etienne lives as an "orphan" and dies as "X." The theme itself is too complex for expression in one "formulable statement" that would cover all elements.

The novel, then, is a "represented action" centered on Phillip, on his "unstable relationships"; truth to complexity is the artistic norm. It requires complexity in Phillip and a thorough delineation of his character, complexity in his various situations and conflicted relationships, and some resolution of his crises that bespeaks theme but does not let it dominate. And it requires sufficiency, realism, and plausibility in what is revealed of the motives and behaviors of the other characters, especially Robert/Etienne. In short, truth to complexity requires most skillful character development through such tools as plot structure, voices of dialogue and narration, prose style, and symbol. Either Phillip is himself the voice of moral meaning, or his insufficiency is supplied by the voices of characters and the narrator/implied author.

Reviewer Mel Watkins saw the novel in two parts, the first a mystery dominated by the eerie presence of Robert X, narrated objectively; the second an account of Phillip Martin's inner struggle, narrated subjectively.[4] What Watkins calls the first half is actually about a third of the text, and the novel as a whole might be better viewed as structured in thirds: the suspense about Robert X's identity and concern with the minister (chapters 1 through 4), Phillip's internal and external attempts to grapple with his son's return (chapters 5 through 8), and his pursuit of Chippo Simon and his confrontation with his own soul (chapters 9 through 11). Each of these thirds has its own part in the revelation of Phillip and other key characters and themes. Watkins, however, is surely correct in noting the loose connections and jarring shifts between the sections, flaws that affect character development.

Taken as a whole, the novel clearly points to Phillip Martin as protagonist

3. Hicks, *Singer's*, 133–4.
4. Watkins, C19.

and to the central questions why he was such a bad father before and whether he can now retrieve his character and familial and social roles. Chapters 1 through 4, however, do not clearly establish Phillip's primary role; they hint at his character but are focused on the mystery of Robert X. That silent and pathetic figure is seen by all the black people in town (except, apparently, by any of the Martin family); he evidently has some personal interest in Reverend Martin; and for all we know, the acting out of his purpose and the revelation and development of his character may be the central issue of the novel. Fixation on Robert is moderated by his own silence and the shift of attention in chapter 4 to Phillip and his fall. Until that juncture, however, all the nervous curiosity of the characters is focused on Robert. There also would the reader's focus be.[5]

Narrative viewpoint is largely responsible for this focus on the secondary character. Gaines asserted that this novel required omniscient viewpoint because Phillip keeps so much inside his own mind and no one else could tell his story without falsity (CEG, 89, 113). But omniscience can allow reader entry into the minds of any and all characters, whether or not they have equal access to each other. We are given entry to the minds of minor characters, to their often false or at least limited views of Phillip. But neither Phillip nor Robert X is seen from inside in these opening chapters. Viewpoint is either objective, as external and dramatic as a scene on a stage, or it is limited to minor characters: Virginia, Elijah, and Shepherd. While each offers a bit of information or opinion about Phillip, they do so without intent to focus on him; their primary attention is on Robert. Virginia hears more about him from Fletcher, and everyone hears from the "grapevine characters": Abe Matthews, Evalena Battley, Dago Jack, Thelma, Brick O'Linde, and "several people."[6] These characters are aware of Robert's hanging around Phillip's church and house, but they make no connection. The one voice that could answer all questions, that of the independent omniscient narrator, offers only bits of information the minor characters would not advert to: Elijah's role in Phillip's family, the teachers' ages and leisure habits, Beverly and Shepherd's relationship, the location and quality of Phillip's house, his and his wife's ages, his appearance, and his reputation in town. While all these bits will be relevant to Phillip's story, they do not at this point have the force to

5. Gaines did lessen the problem by not using the experimental chapter 1, which was published in the *Massachusetts Review* in 1977. That opening began at the bus station, with interaction between Robert, a mechanic, a cab driver, and a Cajun manager. Phillip was not mentioned until the scene at Virginia's, then chapter 2.

6. Ernest J. Gaines, *In My Father's House* (New York: Knopf, 1978), 11–3. All citations are from this edition.

claim priority of attention for him. About Robert X, the omniscient narrator tells only those movements that no one else notices. No comment is offered on either of the two men. The stress of these chapters is on mystery and suspense: what happened in the past and what will happen in the present story.

The mystery, however, is never very mysterious. Even without the title and the dust jacket, and even before the encounter at Phillip's house, the relationship of the two men is readily guessed. A narratively induced "quick intuition" is fine and purposeful if it reduces suspense in order to probe Phillip's character more deeply, even if only by initial hints. But the camera is not turned on Phillip until chapter 4. Nothing indicates that he sees or even hears about the stranger watching his church and house—improbable enough since the young man is right across the street and everyone else knows it. Nothing suggests that he ever thinks of a lost son, recalls his childhood appearance, wonders about him, or has a restless conscience in his regard. Nothing prepares us for his recognition or his reaction on seeing the "thin, bearded face" watching him across the room. Consequently, the suspense of this first section seems contrived; we soon know the essential fact about Phillip. Yet we know too little of him to experience his violent emotion and fall as other than improbable and melodramatic.

One might, however, suppose an alternative to this extended secrecy. *What* Phillip has done is actually much less significant than *why* he did it then and has done nothing about it since then, and *whether* he can or will do anything in the future. Suppose, then, that the time before the novel's opening had been revealed up front. This was actually done in the "in progress" version, published in 1976 as "Chippo Simon." At that time, Gaines planned to use multiple viewpoints. In its chapter 1, Chippo narrates Phillip's background as a "tall, handsome young stud—wild as he could be";[7] Etienne's early and damaging exposure to the incessant "arguing in that house" (Johanna with her mother and sister) over Phillip's irresponsibility; the scene when she rejects his money and leaves with the children; and Phillip's conversion, marriage, ministry, and leadership of civil rights demonstrations. After crediting him with the social changes due to his leadership, Chippo ends the chapter saying, "Then Etienne came back. And everything fell apart" ("CS," 237). So, in that version, there would have been no mystery of Robert X's identity or of Phillip's past, no shocking revelations. Focus and emphasis would have been entirely on Phillip's dealing with his son and with his own past and present—in other words, on his character develop-

7. Ernest J. Gaines, "Chippo Simon," *Yardbird Reader* 5 (1976): 229 (hereafter cited in the text as "CS").

ment. Gaines rejected this chapter for the final novel because he felt the need to switch to omniscient narration. In that final mode, the first chapters were designed merely to interest the reader in Phillip; nothing more would be needed until the confrontation. As an interviewer noted, withholding Phillip's presence from the first chapters does let readers see positive views first and retain some sympathy for him when the truth comes out (CEG, 165–6). But it is still a doubtful justification of the needless mystery.

If, however, readers let go of the fake suspense and attend to the interest of character and situation, they will be helped by the prosaic temperaments and dialogue of the minor characters who present the two major characters. First we see a sensible, steady, kind, and moral woman, Virginia, in her kitchen, a warm shelter against a winter rainstorm. The atmosphere outside her shelter is symbolic—not wildly destructive but cold, gray, threatening, bare, devoid of any real life. Through her, Robert is seen not as hostile to people in general, threatening only by his strangeness and pathetic only by his suffering, haunted figure. Phillip receives extremely good "press" from this woman, whom a reader instinctively likes and trusts, yet it is evident that her knowledge is limited.

Elijah is then introduced as a sort of "son" to Phillip, a young man in his care and his home, by contrast to "the tenant . . . the tenant" (a designation that appears twenty-five times in four pages, 14 through 18), who has no name, no personal identity in Elijah's mind, only a temporary designation by residence, also understood to be temporary. He is a curiosity in the town yet obviously a lost soul who "ain't got long to be here." Elijah, like Virginia, thinks he knows Phillip; the fact that he has been acquainted with him for ten years and lived with him for five lends weight to his opinion. But those ten years cannot include the time before Phillip's marriage and the birth of his ten-year-old daughter; of these Elijah clearly knows little more than he does of Robert X. Ironically, he too is no more than a "tenant" in Phillip's house.

Nor is Phillip really known to the young teachers who are educating other young people, on whom his work necessarily depends for full effect. The one closest to him for a long time (Elijah) and the one who seems to have the most character herself (Beverly) respect and praise him; others lack confidence in the value or continuation of his work, are cynical or indifferent about it and about their race. The scene of the teachers in the Congo Room works effectively as preparation for later scenes. Beverly's praise of Phillip's courage already has a feel of authorial irony, which will be validated when Phillip himself is in bars and at Chippo's, wrestling with the consequences of his past weakness. Chuck's mocking toast to "good old courage" is followed by his "over with . . . no more" speech

(21) and a signal for more liquor. The final sentence of chapter 2, "The bartender brought the bottle," comes down like a heavy chord resonating the sound, meaning, and tone of his speech—virtual despair. Who will be right about Phillip's character? That is the novel's real mystery.

Rendering chapter 3 through Shepherd's point of view partially prepares the parallel of his character to that of young Phillip: careless and uncommitted. Mostly, however, the chapter continues the focus on the mystery and pain of Robert X. Virginia's nervous, jerking dialogue offers just enough realism to offset the melodrama and improbabilities of the dialogue of the two young men. Even if Robert had been pacing, screaming, and crying, even if he had drunk himself to a stupor on cheap wine, it seems unlikely that he would forget his intent to go to Martin's party or would make metaphysical comments on life as alley trash or melodramatic predictions of his death to a stranger. Mills's partial recognition also seems less than plausible; Etienne was a very young boy when he left the area; now he is an emaciated, unshaved, burnt-out man. It must be strong resemblance indeed to recall his granduncle, who left the area thirty years earlier, before the boy's birth.

What chapters 3 and 4 do reveal of major significance to Phillip's characterization is his subtle, unrecognized, inner contradictions of moral character. Setting is a better clue in these chapters than other characters; the minister lives on a "very wide and well-lighted" street, adjacent to a "narrow dark street with ditches on either side" and the old shotgun houses of the poor "only a few feet from the ditches" (16). His dependence on white supporters and his ready adoption of their lifestyle—house, cars, clothing, jewelry—contradict his self-identification with "Poor black people . . . we . . ." (35). His enjoyment of power and praise and his rivalry with his own assistant pastor are more than hinted. Minister and civil rights leader he may be, but he is not one with those for whom he speaks.[8] His exhortation to "Love . . . Understanding . . . Persistence . . . Getting up . . . trying again" (37) will, we feel sure, be tested for validity.

Phillip's ultimate contradiction is captured in the contrast of his peak moment, pumped and applauded as candidate for Congress, to his fall only minutes later at the sight of Robert X. The distinct feel of implausibility in this event is due to the objective outside view of Phillip. The narrative voice says he "looked puzzled, confused"; this is Shepherd's view, as is the incorrect assumption that Phillip "continued to stare at [Shepherd and Beverly]" (39–40). The nearest ap-

---

8. Cf. Jeffrey J. Folks, "Ernest Gaines and the New South," *Southern Literary Journal* 24 (1991): 39–42; he sees Phillip as corrupted by the "boosterism" of the New South.

proach to Phillip's own mind is the notation that he "was not aware . . . was not hearing a thing." Not until the next chapter are we told the chain of thoughts in his mind that sparked his intuitive recognition. That chain makes somewhat more plausible the recognition and the attempt to cross the room to his son. It does not account for his fall.

Given the central importance of that fall for revealing Phillip's character and advancing the plot, and for implying the theme, its depiction must "work." As a symbol, it has value as revelation. The strong man has a weakness somewhere; he has "fallen" in the past. Eventually we will know he "fell" before his oldest son twenty-one years before, sat "looking down at the floor" till the boy was gone (53). Now he is "on the floor" and again unable to rise (41). That past history will explain a lot about Phillip's character and paralysis in this episode. But we do not yet know any of it or his inward movements when he tries to cross the room and falls instead. Simply in the context of realistic setting, action, and dialogue, the fall lacks motivation to make it fully convincing.

What it does foreshadow is the degree of control the white leaders have and will continue to have over Phillip, and the tension already existing between them and the younger black leadership. The white lawyer and pharmacist, supposing honestly enough that they are helping him, hold him on the floor, then make him accept their help, not Jonathan's, to rise. Even in the supposed moral power of his ministry and leadership, Phillip is subject to white power. He cannot get up, claim his son and his responsibility, cannot "stand" in the moment of crisis and choice. And that symbolizes the start of his collapse as a public figure.

The fall does, finally, shift the novel's focus definitely to Phillip. The inner weakness, physical or moral, in the present and implied past, that caused his fall now becomes the "mystery" to be revealed. We must know what the weakness was and is; we must be shown whether Phillip Martin has or can find the grace to stand at last, to voice his truth, to act on this opportunity at whatever cost—or whether an abiding character flaw will degrade him even further. The mystery of the human heart must be probed. For that, we must observe him in new choices, new speech and action; and narrative viewpoint must move inside. These fictional necessities give chapters 5 through 8 a great potential for engaging the reader's interest and sympathetic involvement with Phillip.

The nature of his past action is quickly revealed. Contemporary dream psychology may reduce skepticism about the probability of his reliving Johanna's departure in a dream the very night before Robert X returns; strange intuitions can occur, with strange effects. Nevertheless, Phillip has not thought or dreamed of his first family in more than twenty years of separation. That makes the dream seem contrived to give credence to his subsequent recognition of his son; it is also a vehicle for symbols: Johanna in mourning clothes calling to him, the boy reaching out to him, and himself in a hopeless effort to catch up with his receding past. The version given in "Chippo Simon" by Chippo, driver of the wagon and witness, is realistic and more credible; it could have been rendered in the novel through Phillip's memory, combining his own miserable offering of the "money that's been everywhere" ("CS," 232) and what Chippo would have told him of Johanna's rejecting it. His prior, intuitive recognition of Robert X would have had to be made credible, but that is a problem the dream does not solve.

While Phillip is remembering his final view of his first family, he is also praying. One might suppose that prayer would combine remembrance of past guilt with that of his conversion. But no description of this supposedly central episode of his life is given in the novel. Phillip merely refers to it briefly as the "only other time I ever fell in my life"; he "swooned" when God "lifted the burden of sin from my shoulders" (57). A description was included in "Chippo Simon"; there Phillip does not fall but stands with arms outstretched above his head and calls out, "Yes, yes, I know you live. Yes" ("CS," 234). When asked why Phillip in the novel could not have been made to recall this event as he does Johanna's leaving, Gaines said it "wouldn't have been keeping form together" after the switch to omniscient view (CEG, 166). That is not very convincing, given that the omniscient narrator does reveal other contents of his mind. Without any description of the conversion, without any explanation of what motivated it or proximately followed it, a huge gap stretches between the totally irresponsible young gambler and stud and the supposedly saved, serious, effective, activist preacher and leader. The conversion has no power or reality in the reader's imagination. Perhaps it has none for Phillip; that may be the justification for the omission. Conversion was another fall from which he did not really rise or learn how to live.

The test of any conversion—spiritual, moral, or simply humanistic—is the behavior that follows it, especially in another crisis. Having met his past guilt in memory, Phillip has choices for present action. Chapters 5 through 8 may well be characterized by those saddest of all sad words, "It might have been." In his bedroom, or in his office surrounded with the images of brave and active men, he pursues the "Why? Why? Why?" of his son's return and of his own fall and inability to assert himself and rise. What he does not seem to ask himself is why he did not rise and stop his family's departure so long ago, or why he did nothing about them in the intervening years, or what would be the straightforward, manly, and responsible action to take on this very Sunday. A reader of these chapters, indeed, is apt to be making a marginal list of what Phillip could have done in contrast to what he does.

One can readily believe that moral weakness kept him from marrying Johanna and being a responsible father; we are also asked to believe that he had a sincere moral conversion. After that, he could have tried to find Johanna and make some restitution; instead, he has sent not a letter or a penny in over twenty years. He could have told Alma before marriage that he had other children to find and support, if possible; it seems that he did not tell her his secret and now cannot. Indeed, he seems to exclude her from anything of real concern to him. When she challenges his distance from her, he doesn't know how to answer. "He didn't even try" (71). On this Sunday, he wonders how to contact his son. He could take counsel with his wife or with Mills, his deacon and an older, wiser man; instead, he keeps his secret and acts alone. He knows where Robert X is staying; if he is so eager to talk to him, he could evade his caretakers and go there. Or he could send Mills to bring him to some meeting place. Instead, he spends the day looking out the window for him, wondering, arguing with himself, and finally he tries to have the other young men bring him back as if in a natural group to a party—as if a bottle of fine sherry and a friendly exchange would serve to reunite him and his son in peace. The delay is fatal. Because he did not go get his son from Virginia, he must get him from Nolan. He could then use the lawyer to get him; instead he puts himself in a vulnerable position. He could keep his secret from Nolan and express legitimate pastoral concern for a young stranger; instead he tries evasive half-truth and then lies, and ends up telling the "enemy" what he has not told his wife, his deacon, or any of his own people. He could refuse Nolan's terms of release; instead he "makes a deal with the devil." Probability allows that intuitive recognition of Robert would shake Phillip; it scarcely allows that after three days of doing not even the simplest things to claim him, he would be so desperate as to violate all social responsibilities and relationships.

Above all else, when he has his son in the car, Phillip could be truthful and undefensive about his multiple failures and utterly sincere in his regret and determination to do whatever is yet possible to repair the evil done. Instead, in this one chance with his son, he forgets what he's just asked (what happened to the other children!), is surprised they didn't inform him or think him interested, asks, "Revenge for what?" and how *he* could have destroyed the family, denies he did so, blames "the world" for their suffering and slavery for his weakness, ignores the fact that gambling was the reason he had only three dollars to give them, asserts his past as well as present love for them and his "rights" as father—father "No matter what," though he cannot name the boy who was already six years old when he left. Most revealing of his desperate lack of self-knowledge are his several assertions that he is now a man, has strength, and can stand. In the end, Phillip has not apologized for his past action, only tried to excuse it; he has asked how he can get in touch with Johanna but not pursued the question. He has no moral voice because he has almost no moral character, but he doesn't know that fact either.

With Phillip, Gaines seems to have had a failure of imagination, unless he really intended to make the minister more obtuse than any reader could possibly be. Robert's portrayal, on the other hand, in this scene is fairly successful; Gaines seems to have had a strong imagination of his pain and his words, what he would say and refuse to say. He is clearly the voice of truth in this dialogue, of accurate moral judgment penetrating even the true portions of Phillip's defense. Small wonder the son now rejects his father and goes away for "a good long walk" (104).

When Phillip has seen the last of his son (and not tried too hard to hold him back), his story of weakness, of "could do but instead does," continues. He instinctively begins a journey to the past as source of healing by going to his godmother, Angelina Bouie, at Reno plantation, where his story of falls and redemption began. She has the rights of a "nanane" to know what is troubling him, the affectionate concern and wisdom of an elder to help him, but he is again enmeshed in denials and outright lies. Again he withholds from his truest friends the truth he gave to his enemies. Instead he adopts the false assumption that Chippo Simon will solve his problem. He fails to see that Chippo can tell him if Robert X's story is true or not, but can never change one facet of its horror.

Between himself and his pursuit of Chippo stand the men of the St. Adrienne Civil Rights Committee. They present all the "why not" and "could have" questions and observations the reader has been mulling for several chapters; one may suppose they are authorially presented as validations of a reader's judgments. This scene of confrontation may be the best done in the novel; much of its power comes from the use of Mills as a first-person speaker, from the oral style Gaines does best. In many ways, the scene foretells his next novel; it is a gathering of old men (and one young), here not in defense of the only man who is not afraid of whites but in rebuke of the only one who would and did "fall" before the white sheriff. In *In My Father's House*, as in the next novel, the force of the old men's position is felt in a memory tale that they consider to be "about their cowardice as well as [Mills's] own" (126). Before their collective strength and the bar of their judgment, Phillip is totally exposed in his weakness. He is a house divided between activism for justice and the passive injustice of his private life; no wonder he could not stand. He ditched his public goal for private purpose: "To hell with Chenal. My mind is on something more important. . . ." (116). Now he offers rationalizations and phony reassurances: "I'm only a man . . . and a father" (127); "I didn't have no other choice" (129); "Chenal is a battle, not the war" (128). None of his answers "stand" before their probing questions and analyses. The key words in the scene are Phillip's repeated "I don't know," Jonathan's "disgust," and Mills's "no sympathy." Yet the scene maintains a taut balance of sympathies. Phillip deserves his rebuke and demotion by the old men, yet young Jonathan is self-righteous and pompous, much too personally eager to take power and position, too uncomprehending and intolerant of another's weakness. The reader gives Phillip the modicum of sympathy Jonathan denies him.

When the scene is all over, there is still no indication that the man coping with disgrace by a bottle of sherry in his office has grasped his own guilt or the justice of his "sentence." He does not see the arrogance of judging the old men—none of whom would have done what he did—as "little men." He cannot grasp the truths his wife asserts about his treatment of them or of her, and about his responsibility (not hers) to talk to their children. He is still an irresponsible father; metaphorically, he is "still on that floor" (133). Less than ever can he answer his question, "Who really was Phillip Martin, and what, if anything, had he really done?" (72), though it is more than ever applicable. If there is any accuracy in one reader's opinion that Gaines has debased Phillip very far, too far, in order to make his point to black men, the sequence of scenes with Nolan, Robert, the old men, and Alma are the evidence.[9]

By the end of chapter 8, the reader understands much that Phillip does not and may have small sympathy for him, small hope that he will be redeemed to true manhood or even be considered a grievous loss to himself and others. The problem is a tug between adequate representation and interpretation. Phillip could be credibly degraded, made a tragic failure, but he is simply underdeveloped, underrepresented as an individual; generic interpretation overwhelms him. This is another facet of the power struggle between characterization and theme.

At this point in the novel, a fair character analysis of Phillip can be made. In the terms of Horneyan psychology,[10] his "real" or possible self is a man intelligent, loving, capable of leadership and courageous action—traits totally discouraged in the racist environment of his youth. His first way to cope and defend his inner self was by "moving against" others in the bizarre form of narcissism avail-

---

9. John Doyle to Mary Ellen Doyle, May 17, 1995. In possession of Mary Ellen Doyle.
10. Cf. Paris, chapter 2.

able to a young black man. His chosen self-image was that of strong worker, stud, gambler, fighter in saloons, conqueror of women and other men, but responsible to none. He "bargained" that this stance would prevent any demands on him. The tendency to genuine love and care was suppressed until it surfaced, requiring a movement "toward" Johanna and their children. The result of that inner conflict was the moment of paralysis when Johanna went away. That failure, however, created a despised self whose pride must be restored by "moving away," by denial of responsibility, distortion of past reality, blaming history or other people, losing contact, forgetting even his children's names.

Phillip's pride was restored mainly by his conversion and civil rights leadership. These gave him a new, idealized image as man of God and leader of his people. His new bargain was pray and pray, work and work, organize and lead everyone to do what you see should be done, count on God to be with you and see you through to success and glory (and a seat in Congress). It is obvious to a reader, but not at all to Phillip, that he lacks any truly spiritual relationship with God and trusts only in his own power to win by leading a new fight against social injustice. Marriage to Alma was part of his bargain, more an act of propriety and convenience than of love or passion. The complexity here, which is genuinely moving, is that he really does intend to be a spiritual man, really does believe in, work for, and suffer for a righteous cause, and really does have respect and affection for, if not mutuality with, his wife. He is blinded as only the well-intentioned narcissist can be.

His second bargain collapses when Robert X shows up and desire to cross the room "toward" him collides with desire to protect the image of the strong leader-minister. The paralysis of that moment causes the second and literal fall. And he adopts the same, only worse, neurotic solution—"moving away" from others to rely only on himself. Now, in his time of crisis, he avoids talking to his wife by pretense of sleeping, reading, or being in bed as ordered by the doctor; he withdraws from a relationship by not looking at her, by silence, secrecy, and even by outright lies. On that crucial Sunday, he moves away from Mills by keeping secret the true reason for his fall, from Elijah by half-truths. Phillip's basic tendencies have not changed. He cannot yet effectively "move toward" anyone, not his wife or their children, not his returned son—however much he wishes, or thinks he wishes, to do so. Cornered by the sheriff in his poorly planned attempt to contact Robert X, he allows Nolan to move against him and all his people. When confronted by his people for that failure, he denies the realities that have broken in on him, the implications of what he has done to others. Stunned, surprised, even outraged by their anger, he can only capitulate and move away to another corner, his office, with a comforting bottle. As Alma tells him, he has spent his life "running, and running, and running" away from something (136). It remains to be seen whether this pattern of bargain-collapse-run will end in despair and self-hate, or whether his attempt to find truth by "running toward" Chippo Simon will be his salvation.

The last third of the novel has to make or break the characterization of Phillip Martin, make him the convincing vehicle of a convincing theme; on that accomplishment depends the success of the novel's art. The search for Chippo does have the interest and strength of Gaines's skill in portraying short scenes of "place and dialogue" that reveal the variety of the people he knows so well. It is still necessary to ask if the search also has a purpose beyond thematic preachment, a relevance to Phillip's developing character, if it causes in him any change for better or for worse or creates an explicable, inevitable stasis.

Gaines was asked why the search had to be prolonged by so many encounters, why Phillip could not have simply gone to Baton Rouge and found Chippo. He replied that that would "be too simple," that he must meet all kinds of people (CEG, 165). The reason he must, one supposes, is that the people are offering the common answers on how black men must or should live. The two devout women tell of the killing of the Turner boy, another fatherless son; they lament but accept the destiny of black men with a quiet fatalism. Reverend Peters is a simple old man, pitiable for his weakness, but that highlights the weakness of his simplistic "theological" answer of faith. The denizens of the liquor store are black men in the depths of moral weakness—uncommitted, aimless, laughing off and drinking away their threatened and limited lives. Against them is Billy, seething in anger, offering his militant, violent nonsolution to weakness and his cynical despair of any deep change in society or the relations of black fathers and sons. Finally, Adeline Toussaint, the scarlet-dressed woman of Phillip's past, offers a return to the old solution of the young stud. The answers are all unsatisfactory, all nonsolutions. Granting the thematic patterning in these encounters, the search still seems unduly prolonged and the characters nearly faceless devices for driving home the lesson on the need for a solution.

The journey through Baton Rouge is also supposed to be Phillip's journey into his past. Babb traces his movement as a confrontation with people who remind him of various facets of himself: minister (Reverend Peters), father (Billy), man (Adeline), and alter ego (Chippo). From this progression downward, he then turns upward to the new man. Frank Shelton reads it in the mythic context of a trip through the hellish underworld of south Baton Rouge by night, a trip in search of himself as much as Chippo, until he is made ready to go home to his

Penelope.[11] But Phillip is no wily Odysseus, and this mythic meaning is imposed on a novel essentially realistic in its character and details. At one point, Phillip asks himself what he is doing in Baton Rouge; he cannot come up with any answer except learning his son's true name. That has some symbolic significance, because when he learns it, he will voice Etienne's identity (and Antoine's and Justine's) and give them his surname.

In fact, throughout chapter 9 Phillip is not essentially *doing* anything, just meeting people, talking, and driving on; nor is he *learning* anything essential to his character development that will send him home a truly converted man, be the conversion spiritual or humanistic. Just as Phillip's confrontation with the old men had key words, here each encounter echoes Billy's mantra: "Nothing changed" (169). The chapter ends with Phillip's seeing in the young people "something I shoulda done when I was that age" and Adeline's assuring him that he couldn't have done it then and she'll be waiting for him now (179). Nothing changed. No good and usable answers. And no hint that Phillip has altered his self-perceptions or his moral character for better or worse. On this count also, the encounters seem merely vehicles for the author's thematic exploration of the options for attaining manhood in the post–civil rights era. If any segment makes theme overpower characterization in this novel and makes that theme pessimistic, it is chapter 9.

One may well ask why chapter 10, Chippo's story of Johanna, is in the novel at all. His very knowledge is another strain on the novel's realism; it depends on the happenstances of his recognizing on a bus a much-changed woman he hasn't seen in twenty years, then being interested enough to search for her and finding just the old couple who know the horror of her life. His account of that story is repetition; besides the names of the children and some fullness of detail about the family's feelings, he tells little that Robert X hasn't already told. The main purpose of this chapter seems to be to reinforce the horror in the reader's mind, to verify it in Phillip's and press down on him the "heavy burden" of his own guilt.

Perhaps chapter 10 is a device to introduce Chippo in the flesh so he can act as a foil to Phillip, and in chapter 11 can offer the strength essential to meet the final crisis. He is what Phillip might have become, not mean or without human values, but still a roustabout, a "rover" (214). Having reported the wreckage of

11. Babb, *EG*, 106–11; Frank W. Shelton, "Of Machines and Men: Pastoralism in Gaines's Fiction," in *CRF*, 23. Cf. Audrey L. Vinson, "The Deliverers: Ernest J. Gaines's Sacrificial Lambs," *Obsidian II*, 2d ser., 2, no. 1 (1987): 38–40, for other mythic readings.

Johanna and her family, he first offers as solution his "honest opinion—forget it" (201). But facing the imminent final wreckage of Phillip, Chippo becomes more a man than he has ever been, becomes the real voice calling the minister to real conversion. In urging his old buddy to be different from "somebody like me," from "the rest of them no-'count niggers on East Boulevard" (208), Chippo speaks like a man with real values; he then names his real self, "Erin Simon" (213).

Degrading as Phillip's behavior is in the final chapter, it is not inexplicable or necessarily a condemnation. He is enduring news of the suicide of his just-named son Etienne. Melodramatic and cowardly as the suicide may be (Robert/Etienne was never proposed as a model man), it is inevitable due to his character and necessary for Phillip's finale. Phillip must sustain the ultimate collapse of his bargains and his self-image, face the falsity of both and the failure of all his solutions—and then see if any worthy character can be salvaged from the wreckage. He begins as he had before, in denial ("That's not so"), then self-defense ("I was coming back home to talk to him"), and blaming the messenger (203). His progression from grief to anger to depression and despair is psychologically credible; so is his solution of running away. But with his leadership taken away, he knows nowhere good to go and proposes to fall back on his old defenses: whiskey and a whore, disgusting weakness in a "big man." Yet, ironically, in the passion of his grief, Phillip is still bigger than the morally "small" Shepherd, worrying about whether his arm is broken, getting from the scene his own much-needed lesson of right and wrong.

As so often in Gaines's works, it is a woman who speaks the wisdom that finally gives meaning to a man's life and to the book that recounts it. When the older and younger men, Chippo and Shepherd, know nothing more to say, and when Alma has vented her own grief and anger and gone aside, the words of sanity and possible salvation come from the young woman Beverly. "You have to go back. . . . You wanted too much from man, from God. Too much all at one time" (210–1). She gives his full name, Reverend Phillip J. Martin, which somehow enables him to review his story as he felt it, to express his pain and despair, his anger at God, for whose sake he "gived, and gived, and gived" to others, who "owed" him the son he's now lost. She leads him to look at the change in the others as his sufficient reward and points him toward the future, embodied and symbolized in his living son, Patrick, a sufficient reason to live and hope and work.

Even with Beverly's thematic expression of wisdom and Phillip's seeming acquiescence, however, we are not assured that he will follow through. Her final question, "You won't let us down, will you?" gets no explicit reply. Nor has Phillip ever admitted the error of his self-assessment and of his expectation of God. He may have "gived, and gived, and gived," but not without expecting something back. He expected and got honor and material comforts; the one thing he never gave was reparation to those he had injured. His bargain had to fail, but he never admits it in the novel. And even Beverly, for all her wisdom in turning his mind to his obligations to Alma and his children at home, never sees or suggests that some reparation is still due Johanna, now alone in her grief and poverty. Phillip's going to Alma surely suggests a change essential to his character and his future. Yet his last sad words are "I'm lost, Alma. I'm lost" (214). We have to take her encouraging word that they can start over.

Readers have experienced unease with this perceived irresolution of the novel. Gaines said some of his friends complained of the need for "another chapter"; his interviewer, however, felt he had done well to present the "whole problem but not the whole solution" (CEG, 129). Gaines's sense of a possible solution seems to have progressed over the years. In 1973, during the writing of the novel, Gaines said Phillip has doubts of his survival in his situation and implied that those doubts reflected his own about "man prevailing" (CEG, 62). In 1983, asked whether Phillip's "starting over" might include outreach to Johanna, Gaines replied, "I would think that after this he would . . . go to California, explain to her, then come back and start over with Alma" (CEG, 165). So his creator did not then see Phillip Martin as degraded or finally defeated. By 1994 he was saying, "Maybe even Phillip Martin . . . could do something else" than leave a legacy of irresponsibility and failure (CEG, 321–2). The latter remark at that distance from writing has a tone of wistful hope.

The artistic issue of the ending, however, is not so much the uncertainty of Phillip's future moral stature as a lack of the sense of inevitability that follows from a thorough presentation of character; it is the artistic problem of *Catherine Carmier* once again. Fictional persons may be clearly saved or clearly lost, or may be left in the ambiguity of a personality likely to be forever falling and rising. But if those persons have been solidly, vividly represented, a "resolution"—even by a character's irresolution—has been achieved.

In answering the nagging question of what is askew in this novel, readers and critics of *In My Father's House* have generally said that the central flaw is the presentation of Phillip. The causes of this inadequacy are not in his psychological realism but, as already noted, in the flaws of plot structure, of melodrama and improbability, that cause the simple, formulable, emphatic theme (Black men, be responsible!) to overwhelm and subvert his realistic characterization. In addition, three other factors can be cited.

Protagonists take much of their depth of personality from other characters around them with whom they have nuanced interactions. Secondary and minor characters reveal a principal by their own needs and desires, their traits and behaviors that counter or complement those of the protagonist. In a represented action, minors need not be richly intricate personalities, but they should not all be one-dimensional if the protagonist is to be complex. In a real sense, Phillip is this novel's only character, the one on whom all significance rests. All others seem hardly more than short stick figures around the single large one. Even Robert, for all the effort expended on him initially, takes too little credible imagined life; after one scene with his father, he drops out of the novel, never known in person by his real name or by his experiences recounted in his own voice. For a reader, he has no existence for the twenty-odd years between his childhood moment at Phillip's door and his response to his sister's rape. Robert's potential foil, Patrick, is a nonentity; he appears long enough to shake his father's hand "quickly, bravely" and watch him at the supper table (61, 62); then he disappears. The two adverbs imply much about Phillip and Patrick's nonrelationship, yet how much more might have been made—or at least implied—of Phillip as father by depicting interaction and dialogue with this son. Other characters— the young people and old men, Chippo, and even Alma—exist more as moving shadows around Phillip than people of solid flesh and voice from whom he takes vitality. They come on stage, they speak so he can speak, they exit.

Perhaps Phillip could take life from his own voice, but he hardly does. In his abundant dialogue, we are given his words but very very little of their sound or of his body language. Without facial expressions, gestures, and nuances of voice, the full revelation of words is incomplete. Reporting these can be as important for characterization as depiction of inner thoughts. Even in chapters 5 through 8, where we have interior views of Phillip, we are short of visual revelation; after those chapters, even the interior views decline in favor of straight, spare dialogue. In the important final chapter, the viewpoint is again dramatic; we are told Phillip's movements and read his anguished words, but we don't "see" his face or "hear" his voice; we have no direct access to his thoughts as Chippo, Alma, and Beverly address him. Omniscient narration should allow us ample notation of both the inner and outer person; here it does not.

What we do have throughout the novel is symbolism, the technique Gaines usually employs with such skill. In this novel, it may be very effective, as is his choice of the "miserable, frigid, sunless Louisiana winter"[12] for a story of such chilled emotions and frozen hopes. But at times, the symbols seem "clever," substitutes for a full depiction of character: the cypress gate Phillip means to take down " 'Cause I put it there" (73); the high, gray, muddy river rising like the flood of his past when he meets with Robert X; the muddy gray houses and warped porches, the weeds that have replaced houses at Reno plantation; his old haunts: theater, bars, and rooming house that now haunt his memory and conscience; the pictures in his office of white and black heroes of civil rights with whom he identifies,[13] and gambling Po Boy, with his dollar bill so old and wrinkled it can never be smoothed out. All these would be subtle, suggestive nuances of character, if only the character were sufficiently substantive in himself.

If Phillip Martin is depicted without sufficient complexity of character, of motivation and choice, he cannot be the voice for the theme in all its complexity. He cannot convincingly or clearly speak to readers of the failure of black fathers, the separation and loss of black sons. When Phillip tells Chippo, even near the end, that "a paralysis we inherited from slavery" keeps black fathers and sons apart, a reader with any knowledge of the history of racism and of the way a culture is infused and perpetuated will hear a measure of truth about primary cause. But not whole cause; there are too many solid black fathers in society and in the novel. The same is true for the effects of the civil rights movement; perhaps a Million Man March should have preceded the marches on Washington or Selma. But parents of either gender cannot raise or support children economically or morally, cannot be role models or win respect, unless they progressively confront and overcome the white power structures that oppress both genders and generations. Whatever truths, whatever moral claims or encouragements are to be found in any religion, are not negated simply because one man or many misinterpret or misuse them. Finally, a man, or a full human being of either gender, sorts out motivations, makes choices, and takes responsibility for their consequences. When necessary, he admits and amends the past in so far as he can, stands in his present obligation and opportunity, and starts over. Phillip Martin is portrayed as abundantly intelligent. He could have been portrayed as grappling with these complexities, not always ignoring, simplifying, or denying them in his own defense. On his grappling depends the moral development of his character and the power of his voice; on the portrayal of that grappling depends the com-

12. Larry McMurtry, review of *In My Father's House*, *New York Times Book Review* (June 1978): 13.

13. Beavers, 92–100, analyzes these pictures in the context of Phillip's conversion.

plex truth of the novel's theme. Like father and son, the two major elements of the novel never quite get together.

This limitation on the novel's art is as regrettable as the limitation on life's fulfillment the novel presents. Yet Gaines was not wrong in saying, with reservation, that it is a "good book." Whatever its flaws, it presents a character we can care about, at least moderately, and a situation with thematic questions we can choose to think about with all the passion and creativity of imagination the author intended to provoke.

8

⎯⎯◆⎯⎯

New Visions and Voices

A Gathering of Old Men

The full dimensions of victory can be found only by comprehending the change within the minds of millions of Negroes. From the depths in which the spirit of freedom was imprisoned, an impulse for liberty burst through. The Negro became, in his own estimation, the equal of any man. They shook off . . . psychological slavery and said: "We can make ourselves free."
                                   —Martin Luther King Jr., *Why We Can't Wait*

WRITING IN THE early 1960s, Martin Luther King capsulized a historic move-ment involving millions; in *A Gathering of Old Men*, set in the late 1970s, Ernest Gaines depicts the same change in the minds of about twenty people. His search for a definition and example of authentic manhood expands in this novel to a group, each person experiencing "an impulse for liberty" from old fears and fail-ures, each influencing the others to an action that will make them all free. Asked about the origin of this novel, Gaines replied semiseriously that the "easiest way to explain" it was as the need to write about men, since he had written one book about a woman. Very seriously he explained that in his returns to the South, he had talked much with the old men gathered on porches, the survivors of the old system, had heard them talk of the prowess of their forebears in lifting cane and cutting logs, but he had also seen in their eyes, heard in their voices, a desire for a different prowess, for bravery, for the "thing that really makes man. That is: being able to do that thing that you said you cannot do" (CEG, 271–2). The one thing above all others that blacks traditionally could not do in the planta-tion culture was to "stand" in opposition to white power, to defend themselves or others against it. But, said Gaines, though one cannot make up for the past, there "comes a time in one's life" when "dignity demands that you act . . . when it is necessary to be human . . . when you refuse to back down." That "moment" is "manliness," yet it is as available and compelling to women characters as to men (CEG, 242). It is "humanity." He had shown it repeatedly in Miss Jane Pittman; she had taught or aided young men in reaching it. Now he must give to old men their moment, their day to stand.

The victory of Gaines's old men, like that of their race, occurs first in a change within their own minds, a new way of seeing themselves and their people, as well as the white race in all its historic power, benevolent or brutal. Transformed vision, both King and Gaines imply, releases the voice, enables speech and action, a "stand" for justice. All this makes real social change possible if both races can see and hear themselves and each other as individuals and as community. Readers, presumably, can be induced to share this vision and hear this collective voice through the novel's art.

Before their stand, the old men have seen themselves and their race in stereotype, as oppressed, terrified, and helpless before whites, needing white protection against white violence, always done in by it in threat or reality. They speak to whites rarely, respectfully, about neutral or trivial topics, never in daring or open truth. Only within the shelter of their own quarters and culture can they acknowledge their individual differences of character, be friendly, respectful, and casually supportive of each other, share their stories and food, the truths and enjoyments of their life. They do not see themselves as "men," assume they cannot be, because never in their long lives have they been allowed to be or asserted a right to be men. Mathu is the exception; he is not fearful of whites, but he cannot enjoy life with blacks whose cowardice he despises. Not until near the novel's end does he "see" a cause to speak to them.

The black men see whites variously but always according to defined group expectations: benevolent protection from Candy and her class; competition and displacement from the Cajuns; verbal scorn and physical brutality from "the law" and from most Cajuns, especially "Fix and his crowd." They have little awareness of the changes represented by such younger people as Gil, Sully, and the teacher from USL. Black women mostly share the views of the old men; black children are also picking up the stereotypes, though they are still both confused and open-minded enough to adopt new views through new experiences. Change in the blacks begins when they are ready to challenge their own fearful concepts of both races: "whites think we think they are too powerful to challenge: we'll show them."[1]

---

1. William Hugh Jansen, "The Esoteric-Exoteric Factor in Folklore," in *The Study of Folklore*, ed. Alan Dundes (Englewood Cliffs, N.J.: Prentice-Hall, 1965), 45–8, explicates the intricacy of con-

Whites, of course, see blacks only in biracial contexts and so in the stereotypes blacks have been conditioned to accept. For Candy's class, they are children to be treated well and protected in expectation of labor and subservient respect, then cared for in old age. Almost all other whites see blacks as degraded laborers and sex objects to be exploited, controlled by battering, treated well if they accept their "place," and occasionally knocked about just for fun or "training." The only difference in the initial views, voices, or plans of Mapes and the Cajuns is a matter of degree and legality. What the whites "don't see," have never been told, is the blacks' real view of whites or of black life in their own community. This blindness leaves them vulnerable to blacks' use of their knowledge of white expectations, which cost Beau his life and give all the other whites a shock that must permanently alter their vision and racial relationships. The blacks can and do take advantage of surprise to "fool the white folks."[2]

Whites' images of themselves are tragically molded by their views of blacks; failing to see either race accurately, they are themselves oppressed by themselves. Candy sees herself as "quality," the protective and benevolent mistress of the plantation in place of her inebriate uncle and aunt, distinctly superior to the Cajuns and even to the law represented by Mapes. Like him, she assumes unquestionable authority and the power, by her own cool management, to shape and control the bizarre situation she has created. Like Lou, Gil, and Sully, she has liberal views but also a margin of "don't see"—that she, like Mapes, has lost control of people who have freed themselves from her. Once she does see that, she doesn't know why this has happened or how to respond. The voice she has always had in the quarters loses force, becomes a querulous protest, and finally fades away. Ironically, the Cajuns—the Boutans and their friends—have the most accurate, albeit suppressed, view of themselves. They see but "don't see" that they are the white serfs of their society, validated only by the racial link to their "betters" and by control of blacks. They believe themselves able to get black labor on demand and to terrify and kill with impunity while claiming protection from the law if in danger from blacks; that is, in fact, what they have always done. Gil, the one Cajun who can change, has to learn to see the blacks, and even the murder of Beau, in new ways, in terms of a moral social order. Until he does, his response remains an issue of personal ambition versus family loyalty

cepts and stereotypes one group can hold of itself and of another, and the ways groups use these perceptions.

2. For analysis of the white characters, especially Candy, cf. Babb, *EG*, 123–8; Beavers, 172; Sandra G. Shannon, "Strong Men Getting Stronger: Gaines's Defense of the Elderly Black Male in *A Gathering of Old Men*," in *CRF*, 207–9.

and duty; he remains torn, and his voice descends from the authority of a "son" in "the family" to the pleas of an outcast child.

All these stereotypical attitudes and assumptions are so obvious that presenting them might produce only a stereotypical novel; some early reviewers, students, and critics have seen it that way (cf. CEG, 175–6). What lifts this work to the significance of art is its devising a reversal of stereotypes so motivated and credible that it can occur in the minds of both characters and readers. The novel presumes in readers a greater vision, or at least wider eyes. Readers may be like the blacks in seeing the reasons for fear but have a sense of black dignity and potential, and more hope to see them achieved. They may identify with Lou Dimes in both his liberal views of what changes must come and his uncertainty about how and when they may come. They may share both Lou's and the blacks' views of Candy, Mapes, Fix, Luke Will, and all they represent, but they remain unsure of the hope that they can be put in Gil's and Sully's generation. Like Gil, readers ask the question, "Won't it ever stop?" (122).[3] How many must and can be expected to "see" and speak up before it stops? And further, what can effectively make it stop?

This uncertainty raises the novel's major ethical issue, a chief element of its theme. It seems to say that one must expect to see change achieved only by courageous black readiness to match black guns against white. Readers convinced of the futility of circular violence or morally committed to nonviolence can be puzzled or disturbed by the novel's apparent ambiguity on this issue.

On one hand, Mathu, in twice pushing a gun into Charlie's hand, is urging courage and self-defense, not specifically murder. The gathering on the porch is clearly a superior choice to "crawling under the bed," as courage, loyalty, and respect are superior to fear, abandonment, and contempt. In the real world of 1970s bayou Louisiana, it is not evident that a gathering without guns would have intimidated, morally impressed, or stopped the likes of Fix and Luke Will. When Luke arrives, he prevents peaceful dispersal by shooting first. When he later offers to turn himself and his cronies in to Mapes or Dimes, the moral issue is "discussed" under the pressure of battle. Charlie refuses a "deal"; Lou tells him he is moving from self-defense to murder. Gaines was asked in an interview why he did not allow the fight to end at Luke's offer; he replied that though Luke did mean to give up and get out alive, Charlie could not know that, would never have trusted him to stop, and did not trust, either, the justice of a white jury; the

---

3. Ernest J. Gaines, *A Gathering of Old Men* (New York: Knopf, 1983), 122. All citations are from this edition.

last point was expressed in dialogue the author later cut (CEG, 169–70). One reader at least has shared Charlie's view, "had no doubt . . . Luke Will would go home when he had either shot or lynched Charlie and not before."[4] Charlie's mistrust is justified by Luke's refusal to give up his gun first. And Charlie's rush on Luke's group seems less a desire to shoot for murder's sake than to perform one insistent act of courage and die in that act rather than in the chair, to make his death meaningful rather than pitiful.

Gaines also discussed the possibility of multiple deaths, saying that they could not occur "because the old men couldn't see anything and the other bums were drunk" and that he had devised both factors to prevent "complete chaos" and keep the focus on the old men's "stand." In the end, two people die, not twenty: one gets what he came in hatred to give; the other "redeems" himself by his death from a life of cowardice and self-disrespect. It is hard not to recognize hero-ism in Charlie as well as in the other risk-taking black defenders—and in the plot's outcome as the author devised it.

On the other hand, Gaines has often referred to Martin Luther King Jr. as one of his heroes (CEG, 91, 131, 164), and King's way would have been to orga-nize a gathering without guns or, given the existing gathering, to end it by a cou-rageous act of negotiation. That is, in fact, the role of Clatoo in stopping the potentially violent confrontation with the sheriff. And it must be said that the ending devised for the television production, in which the rednecks back down and depart, Charlie walks in dignity to his legal accounting, and the men cele-brate a victory of courageous standing, is the one a peace-minded reader would desire. Yet it came off as far less dramatic and also less realistic and probable.[5] The resolution, if there is one, of this thematic dilemma is first in Clatoo and then in the secondary hero, Gil Boutan, who stops the larger planned lynching by his refusal to participate in it, then or ever. He still needs Russ to articulate the moral meaning of his choice for his and others' future, but he "want[s] to think. . . . just want[s] to think" about it (151), as must his entire generation, and as readers are invited to do.

If Gaines cannot be said to have adopted Martin Luther King's philosophy in full, he has pointed toward better, nonviolent solutions in which eyes and voices have more power than guns. Blacks must "see" what Charlie has "seen

4. John Doyle to Mary Ellen Doyle, February 15, 1996. In possession of Mary Ellen Doyle.

5. Gaines said that he did not much object to the film change; he had tried to prove a point about the old men standing (CEG, 200–2). For a full discussion of the film adaptations of Gaines's works, see Charney, in CRF, 125–35.

in them swamps" (208)—a life free from the inner oppression of fear and self-depreciation—and must assert by voice and action their right to it. Whites must, like Russ, see the need "to plow under one thing in order for something else to grow" and must articulate that need to the younger generation who can, if they choose, voice it in defiance of the strongest, potentially most violent authority in their own society so they can "help the community" attain a just social order based in nonviolent moral order (151). Readers must be moved with Lou Dimes, the blacks, Gil, and even Candy to see all of this and its implications for themselves.[6]

That is an immense change from blindness to vision, and from vision to voice and action. Within one story, a credible change requires the rhetoric of powerful techniques of plot, characterization, and narration, as well as symbols that subtly pervade every part of the work.

Though this novel was chosen for a television film, a form whose prime requisite is usually dramatic physical action, the story has, in fact, very little such action prior to the big shoot-out at the end—ironically, the one major scene not used in the film. Snookum runs through the quarters, the men and other characters drive or walk in there, and Beau's body is carried out. Mapes slaps some men; and Miss Merle serves sandwiches. Otherwise, they all wait for the expected action to begin. In this plot, images and linguistic references, silence and dialogue, mark the movements of outer and, especially, inner action. Vision and voice enable each other in an empowering circle of influence.

Not to see, or to be unseen or disregarded by others, is almost invariably also to be voiceless, unheard, or unheeded. It is also true that to begin to "see" is also to "hear"; to "hear" is to "see" what can and must be done. Reverend Jameson looks down the quarters but "couldn't see a thing . . . for all the weeds" (7); he will remain a "don't see" character, blocked by the weeds of the past, a man at whom and to whom the others do not look or speak except to silence him. Miss Merle, driving into the quarters, does not see any blacks and assumes they are in hiding like "frightened little bedbugs" (12, 15); the action of the novel will be the blacks' emergence from life "under the bed" (28). Mat and Chimley, who have lived in fear, perform a whole ritual of not looking at each other so they won't "see" each other's thoughts or fears or have to call each other to a high-risk action. Mat, once changing, looks at his wife as if he doesn't know her; he

6. The representation of progressive responses to violence is discussed in CEG, 44; Reynolds Price, "A Louisiana Pageant of Calamity," *New York Times Book Review* (October 30, 1983): 15; Lance Jeffers, review of *A Gathering of Old Men*, *Black Scholar* (March 1984): 46.

keeps looking until he sees both her and himself differently and can passionately voice his truth. The graveyard scene reveals how various families of blacks have always seen each other: the Creoles as "quality," despising and despised by other blacks, Dirty Red's people as "trifling," and Billy as just inept (44–6).

Central to the novel's meaning is Johnny Paul's "don't see" diatribe, which states the novel's primary motif as it launches the storytelling that both energizes the blacks and moves others, including readers and even Mapes, toward a genuine "I see" (87–92). Gaines said Mapes had never seen the flowers because he never saw "the people, the history, the soul, and spirit." Now, he is so focused on solving a crime that he cannot see the "presence of the unseen, the unspoken, the unknown . . . so powerful, so pervasive" (*CEG*, 257). By listening, however, he is "starting to feel what was going on" and "knowed he had to wait" (93); his voice thereafter becomes almost as respectful as ironic in his exchanges with the people. Gil, the most open-eyed Cajun, has his terrible moment of refusing to look at or speak to his black partner Cal, but overcomes it. His father, by contrast, opens his eyes wider at news that blacks await him with shotguns but then narrows them again "to where they were almost closed" (146). Black Charlie, having run to avoid being seen, returns transformed by what he has "seen" in the swamps. Finally, Miss Merle's exasperated "Jesus, will you just look at this. . . . Jesus, you ever seen anything like this in all your born days?" (128) is a provocative narrative question. No, not even Jesus has ever seen such action, but social change depends on blacks, whites, and today's readers seeing and "seeing," "hearing" and speaking out; the novel's imagery makes that clear over and over.

When the men, beginning with Mat and Chimley, glimpse a possible new self-image ("now when we're old we get to be brave" 32), then they begin to speak and motivate each other to take their "last chance." Their totally unexpected action of gathering in mutual defense and assertion is only the first of many unforeseeable changes in behavior laced through the plot to force a new way of seeing the races. Besides their customary fear, these men are too old to do anything daring—so everyone thinks. To their own wives, they appear "old fools" "gone crazy" (32, 36–7); to Candy, child-men following her directions; to Sully, a weird scene out of *Twilight Zone* or a Brueghel painting; to Miss Merle, Mapes and his deputies, and all the Boutans, a reversal of expectations beyond belief. Even to readers, the old men represent such a reversal. Sandra Shannon notes that the literature of the civil rights movement implied that all change would come through the angry and courageous young; the old were passive, resistant, or, at best, irrelevant. But David Estes has noted that if these men begin as Sambo figures, they become tricksters, subverting the old way by cunning and courage. Like good tricksters, they derive their courage and use their cunning chiefly by their voices.[7]

The old men's fundamentally altered way of seeing themselves and their un-characteristic behavior in gathering in turn cause role reversals in others, both white and black. Mapes assumes he can knock a true account out of weak Uncle Billy or some other man until they all begin to "sass" him and grin at his failure. Later, when Tucker dares Mapes to lock him up and Deputy Griffin to stop his defiant talk, it is Griffin whom Mapes puts down; it is Tucker who says to Griffin, "You through, boy?" (95), a stereotypical white-to-black address, as dangerous as a black could make to white authority. Some of the women come to stand with the men and speak up just as defiantly to their own Reverend Jameson and to Mapes and his deputy. Reverend Jameson is told to "shut up. Go on back home. . . . Nobody listening to you today"; he is called "old bootlicker" and "old pos-sum-looking fool" and is even physically threatened (56, 105–6), unlikely enough words and behaviors from a black man to a minister, unheard of from an older black woman. Old, jail-toughened Beulah extends her defiance of Deputy Griffin to calling him "boy" and telling Mapes to silence him "if you want him around much longer" (108–10). The treatment of Jameson is not presented as necessarily admirable but more as comprehensible in the heat of desire to cast off all past symbols of subservience. Estes sees Jameson and Griffin used to mea-sure the growth of the men and the humiliation and defeat of white power.[8]

Mary Helen Washington has criticized Gaines's presentation of the women in the novel; she says they are allowed no right to suffer, be heroic, or even talk.[9] Granted that they are sidelined to let the old men stand out and that some are presented as immensely fearful, still one cannot undervalue Corrine's, Glo's, and especially Beulah's roles and words. Perhaps Jameson's fear is seen as similar to that of the wives who stayed home, and so it is given to the strongest one who came, ironically carrying a stereotypical name, to insult and silence him. Finally, the uncharacteristic behavior extends even to the children. When the men whom Berto's "sissy-looking boy" Fue had mocked for their cowardice actually stand and speak up, even the youngest child, Snookum, imitates their bravado and dares Mapes to jail or beat him.

Gaines could have set up the altered vision, voice, and action of the blacks as counter to rigidly stereotypical behaviors of whites, especially the redneck Ca-

7. Shannon, in CRF, 204–6; Estes, "Humor," in CRF, 243.
8. Estes, "Humor," 243–5.
9. Mary Helen Washington, "The House Slavery Built," Nation (January 14, 1984): 24.

juns. If readers are to love to hate them (or at least their proclivity to lynch), let them be unremittingly hateful. But Gaines, in Alice Walker's comment, "cannot bear to reduce even the ugliest, cruelest, and most loathsome redneck to a stereotype."[10] In fact, Gaines sets readers up to expect the best from the liberal whites, Candy and Gil, and only the worst of Luke Will and Fix Boutan; then he startles us with unexpected reactions from each. Candy is quickly seen as suspiciously benevolent, determined to protect on her own terms. This oppressive blind side in her character is exposed under floodlights when she demands to be present at the old men's conference. The confrontation erupts vocally: everyone is arguing, asserting, threatening, defying, or mocking. Candy, who can't "see" that her authority has been transferred to Clatoo, can "hear" only one voice, Mathu's: "Quiet. Soft. The way he used to talk to her when she was a little girl" (175). She, not the blacks, is now the "child." Symbolically, as she clings to Mathu, he "covered her hands with his . . . and pulled her free" (177). Only at the novel's end, again at a word from Mathu, does she wave good-bye to the men and "search" for the hand of Lou Dimes.

At the opposite extreme from Candy's liberalism is the trigger-happy racism of Luke Will, apparently a man without feelings for anyone, incapable of understanding even the family motivations of Fix Boutan. Yet when the shoot-out gets heated, it is Luke, not his cronies, who recognizes the change in Charlie's personality and authority, begins to respect his enemy and the seriousness of his own position, even offers to "turn ourselfs in," and asks Sharp to "look after Verna and the kids" (205–6). Gaines said he could not, in fairness, deny Fix or Luke Will their humanity; yet he had written several drafts before including Luke's speech expressing concern for his family. "Maybe I was feeling good that morning" (CEG, 168). Though Luke is not finally the animal we thought, he is incapable of the change required for lasting societal reform. Hope of that rests on the tug of motives between Fix and Gil Boutan.

If there is one character we are prepared to stereotype and detest, it has to be Fix, doer or instigator for decades of all the "dirt" done along the St. Charles River, against whom every black has certified reason for vengeance. Yet when we finally see this lynch-ready monster, he is "sitting in a soft chair by the window," tenderly holding his now fatherless grandchild in his lap, "and you could see that he had been crying"—he is merely a grieving father and grandfather (133–4).[11]

10. Alice Walker, review of A Gathering of Old Men, New Republic (December 26, 1983): 38.

11. In the film adaptation, Fix is not seen with his grandson, and the effect is different; the redneck stereotype remains.

Even when he argues vehemently with Gil about vengeance for Beau, his speeches reveal motives that have little to do with race and everything to do with notions of family honor: "There will be no split in this family. This is family. Family" (145). And though he himself splits the family by ordering Gil away and closes his eyes and ears to any pleading faces or voices, we can never quite forget that he is less a monster than an old man with a distorted sense of justice.

The future, however, has to depend on his son and his son's generation. Gil, before we see him, is presented by his college friend Sully as the hope of the LSU football team, along with his black partner, Cal. Literally and symbolically, he embodies the hope of being "All-American . . . black and white in the same backfield—and in the Deep South, besides. LSU was fully aware of this, the black and white communities in Baton Rouge were aware . . . and so was the rest of the country" (112). Yet his first action in the novel is the visual and verbal rejection of Cal in reaction to news of Beau's murder. It is perhaps the moment of highest risk in the novel's look-see-speak pattern: Gil has been seeing race in a positive way far in advance of his family; he has even had a notion that being All American with a black partner would have some wider social meaning. Now he loses sight of that and seems to revert to the family's generalized hatred. Only after he has accepted rejection himself can he begin fully to see that what he does on the football field has wider implications than his own fame and glory, that his real family obligation is to his nephew Tee Beau, that by beating Luke Will, he will "help Tee Beau" and so "help this country" (150–1). Daniel White says that white fathers and sons must separate until sons can be free of the old codes and become a new kind of father (as Gil to Tee Beau); then they may reunite.[12]

None of Gaines's novels has received more critical praise for the abundance, realism, humor, and pungency of its dialogue. It perhaps also most satisfied his desire to capture "the way my people talk." The dialogue is not only rich in itself and apt for characterization, it is also the very effective engine of the plot. The essential action of the plot is not only the gathering of the men, nor the shoot-out, it is a deeply significant shift in the dominant voices. Those who are heard or not heard in dialogue reflect the "change in the minds," the changed "seeing," and the resultant change in personal and power relationships.

In the beginning, dialogue *is* the action: Snookum notifies the folk of Candy's call; Janey calls for Miss Merle and Lou Dimes and talks desperately to herself

---

12. Daniel White, " 'Haunted by the Idea': Fathers and Sons in *In My Father's House* and *A Gathering of Old Men*," in CRF, 178–9. Cf. Beavers, 169–70.

and Jesus; Miss Merle engages in verbal battles, with Candy for the truth, with Bea for a sensible response, and with Janey for "answers" about who "don't like Fix" (chapters 1 through 3). The children are the voices of ignorance and triviality; contrasted with their concerns about turnips and teacakes are Candy's urgent "get here quick" repeated six times and Janey's frantic "that shot I heard?" repeated three times (5, 9). Janey and Miss Merle are the voices of fear; intense, experienced, knowing, and credible. Candy is the voice of command: however "wild and scared" she may look or be, she intends to manage the action for her determined purpose—which has everything to do with the protection of Mathu and "my people" and nothing to do with an increase in their freedom. The dialogue is somewhat obscure about how the gathering took its final form: Candy sent for the quarters people first; Rufe seems to have come with a gun, Johnny Paul to have gone home to get one; it is not clear whether she or they devised the idea of many people from all over the area gathering with identical guns and taking "the credit" for shooting Beau. If the men originated that idea, then they are beginning their own part of the action, and she is following them.

By contrast to the incessant, rapid, panic-laden or irrelevant rantings and repetitions of the children and women, the dialogue suddenly grows sparse, slow, and quiet as the men decide to gather and make their way to Marshall. Very little is actually said. Mat and Chimley look at each other for questions and answers; their eyes do the most important "speaking." Neither Chimley nor Mat chooses to communicate their plans or reasons to their wives; as yet they assert themselves "bravely" (and safely) only within their own houses. Mat's phone calls are reported indirectly; in the truck and graveyard, few and mostly trite remarks are exchanged; at Marshall, the men are mostly quiet except to state their "guilt." The only pieces of real dialogue are Mat's explosion to his wife, Cherry and Dirty Red's exchange on their ancestors as motive for the present risk, and Jameson's ineffectual protests and pleas. The scarcity of dialogue in this section makes the significant pieces stand out, makes the men's motives and moods—fearful, reticent, passionate, or laconic—all the more memorable and moving. Clatoo speaks one line for all, "I come here to stand, not to talk" (55).

As soon as the men have gathered, Candy's limited importance declines further. Only a third of the way through the novel does she get to speak her story, first to Lou in indirect dialogue, then in her own voice to Mapes. By that time, everyone who dares has told her she's lying; everyone the readers will believe has assured us Candy's power is of no real consequence now that the men are present to take their stand. Mapes goes past her to take control his way, which consists of few words, a few orders and questions, and blows when words are futile. He fails. The one character who speaks up and talks with Mapes is the weakest of the men, Billy; for him, words of defiance and remembered pain are a source of new strength. He now "sees pretty well . . . pretty well indeed" (79); those who see him standing line up for their blows. At this point in the narrative, action has switched from talking to standing.

Mathu will speak to "the man" though he's white, but not to the other blacks. He seems about to address them at Mapes's request when they break in and begin the storytelling. They thus delay any action that Mapes might other-wise take, force him to listen to them and force his deputy to listen, until he gradually slows and stops his ironic put-downs, essentially changes to their side (where he says Jesus is), and is finally drawn into serious dialogue with them about their racial experience. Their memories poured out in speech are the ac-tion of this section, their take-over of power. By reviving old visions of who they were, they assert their right to be who and where they are. They kill old pain by asserting that they have killed the old racist power that caused their pain. Having once more looked hard at their lives, they free themselves by voicing pain and truth in the face of the current white power figure, the one before whom they would most be expected to keep silent or to give the expected answer. Having refused to say what Mapes wants to hear, they force on him the truth he does not want. And the truth sets them free. Through their voices, the balance of power at Marshall has shifted.

The same shift must occur in "Cajun country . . . Gil's country" (131). Gil, at first, is as lost for words as the old blacks; he speaks nothing to his partner Cal, minimally to Sully, and only abrupt questions to Mapes. His one question, "What's going on here?" (repeated seven times), is thematic; the reader, too, must ask it. The answer comes when Gil is moved to turn on Candy and assert Cajun dignity vis-à-vis upper-class whites; in challenging her sense of superiority and condescension to his people, he seems to release his awareness of blacks as his equals, of Cajun injustice to them, expressed in his passionate and repeated wish to "stop it" (chapter 10). All the way home, Gil is silent again; once there, he can't say "what I want to say," what only he can and must say to his father. Young, confused, and grieving, he cannot separate his instinct and desire for a better, a just social order from his personal desire to be the All American hero. But having "seen" the old men, what "none of us in this room has ever seen before," he is enabled to say how he has experienced his family's history and rep-utation, and to say the one necessary line: "I won't go along" (136–8). His defi-ance sets off another long dialogue (one of Gaines's most insightful) among many characters, which again constitutes action while assuring the essential nonaction, the shift in moral power to Gil's generation. This long dialogue creates a series of foils: Gil versus his father, Gil versus Luke Will, Russ versus Fix and Luke. Gil listens, talks his way through his own inner movements—refusal to lynch, grief at expulsion from his family, valuing family over football. At one point he sounds very much like his father: "I'm talking about my family. Not the damned public. My family" (150). Russ talks him toward a new view of "family" in a new human social order. For this inner action to be complete in Gil or his generation of whites, he and they must "think . . . think." He falls silent in the novel; his is not the final voice of the future.

To complete the novel's action, some stunning parallels and contrasts are set up by the dialogue. At Tee Jack's bar, Jack Marshall voices irresponsible denial and inaction; Luke Will and his "boys" speak crudely for the old order, what Fix should have done. When word reaches Marshall of what Fix *has* done, highly ironic role reversals occur. Johnny Paul, almost like Luke Will, also speaks for the old order, seeing Fix as Fix sees himself: as a necessary avenger of his boy's blood, while Mapes, like Gil and Russ, articulates the new order and gives the black men credit for it. The black men fall silent, then become almost another gang, demanding their chance to fight and shoot. Clatoo, also like Gil, becomes the voice of reason; he tries dialogue over violence and attempts to avoid a useless fight. He also frees the men from Candy's interference. Dialogue during the physical action of the fight is necessarily minimal; it serves to show the fake power of Luke's gang and the comic improbability of any serious killing by the old men; it ludicrously diminishes Mapes as a power figure and seriously affirms Dirty Red and the other men.

The most potent dialogue of the novel occurs in these final chapters at Marshall; it completes the thematic shift. Once Clatoo and Mathu have silenced and dismissed Candy, her voice is heard briefly only once again, in Lou's car, where she can't see, literally or figuratively, but stares silently ahead into the darkness. At the end, she will turn willingly to Lou; she will have "seen" her new truth, but she will never have the voice of command that was hers at the start. Mathu has become the voice of the "law" of the new order, first judging himself and then exonerating the men of their past. But the final voice, the final power figure in the novel, obviously if ironically, is the newly made man, Charlie. To him is given the major speech of the book, affirming that he is a man, is free of a "heavy load," that he is ready to go of his own volition, and that the old men "did all right today" (193). Even though the fight and the trial must follow, the novel's movement toward change is essentially complete.

What implications readers see in all this imagery, unusual behavior, and dialogue will depend, in great part, on Gaines' arrangement of the plot, which flows with a smoothness that virtually conceals its significant pattern. Because the blacks must first see and speak differently for themselves, must be their own chief source of liberation, the first nine of twenty chapters are set at Marshall and focus on black decisions and movements. Candy and Miss Merle are the only whites present or at all active (Candy's aunt and uncle are at the house but no more "there" than ever). Lou Dimes and Sheriff Mapes arrive in chapter 8, followed briefly by the coroner. But Lou at this time is merely an observer and ineffective emotional prop for Candy; the purpose of chapters 8 and 9 is to show that Mapes cannot manipulate the blacks anymore: not by persuasion, sarcasm, or blows. They will gather; they will bolster each other's courage even as they deny each other's claim to have killed Beau; they will line up to be slapped; they will demand time to tell their stories. And they will not go home.

Only when the old black men's vision of themselves has begun to change radically by what they have seen and heard of each other, when their stories have been told, when they are in control of themselves and the Marshall quarters, when they have nothing further to do but wait for Fix and family to ride, only then can the novel take us to meet this once feared white clan. We meet them first, however, at LSU and at Marshall, in the person of Gil Boutan, All American—if he can resolve his new moral and emotional dilemma, if he will now do "all I can to stop" lynch-mob power. He thus preempts his father's role as focus of the "gatherings" of white men, old and young; his refusal stops his brother and thus the family. He is not present at Tee Jack's bar but is made a foil to Luke Will, who is not a Cajun and has not even their code, can persuade only by vulgar name-calling, imbibing Old Crow, source and symbol of his false courage, and intimidating a few followers as trashy as himself to do what Gil has refused to do. Readers may share Tee Jack's apprehension, but we have seen true determination and bravery in old black faces and now in one young white one, have "seen" what that will have to mean for the immediate and long-range future.

Between Gil's confrontations with the old black and old white men, a little seven-page interlude at Marshall (chapter 11) serves several purposes: it uses the trivial dialogue and movement around the outhouse to build a mood of tense expectation, and it reveals that Lou still has no real clue to what the old men will do or how they have changed. It offers essential comic relief by Miss Merle's "dishing out the sandwiches . . . and fussing" (125) and by Griffin's ludicrous butler/cop image "standing there with an empty basket in one hand and a loaded revolver in the other" (126); Shakespeare's Dogberry is not a better assurance of a safe outcome from potential tragedy. More seriously, the sandwiches provide a shared meal that binds everyone into a kind of community ("Mapes, Candy, Mathu, Griffin, the old men, the old women, the children—everyone was eating" [126]) as well as a kind of conspiracy of blacks and whites (Griffin and Jameson excepted) for mutual protection from a common enemy. Yet Miss Merle's comic repetitions also indicate the level of stress in the one with least reason for personal fear, which, along with the final dialogue of Mapes and Lou ("What's going to happen?"), renew a legitimate suspense in readers. We too have to wait and follow Miss Merle's insistent "Just look!" if we are really to "see" what others will see in the coming action.

When the two gatherings, black and white, have been rendered separately but not equally, the climactic chapters are a drama in black and white, with shifting focus. The conclave in Mathu's house is all-black; then the whites join the blacks to hear Charlie's story. The shoot-out is also biracial, with blacks dominating. Finally, the epilogue is a white insider's report of the trial and of all the changed relationships the "gatherings" have caused. Everyone has seen what could never have been foreseen, heard words never spoken before on the Marshall plantation or in St. Raphael Parish; no one will ever be the same.

The credibility of any plot, of course, depends in large part on characterization. A plot that foreshadows radical social change depends on characters who are more or less individualized according to the degree to which they are capable of change. This novel, however, presented Gaines a special challenge in that its protagonist is not a single but a collective person; he himself identified the protagonist as the group of men. In an early version, it was to have been a mulatto cousin of Candy's; then he saw the real interest and importance of the men and concentrated on them (CEG, 167). They must, then, be a "gathering" with a common cause sufficient to create a unified personality capable of extraordinary group action. Yet Gaines also had to avoid the stereotype of blacks that "they're all alike" and give reason to "see" and respect his people as individuals, a requisite for social change. This balance he accomplishes by varying the personal traits and the degrees of delineation of his nineteen old men.

Color is the most obvious and symbolic visual trait distinguishing the men; not only whites but also the blacks themselves, especially Mathu, must learn to distinguish "not by the color of their skin but by the content of their character." The colors noted range from Mathu's African "blue-black" (51) to the black of Chimley and browns of Mat, Clatoo, Johnny Paul, and Tucker, to the colors Mathu despises: Cherry's "between red and yellow" (39), Rooster's common yellow, the Creole yellow of the Lejeunes and Jacob, and the Albino milk-whiteness of Clabber. However, when Mathu names those he had most despised for weakness of character, his list does not correspond exactly to his color code. Rooster and Dirty Red (presumably named for his color) qualified for his contempt, but so did Billy Washington (old and nervous but not color-identified) and black Chimley. And Jameson, scorned by all, is "jet black" (54). The issue of respect is not drawn in color alone; when the men go beyond it altogether in their interaction, only then can they become a cohesive, mutually supportive corps with purpose and power.[13]

Moral weakness and strength are defined, rather, by consistent traits, perhaps culturally induced, but over which a man is presumed to have some control. Reverend Jameson unquestionably is presented as weak and despised by all, including, it seems, his author/creator. One must question Gaines's fairness in making Jameson the only man who falls down when Mapes strikes him. He has, after all, taken the same abuse without talking to the sheriff. His weakness thus seems to be more a function of his church calling and his rejection of a gun-bearing assembly than the truth of his character. Gaines admitted to John Lowe that the film actors of the old men insisted on changing this scene: "He may disagree with us, but he shouldn't fall . . . maybe they were right" (CEG, 309).

Billy Washington's character is ambiguous: others see him as weak, comic, or pitiful because he can't shoot a rabbit at his feet, yet at age eighty, he has come a distance to stand with them, quietly defends himself against their teasing, is able to stand under Mapes's blows, and is the first to give a story as reason for the killing he claims to have done. Clearer cases of weakness in process of change are evident in Rooster and Chimley. Rooster has long endured insults and possibly even cuckolding, not out of nonviolent principles but out of fear, and not even fear of whites but of his own wife and of Mathu. His wife was the one who sent him to get a gun, but once having done so he feels power in himself, which takes the form of a need to fight until he has heard Mathu's affirmation of his change. Chimley is a thoughtful, serious introvert, follower of Mat and the others. He needs Mat's courageous decision before making his own, looks to him, responds to his comments and plans. Only with his own wife can he be assertive. Later, narrator Cherry Bello groups him with Billy and Dirty Red, none of them looking "ready for battle, that's for sure" (43). Dirty Red may be the best example of moral inertia; he lacks initiative, energy, and will to exert himself even enough to knock ashes from his cigarette. He speaks only to tease Billy, the only one as inept as himself. All the men see him and his family as "too trifling" to

13. Griffin, "Creole," in *CRF*, 38–44, discusses the negative results of Mathu's sense of color superiority; Beavers, 171, explicates his transformation.

mix with. But Dirty Red is there, chiefly in memory of his family in the grave-yard; with a quiet realism, he is ready to die himself. As the mood of the event enters into him, he speaks up to Mapes, claiming his part and the change in him-self. His final validation comes with Mathu's assurance that his parents are proud of him, and he is next to Charlie during the shoot-out, wanting "that stuff" Charlie found. Charlie assures him he "already got it"; thus he represents all the men who came in fear and stayed to lose it (207–10).

Of the "strong men getting stronger," Mat is the first we meet. Not without fear, quiet but expressive, he has strength of memory and moral motivation: "If he did it, you know we ought to be there. . . . Mathu was the only one we knowed had ever stood up . . . 'bout . . . crawling under that bed. . . . It's too low, Chim-ley" (30–1). Having thus initiated a response and enabled Chimley to look di-rectly at him and so at previously unheard-of action, Mat takes the lead, gives directions, and makes arrangements. He rejects and subdues his wife's fearful in-terference even as he acknowledges with hot tears his past abuse of her. At the end of the day, he wants to stay at Marshall or follow Mathu to jail out of a need to finish their plan; he senses this may be their last such brave gathering. Mat has courage and influence, but he lacks the force of reasoning possessed by Cla-too, the strongest of them all.

Clatoo is the most developed black character, presumably because he is the leader. He can assume that role not only because he has the truck to transport them, but also because he knows his people and their history and has a leader's strong self-image; his clothing "let you know he was a businessman" (38). He organizes and directs the advance on Marshall like a sergeant, allowing for depar-ture of the too fearful, commanding straight posture from the faithful, "like sol-diers, not like tramps" (49). And he has brought the shoebox of real shells in expectation of their moment of real and fearless manhood. A clear observer and analyst, he knows not only that Candy is lying, but also why, and how to inter-pret the signs of her falsifying: "I knowed what Mathu meant to that family. . . . Besides that, she was trying too hard . . . daring you to think otherwise. . . . She told it too fast, too pat—she had practiced it too much" (50). Candy talks to Clatoo as group leader, and Mathu speaks to him, however briefly, while ignoring everyone else. Clatoo explains Mathu's color bias, interprets Glo's long hand-shake, giving "two reasons" (51), and notes Mathu's repeated looking toward the fields (presumably Charlie's hideout). Jameson begs him to persuade the others to go home; he can refuse the preacher. He speaks boldly to, then stares straight back at, the sheriff; he owns his long-suppressed militance. His public defiance is new; his character has not changed. By the end of the afternoon, he assumes the command Mapes ironically relinquishes to him and orders Jameson's silence as if he were now the sheriff. His most important and effective leadership is asserted when he stops the foolish and dangerous threat of a shoot-out with Mapes, calls for the conference in Mathu's house, forbids Candy to participate, and then uses reason with the men to get them to leave peaceably. Here his militance is Martin Luther King–like and suggests the desirable social order to come. When Will Luke forces the final fight, however, Clatoo leads the troops out of the house and takes command of strategy like a general eager for the enemy but concerned for the survival of his men.

In the end, of course, Mathu and Charlie prove to be the strongest men. Mathu has always been brave enough to challenge whites, but he has never really understood other blacks. Without that dimension of mental and moral vision, he sees no reason to take a vocal role in the drama on the porch or to interfere with Candy's attempts to direct it. Not until the other black men have taken over as directors does he "see" himself with his own manhood limited by mean-hearted, bitter contempt; his house is the real courtroom, where he is self-judged and self-convicted. Then he is able to pull himself apart from Candy; it is his word, not Clatoo's, that would have sent the men home peaceably.

From Mathu's dark kitchen, Charlie has listened to his voice, to the voices of the men. These have echoed the voice he heard back in the swamps, that place literally and symbolically at the end of the road, beyond the community's quarters, a place where no good crop grows and no work sustains life or dignity, historically the hideout of fearful runaways; in that place, Charlie has heard "a voice calling my name . . . calling me back here" (192–3). Reversing the vision-to-voice pattern, Charlie listens, hears, then has his vision of himself made new as a man, achieves that "something . . . that you see in the faces of people who have just found religion" (193), and is empowered for his peak moment of courage, confession, and self-assertion. In that moment, one more tale must be told, for all the same reasons and effects as in chapter 9—Charlie's tale of fifty years of abuse and one moment of felt power, a day of shameful fear and the conversion that created the "man" before them. First described by Lou as physically "the quintessence of what you would picture as the super, big buck nigger" (186), he now defies stereotype, is seen as Gaines's picture of "a man . . . a man." "Big Charlie, nigger boy" is "Mr. Biggs," doing "what he think is right . . . what part him from a boy" (187, 85).

As always in Gaines's fiction, the rhetorical impact of plot and characterization is felt most intensely through his special techniques of narration. In this novel, narration has special importance because character changes and new visions of race must be vocalized. What is seen must be said; what is heard affects what is seen next. Two factors of narration make it especially effective: the choice and arrangement of narrators and the use of both retrospective and immediate modes of narration.

This novel could hardly have been narrated by a single character. To interviewers, Gaines cited several times his initial intent to assign narration to Lou Dimes, the "liberal white guy," "the most *decent* person in the entire book," who would know the relationships of Candy and Mapes to Mathu and would try to learn, understand, and tell all. Gaines soon realized, however, that he would thus lose the whole gathering scene, that Dimes could not get all the necessary information nor the rhythmic language desired, especially not Snookum's and Janey's; he "could not reveal their inner thinking to the audience as they could themselves" (CEG, 167, 123–4, 188, 243).

But neither could the single voice of an omniscient narrator have served the novel's needs. That narrative persona, though knowing the multiple movements and visions, exterior and interior, of all the characters, would have been awkwardly withholding information to create suspense; the detachment of that voice would have eliminated the special emotional effect of orality, the revelation of inner turmoil and transformation within the old men, what readers need to "hear" in order to "see." The switch to multiple narrators is possibly the single most significant decision Gaines made in executing this novel. Several critics have detailed its advantages: a range of perspectives to describe, probe, and evaluate the action; achievement of communal focus and the wisdom of myth.[14]

Having chosen the multiple mode, Gaines had to select his speakers and arrange their order of performance. The first three are a black child, a black woman, and a white woman, all of them confused or terrified or both; all of them see yet don't see what has happened and cannot imagine what will. They are, as noted, the voices of ignorance and warranted fear. Readers may be amused by the comments and style of each; one audience at least rocked with laughter at Gaines's rendition of Snookum's frustration and Janey's incessant pleas to the Lord Jesus. Yet no reader or listener can miss the potential for a real bloodletting disaster. Comical as is Toddy's power over Snookum, it mirrors the adult world of "you can't retaliate no matter what I do to you." The whole novel will be about boy-men who break out of that culture of fear and repression. At its end, however, the child's "sentence" to one year of "couldn't do him nothing" will

14. Babb, *EG*, 117; Byerman, *Fingering*, 95; Phil Ward, "Artistic Story Compels Quick Reading, Thought," *(Baton Rouge) Advocate* Sunday Magazine (October 30, 1983): 16.

be seen to have forecast with comic irony the men's legal but mostly meaningless sentence to five years without guns. At another level, Snookum's satisfaction at having seen what Toddy has not (Beau's dead body), his inability to see what is really before him, and his reduction of its importance to the level of nickels and pralines, all serve to invert his viewpoint in the reader's mind, to magnify the adult event and legitimate the women's terrified "seeing" of Fix and the Cajuns. As for the women, black Janey and white Miss Merle, they authenticate the danger by the commonality of their fear and prayer and their irritation at Candy's irresponsible, besotted aunt and uncle. Yet they, too, react out of the old racial code: Janey crying and pleading like a child, Miss Merle slapping a black person in frustration, as Mapes will do later. They are a preview of Mat's realistically frightened wife and his threatening response.

Chapters 4 through 9, the gathering at Marshall, belong to five black narrators and only one white. Chimley and Mat represent the decision making required of all; Cherry Bello, lifelong resident and owner of a liquor and grocery store, knows the characters of all the gatherers and the history represented by their colors, family groups, and graveyard plots. The entry into Marshall is Clatoo's story; just as his leadership gets the men there, his intelligent, intuitive mind reflects in factual style what is found there and interprets the attitudes and words of Candy, Mathu, and Reverend Jameson (who is Clatoo's foil). Rufe, his own personality submerged, serves as "camcorder" for the thematic dialogue of Mathu and Mapes and for the storytelling that galvanizes and unites the community. One chapter at Marshall (chapter 8), which presents the first actions of Mapes and other white men, is narrated by Lou Dimes, a man with whom Mapes would think out loud about his options for effective legal action. Dimes is also a journalist, observant of physical detail and dialogue and reasonably objective in reporting them. However, he has significant limitations in journalistic objectivity and judgment: he immediately rules out Charlie as the killer, just as Mapes does; he assumes that the quarters are empty because all the people have "suddenly picked up and gone" in fear, and that that old mode of response is "the smartest thing to do" because "Fix is going to demand a nigger's blood" (59, 62). Since all his interpretations are erroneous, his narration serves to create a contrast and point to the greater accuracy of the blacks telling their own story.

Of the whites and blacks present at Marshall, two, of course, cannot be narrators: Mathu, who knows the real killer, and Candy, who thinks she knows and does know that her own version of events is a lie. For readers of the novel as a "whodunit," Mathu is too obvious a suspect, and Candy's moderately plausible account, perhaps *because* other characters don't believe it, just might be true.[15] Gaines also believed that observer characters would be better narrators than those most involved—though in one draft he did have Mapes narrating after he was called to Marshall's (*CEG*, 167–8).

When the focus of action shifts to whites in chapters 10 through 13, so does the narration. Sully provides a close view of Gil Boutan in the context of his fairly progressive urban university and his strictly traditional rural family. Like the TV for which he is nicknamed, Sully presents events just as his inner camera has caught them; he is not always able to understand or explain them. A reader, for instance, knows the reason for Gil's hostile turn on Cal before Sully knows and guesses that Gil will not be like his father when Sully interprets his words to mean that he will. Lou Dimes, in the interlude at Marshall, offers the key question, "What's going to happen?" (130). And Tee Jack, simply by his person, his thoughts and words, represents the morally failed society that breeds and "explains" Luke Will and other "regular customers."

The climactic events equalize and level black and white; this effect is reflected in the arrangement and paralleling of narrators: first a grouping of a black, a white, and a black man; then a black child in the center; and another grouping of a white, a black, and a white man. The adults are equal in number; each is either representative of or essential to the action and meaning of the situation he narrates. In the first group, Rooster represents all who have endured out of fear and now need to fight and to hear Mathu's affirmation. Lou tells his own final stand with Candy and interprets, as he can best, his own and Mapes's responses to Charlie; both, like Charlie, have seen a "vision," heard a "voice," and been changed. Coot, the old soldier in uniform, records the fight, giving it a semblance of strategy and overdue honor. Snookum, child-narrator of Mapes's abdication of power, reduces the big sheriff to comic size; the little boy and the bully-boy, parallel to Jameson and Griffin, cannot fight. In the final group, Sharp, representative redneck, "lieutenant" to Luke as Coot is to Clatoo, records Luke's last stand. He can admit, as Luke cannot, his sense of failure and fear; unlike Luke, he is enough in control to be a witness to his own and others' moods and actions. Dirty Red, probably the most changed by Charlie's new-found "stuff," is the appropriate narrator of his hero's final stand and death. Lou, journalist, friend, and lover, familiar enough with both races, with court procedures, and

15. Dorothea Oppenheimer, Gaines's agent, noted the dual nature of the story: "It is both a who-done-it and a sort of tragi-comedy-folk opera . . . combined. Quite unique. Keep it that way all the way through. Never mind if it's different. . . . This is yours" (quoted in Simpson, 312).

with Candy's relation to Mathu and himself, reports the trial with details that allow a reader to perceive its implications.

Black and white men are in a level shooting match in the dark; the alternation of racial narrators works like an exchange of shots. At the trial, they are equalized in their battered appearances, their supportive audiences, and their sentence. And though all three black narrators shoot while only one white does, Lou's double narration fits his double role as the white who really sees what the blacks have seen in Charlie, and as the reporter who sees more than the other media at the trial.

Who narrates *what* and *when*, rhetorically important and successful as these choices are, may be less crucial to this novel than the *how* of narration. Understanding and change depend on believing; believing requires seeing what never would have been believed otherwise; true moral "seeing" also requires "hearing" with ears and heart; seeing and hearing enable speech and action. Consequently, the novel needs not only varied narrators, but also varied modes of telling: both the release of long-suppressed emotion by retrospective first-person storytelling to a defined audience (like Miss Jane Pittman to her neighbors and the young history teacher) and the perception of immediate outer and inner experience by the mode already described as narration by "camcorder" (see chapter 3).

This latter mode of narration is substantial in this novel; it places readers continuously within the minds of the fifteen participant-narrators, seeing and hearing through their senses, conscious of their thoughts, and moved by their emotions. The style is characterized by immediacy; it uses minute details most unlikely to be remembered and recounted later but experienced internally, in the heat of the event as it happens. It is not an oral account to any audience. However, it is too clearly organized and written to be considered stream of consciousness. The novel's editor struck on the distinction of modes without defining it. Since Gaines wanted to show the people's lives before their "stand," his editor advised him to have each one "thinking back" while en route to Mathu's or have each one "speak . . . on the scene and . . . tell what he was doing" (CEG, 213).

That the narration is not strictly after-the-event storytelling is apparent when the novel opens with Snookum and Janey as narrators. The boy's experiences are rendered moment by moment in details he might well notice at the time but could neither remember nor articulate later in such a complete and coherent way: his own running "spanking my butt the way you spank your horse" (6); Candy's and Mathu's clothing; and Rufe's, Corrine's, and Janey's facial expressions. What he sees in faces he intuitively interprets: "looked wild and scared. . . . looked at me a second like he was trying to figure out what Candy wanted him for. . . . looked old and tired-looking . . . looked at me hard . . . how they do when they want you to remember something. . . . mad at first, now she was scared" (5–8). Dialogue, however, is recorded in strictly "she said. . . . I said" style; child that he is, he does not interpret the nuanced sounds of voices. As for Janey, her panic-stricken, repetitive prayers interspersed into each action, and her direct, rapid-fire dialogues with "City" and Miss Merle, are nothing if not immediate. Together, the boy and the woman pull readers into a highly volatile unfolding event, into the intensity of suspense and fear it arouses. By the very difference in their awareness and emotions, readers see its implications.

The adults certainly could narrate a tale after an event, and several of them do, but the style of the basic narration of the chapters is like Janey's, though less emotional; it is not the same as that of the interpolated oral tales. These old narrators are not speaking aloud, but their sense impressions, thoughts, and feel-ings are recorded in the only style natural to them—the one they use in talking to themselves or aloud.[16] Three examples will illustrate differences. The first is from Rufe's narration of chapter 9:

> That little spare-butt, slack pants deputy left the yard, walking all tough like he was ready to take somebody in. He probably couldn't take Snoo-kum to jail. . . . After he was on the radio a few minutes, he came on back in the yard and told Mapes. . . . Mapes told him. . . . That little deputy took in a deep breath and went back to the road talking to himself.
>
> I had been watching that little deputy so much I didn't hear Gable when he first started speaking. . . . It was Glo I heard first. I heard her saying: "Careful, Gable. You know your heart. Careful, now."
>
> Gable was standing on the other side of the steps, near Glo. . . . Last person in the world any of us woulda expected to see today was Gable. . . . "Be careful, Gable," Glo told him. She reached out her hand to touch his arm, but he was too far away from her. . . . His voice choked and he stopped. I wouldn't look at him. I was thinking back. (100–1)

This passage has the immediacy of Rufe's observations and judgments of the dep-uty's appearance, movements, and incompetence. It elaborates his shift in atten-tion, his thought "today," his memories of Gable, and his felt responses to the gestures, expressions, and direct speech of Gable and Glo. Compare this with Gable's own retrospective account of his son's execution:

---

16. All critics who discuss this narration assume that it *is* oral. Cf. Babb, *EG*, 10, 11, 114; Fork-ner, review of *A Gathering of Old Men*, *America* (June 2, 1984): 425; Price, 15; Ward, 16.

They knowed what kind of gal she was. . . . But they put him in that chair 'cause she said he raped her. . . . Called us and told us we could have him at 'leven, 'cause they was go'n kill him at ten. Told us we could have a undertaker waiting at the back door if we wanted him. . . . Is that something to say to a mother? Something to say to a father? 'Come get him at 'leven, 'cause we go'n kill him at ten'—that's something to say to— . . . Saying how they hit that switch and hit that switch, but it didn't work. . . . Monk Jack said the boy said: . . . Said the boy said: . . . Said he said: . . . Monk Jack said they told him: . . . Monk Jack told us how . . ." (101)

This passage, within Rufe's chapter, is from Gable's long, direct, retrospective, oral account to a clearly identified audience, one of whom interrupts him. Fewer details are noted—not the minute and immediate but only the most memorable or emotionally wrenching; speech is minimal, one-sided, and reported indirectly, Monk Jack to Gable to his listeners. Details and speeches, however, by their involuntary selection and frequent repetition, mark the intensity of pain and the need to exorcise it by oral recount.

Some of the oral style enters on occasion into the camcorder mode, as when the men are paused en route to Marshall and Cherry Bello sees Jacob Aquillard enter the graveyard:

I seen him pulling up weeds from Tessie's grave. Tessie was his sister. . . . The white men . . . killed her. . . . But listen to this now. Her own people at the old Mulatto Place wouldn't even take her body home. . . . Them, they're quality, them; but they wouldn't even take her body home. Buried her with the kind she had lived with. (45)

Here, Cherry is remembering and reflecting as he watches. His style, however, is marked by traits of orality: the explanatory tone, the admonition to listen, the reflective repetition, the sentence with an implied subject. One might say that oral style in this passage is inconsistent; it might also be true to the way some people think by talking to themselves when their movements and emotional responses have slowed.

Since the camcorder is so effective a means for drawing readers into the intensity of each felt event and the insightful mental notations of the various narrators, one may well ask why the interpolated oral tales are needed at all. Most critics, assuming all the narration is oral, have not distinguished these stories from their context, only commented on their emotional force. They are, certainly, part of what the particular narrator is hearing and the camcorder is putting on tape, yet they stand out from their surrounding narration with enormous and indispensable power. Their rhetorical effect on readers stems from what they reveal of yet another character's inmost memory and emotion, and still more from what they accomplish in the community of black and white listeners. Memory unspoken is individualized and too "safe"; events seen anew must be voiced—to blacks for understanding, consolation, affirmation, or absolution; to whites for their "seeing" and "hearing," their indictment as part of the "corporate" Fix Boutan for the deeds of a racist society, and their call to conversion of self and society, to reparation by collaboration, if possible, with this black action, at least by getting out of the way of black self-assertion and dignity on this day. Chapter 9 is a powerful and necessary breakthrough in the dammed-up knowledge and anguish of the speakers; it is the torrent of truth and righteousness that awes the white hearers, even Mapes (*especially* Mapes) and carries the blacks in shared courage toward their climactic action.

Just as the men must have character traits in common yet be individualized, so must they have a story in common, a story of abuse that is the root of their common motivation to stand, which yet branches out into separate tales. Gaines had gleaned many such stories in conversations with old men. Now he had to select among them to get both variety and commonality, something that had hurt them all (CEG, 272). This "something" Fix Boutan represents, and these stories the people must share. The stories emerge first in memories: Miss Merle's of Clatoo's sister, Chimley's of Mathu's fight with Fix, and Cherry's about Jacob's sister. Mat's anguished cry to his wife about their son Oliver is both immediate passion and oral recall. Billy Washington's account to Mapes of his son beaten to insanity is recorded by Lou Dimes. The main remembering and telling occurs in Rufe's chapter (chapter 9) while the people wait their hour to "stand," beginning with Johnny Paul's powerful eulogistic remembrance of all that black people "don't see" since Cajun tractors invaded the land like insects, devouring flowers, houses, jobs, community, and a way of life. His lament is followed by the horror stories of beating and killing, botched execution, skilled work made obsolete, insult and injury to veterans and to women, all the "dirt" done by those who lived along the St. Charles River and took it from the blacks, for whom it had been the "river of life," providing food, pleasure, and religious ritual.

Hearing these incantatory or defiant recitations one after another, the black men and women see new significance in events they have long known about; they see not only the familiar horrors but the moral and psychic debility caused by fear and embittered acquiescence to oppression. Each individual's story, which had before claimed only the sympathy and anger of his neighbors, now is claimed by every person and thus becomes part of a collective past, a community history. The people's silent refusal to comment in judgment on Tucker constitutes a sort of public confession and communal absolution for all. Yank's demand for use and correct spelling of his full name, "Sylvester J. Battley" (98–9), is the demand of all for a recognized and respected identity.[17] In this new communal vision, in many voices made one, the people are purged of fear and guilt, empowered by compassion and mutual forgiveness, prepared and strengthened anew for collective resistance.

Eventually, being forced to listen to the accumulation of tales has made even Mapes "see"—though he has the sense not to say so again and tries to make the people exonerate Fix of specific crimes. It is not quite true, however, that Gaines agrees with him;[18] what Fix *has* done can stand as typical of "everything." Before the story turns the camcorder on the Boutan world, readers have also surely seen in the black characters and heard in their "short stories" what most have never known or understood before—or never so clearly and intensely. Here, as in *Miss Jane Pittman*, episodes, short tales, have been woven into the fabric of a novel to reveal, if one has eyes to see and ears to hear, both an oppressive way of life and a way to change it.

In the end, most of the novel's characters know themselves and others as never before. The trial scene has been called anticlimactic, and Gaines himself diminished its importance by saying that he "had to get them buried and have some kind of hearing; but as far as [he] was concerned, once they walk around and touch Charlie's chest, it's over" (CEG, 170). The comedic elements have also been criticized as inappropriate after the almost mythic tone of Charlie's death and the ritual over his body.[19] Nevertheless, neither the significance nor the humor of the trial can be casually dismissed. In the courtroom, a sort of final judgment on past and future is given, not by Judge Reynolds but by Gaines. It is a judgment of hope, based on the visible rearrangements and radically altered perceptions of intra- and interracial relationships. No single character or group is "seeing" as in the previous week. The black men, a solid unit, have lost their old views of themselves and of whites. Clearly they now have no fear of legal reprisal, no expectation that "Fix and his crowd" can ever threaten again. If they exaggerate their testimony, it is only "now and then" and more from new pride

17. Cf. Joseph Griffin, "Calling, Naming, and Coming of Age in Ernest Gaines's A *Gathering of Old Men*," *Names* 40 (June 1992): 90–6; Babb, *EG*, 115.

18. Ward, 16.

19. Estes, "Humor," in *CRF*, 246–8; Babb, *EG*, 130; Price, 15.

and a sense of power than from the old pattern of making the white folks laugh to save their own necks. If they will have no tangible weapons, they will have self-respect and be beyond petty whites' power to harass. The court trial is their opportunity to affirm publicly their new power and to enjoy doing so; in that enjoyment is their humor. Only the outside journalists, who have not been present for the actual event, fail to see its revolutionary implication; for them it is "astonishing but not serious," and the trial is an old-fashioned minstrel show. Lou, who narrates it, seems clearly to distinguish himself from the media and their incomprehension, to be one with all the locals who did not laugh "nearly as much as the news people" did. He knows that "the whole thing" *is* serious, as well as astonishing (212–3).

As for the whites, they are less a powerful unit than before. "Fix and his crowd" may never see black dignity, but they have been forced to alter their expectations. They know that they cannot exploit, batter, or kill as before, less because the law will prevent or punish them than because the blacks themselves will. Gil is with his family at the trial; he has not, after all, been expelled. But he is no longer subservient to his father's mores. He has seen the larger vision Russ presented to him; he and Cal have fought and won together a larger victory than a football game. Candy has hired a lawyer for the men, but she has otherwise surrendered control; she offers Mathu a ride home but lets him go with his people without protest and herself seeks the hand of her proper partner in life.

Mapes, as the figure of previous expectations of "the law" for blacks, is reduced to a comic buffoon. But his personal reduction at this point is subject to criticism as unfair. His powerlessness during most of the porch scenes was effective satire, but he distinctly changed in his "seeing," reflected in his respect for "Mr. Biggs" (193), and he went outside alone to stop Luke Will (195). Though knocked out of the fight, in his brief part he had essentially changed racial sides. The humor of his overweight inability to get up when winged and his abdication of authority to Lou hardly seem to merit such a public humiliation. It is the one paragraph on Mapes, more than that on the old men's testimony, that gives the trial a possibly excessive comedy that dilutes the content of its serious judgment. The tone of humor at the end may be designed and desirable as relief from the heavy violence of the preceding chapters. And the court's imposed sentence, impossible to enforce—"like telling a Louisianian never to say Mardi Gras or Huey Long"(213)—is a satiric comment on the gun culture of both state and nation. Still, it implies a reversal in the symbolism of the guns; what was a symbol of a "real man's" power to defend or to deceive or destroy is reduced to a symbol of mere violence no longer sanctioned nor needed by men who are no longer afraid.

The phrase stands as an implied requirement on "black and white alike" (213) to abandon violence, to enable a new culture of race relations to be achieved by the Gils and Sullys, the Snookums and Toddys, the Lous and Candys, when black and white alike have seen the vision of it and raised their voices to call for it. That is no laughing matter.

At the end of a close reading of the novel, one may say that its art flows from this vision of hope seen in a kaleidoscope of many scenes, characters, and symbols, from the prophecy heard in dialogue, multiple narratives, and oral tales. All elements have added up to an immediate experience of the history of a people, a work with power to make the "blind" see and the "deaf" hear. In the understanding of that people, black and white, is our hope for understanding and abetting the historical movement of which Martin Luther King spoke, of which the people are both a fictional and a real part.

9

Many Teachers Taught

A Lesson Before Dying

READERS OF GAINES'S latest novel seem to have a different initial experience of it, depending on whether they have read his other fictions or only this one. The novel unquestionably works over most of the same issues as did those that preceded it: definitions and possibilities of black manhood; relationships between the generations, especially of young men and older women; the conflict between secular progress and traditional religion, especially as the latter is embodied in ministers and traditional forms of worship; questions of what behavior constitutes authentic and enduring love between men and women; questions of black migration, of the need to leave the Deep South for the North or West, where blacks, especially black men, can find—maybe—opportunity for education and life choices; and the struggle to obtain justice in the labor and penal systems, to maintain and assert some dignity and freedom of action in the face of raw southern racism. Along with problems, character types have reappeared. Sheriff, minister, convict, white landowner, black schoolteacher, Creole woman—each has been drawn from the lineup. So the longtime reader of Gaines has an initial sense of familiarity.

This last novel, especially, reminds one—with significant differences—of the first. Jackson Bradley is reincarnated in Grant Wiggins, Aunt Charlotte and other elders in Tante Lou and Miss Emma, Catherine Carmier in Vivian (though only insofar as she is a desired Creole lover). The action seems to begin where that of the first novel left off: Grant has repeated Jackson's cycle of Louisiana-California-Louisiana but has settled, at least for the time, in his aunt's house and is teaching school. Vivian is far more mature than Catherine, but the gnawing questions for the lovers are the same: Can Grant remain in Louisiana and be happy, feel useful and productive of change for his people? Can he find happiness if he leaves? Has he found the one woman to whom he can make a lasting commitment in love? Should she trust it and leave with him or encourage him to stay?

It is the differences in the two novels, however, that account for the experience of A Lesson Before Dying by first-time readers of Gaines, and also his long-time readers when they move beyond the familiar and surrender to the startlingly new. Invariably both groups, students and others, academics or not, speak of intense, gripping emotion: feelings for, with, and about characters and situations; heartbreak such that they must stop reading a while; yet in the end, hope—hope for the whole community of the novel, young and old, black and white. And they speak of a message that is powerful, believable, necessary, yet never contrived, a voice that speaks to heart and mind alike. First-time readers of Gaines want to go from this novel back to others; familiar readers sense a pinnacle achieved and issues brought to a measure of valid resolution. And Gaines has cited with pleasure the letters from ordinary, even reluctant, readers all over the country, from white Southerners who state the novel's importance to them, and from students who cite what they learned from it. "They all say they cried while reading it" (CEG, 295–6, 314). A critic is compelled to ask what qualities of plot, character, and theme, of structure, symbol, and voice Gaines displayed that won such universal praise and the National Book Critics Circle Award.

A Lesson Before Dying has a very different and emotionally more demanding plot than any preceding it. It also has key characters not paralleled in any other work: Vivian, who would perhaps parallel Alma Martin, had Alma been developed, but who is distinctly beyond Catherine Carmier or Mary Agnes LeFabre in life experience, maturity, and self-possession; Paul Bonin (whose name in English means "good"), the white policeman; and, above all, Jefferson, who is distinctly different from Marcus Payne and Proctor Lewis. These characters differ from earlier ones both in type and in development. Along with Grant, they have complexity of thought, impulse, and choice. With them are minor characters of a new type: children seen and heard in a schoolroom, the school superintendent, Grant's mulatto former schoolteacher, and a minister who (at last) is neither a fool nor a knave.[1] Characters of a wider diversity can deal with issues of wider, deeper complexity and more exacerbating emotion, even as they are gathered in response to one focusing event—the unjust condemnation of Jefferson.

In earlier novels, Gaines's own experiences at River Lake plantation or New Roads, the people, the stories, the songs he knew, provided ideas and the materials for his plots. Only *Miss Jane Pittman* seems to have required extensive research. *A Lesson Before Dying* seems, from his interviews, to have begun in his imagination of a character he had never encountered, a convict sentenced to die. He seems to have wanted to explore "manliness" in its least likely incarnation—one with maximum personal limitations and deprivations, with a "mask over the brain," with little past chance and less ability to come to awareness of what a man could know: a beach, a birthday, "a day all your own," the Constitution or Bill of Rights, or heroes like Frederick Douglass. To learn what such a character would experience in such a situation, Gaines then researched prison life by extensive interviews with death-row lawyers, sheriffs, and deputies who had worked with such convicts (CEG, 198–9, 291).

Given his convict's deprivations, Gaines evidently saw that he had an issue not strictly of masculinity; he framed his question for a wider answer: "How can you make this young man here a true human being?" (CEG, 199). To find out, he would take such a person and put him in the most demeaning of situations, on death row for a crime he merely witnessed in terror, and with almost no time left for any change in status. Though he denies any conscious choice of significant names—"not the point at the time" (CEG, 301), David Vancil notes the apt irony of Jefferson's; he is neither free nor equal.[2] He is not even acknowledged socially as a man or a human. Then, in a classic irony, Gaines would send his convict an unwilling teacher of the kind who existed when teaching was the only profession blacks could achieve in the South, one who hates his role and is unsure of his own worth and manhood. Finally, he crowned the lesson in humanity by commissioning the teacher through the insistent voices of women.

A Lesson Before Dying, however, is not centrally about Jefferson and his lesson in manhood/humanity before his electrocution. It is not even primarily focused on Grant Wiggins, forced to become mentor to his failed former pupil, slowly yet at last willingly becoming his student's student. Mary Helen Washington, in

1. Gaines admitted he began the minister as the stereotype, old and doing odd jobs, but ended by making him stronger than Grant (CEG, 324).

2. David E. Vancil, "Redemption According to Ernest Gaines: Review of *A Lesson Before Dying*," *African-American Review* 28 (1994): 490.

a letter to Gaines, noted that "the purpose of prisons is to disrupt community; while the project of your novel is to re-establish these communal ties."[3] The accuracy of her reading is corroborated by Gaines's report that he first intended to set the novel in 1988 but changed to 1948, a time when executions were still done in the parish where the crime was committed, when a portable chair was transported from one parish to the next on the bed of a truck, in sight of all, and when visits would be arranged by local people with the sheriff rather than by an attorney with the warden of the penitentiary. All this detail mattered "because I wanted the community in some way to be involved" (CEG, 198, 306).

Both Washington's and Gaines's comments imply a protagonist status for the community. Not only Jefferson, not only Grant, but the entire local populace must be instructed, must be changed radically by the impact of the event that disrupts their days and ways of thinking about and relating to each other. All will learn how to live better as Jefferson learns to die. Like the old men of A Gathering of Old Men, like that community, these people must come to "see" each other differently, especially the weakest and least manly among them; they must come to speak to, with, about each other differently, use their voices to assert their stories and their values. In this sense, Gaines has explored again and brought to a new degree of resolution in this latest novel all the issues he had explored before.

To accomplish his communal project, Gaines brings together by forces within the community its two most alienated members, has them learn from each other while interacting with the community; by their painful process of learning, they teach their lesson to the community. Grant is central to the project and the story because he is professional teacher, survivor, and narrator, but Jefferson is much more than secondary to him; he is more crucial to the story even than Vivian. Jefferson is the shadow side of Grant—uneducated and unambitious, without honor in his own black community and without imagination of anything beyond it, a pupil who never learned, much less came back to teach, victim of socially encouraged ignorance rather than dangerous achievement. Together, Grant and Jefferson are two versions of one imprisoned person, of one damaged black man. The thematic resolution must encompass both of them and, through them, their people.

Mary Helen Washington has questioned whether the story does not set Jeffer-

3. Mary Helen Washington to Ernest J. Gaines, March 10, 1996. In possession of Mary Ellen Doyle.

son up as a sacrifice for Grant's manhood, "the sacrificial victim for the more important character's growth."[4] I think not. A crisis is Jefferson's only way to achieve manhood. Nothing in his life becomes him like the leaving of it. Without his incarceration, that life would have continued to be an aimless trip "on his way to the White Rabbit Bar" (a name full of symbolic nuances).[5] Impending death is the occasion for his growth into meaningful life, however short.

Washington also asks whether the novel even questions the "acceptance of a system of exploitation that necessitates, even guarantees that young black men like Jefferson will become convicts."[6] That problem is trickier. Certainly the community in the novel is geared to such an expectation. And expectation is a form of acceptance. If the authorial voice is to oppose that, then the entire community must learn otherwise or else be shown as failing its most important educational opportunity. By seeing unexpected behaviors in Jefferson, the black community must be led to new ways of relating to its "lesser" members—whether lesser by age, education, poverty, or talent. And in some credible measure, white society must be incorporated into wholesome community. Any hope of future justice and decent interaction requires the powerful to move toward compassionate imagination and toward recognition of humanity in the vulnerable, in this case Jefferson.

Together, then, Jefferson, Grant, and the entire community must learn the lesson that all Gaines's protagonists struggle to learn: that no one is anyone's "hog," that "manhood" is really strong and sensitive humanity, which includes perceptive and reactive comprehension of others' acts and feelings, and the moral and relational values that enable one to learn and love, make commitments, and survive as an integral personality wherever one is, regardless of external circumstances or even impending loss of life. When Grant has opened his own mind and heart to that lesson, he is fit to go on teaching. Neither California nor Louisiana offers him escape from racism's indignities; if he ever does go away again, it will not be in that false hope. By contrast, when Jefferson has learned and practiced the lesson, he finds his voice, no matter how broken his expression or how brief. He has escaped indignity even as racism is taking him to the electric chair. And when the whole community has learned, as much as each mem-

---

4. Mary Helen Washington to Mary Ellen Doyle, 1997. In possession of Mary Ellen Doyle.

5. Ernest J. Gaines, *A Lesson Before Dying* (New York: Vintage, 1994), 4. All citations are from this edition.

6. Washington to Doyle, 1997. In possession of author.

ber can, there is hope for the children, hope for race relations, hope for a more human world.[7]

The novel is structured to reveal aspects of this theme, its "lesson" of individual humanity experienced and developed only in wholesome community relationships. The structure might be described as two concentric circles. Within one, the plot is worked out: Grant and Jefferson interact with each other by resistance and then engagement, and the entire community gradually and increasingly interacts with both of them until all have learned the lesson. Each significant character is seen learning; each changes as the chemistry of human relationships is altered in the laboratory of the community, with Jefferson's impending death as catalyst for reactions. Around that circle of learner-teachers, Grant, as narrator, draws another. By his manner of telling the story (including Jefferson's voice), he reviews his own lesson and teaches readers what all the community has learned.

The novel's "inner structure" of thematic relationships may be described in three sections. Chapters 1 through 8 introduce all significant community relationships "as they are" at the time and in the context of Jefferson's condemnation. With the introduction of Jefferson in chapter 9, those relationships begin slowly to expand and change; incomplete but distinct alterations in him, in Grant, and in the community are achieved by chapter 19, the Christmas program. Chapters 20 through 28 hasten and achieve the essential lessons and character changes, described, ironically, more by Jefferson himself than by Grant. Chapters 29 through 31 witness to the achievements of Jefferson, the community, and Grant; they constitute a sort of report card or "grading" comparable to what Grant gives to Jefferson's diary. Action before chapter 29 is mostly in painful stasis; so little can be done, so limited is the space for movement. Characters go from blacks' houses to the big house, from house to school, school to houses, to Bayonne only to another school, a bar, or the jail, where one can visit, attempt communication, but never set another free. Jefferson's confinement is hardly more restrictive than everyone else's. All the world's a jail. There is nothing to do in it but walk, look at each other, and try to talk. The chief evidence of change throughout, in this novel as in *A Gathering of Old Men*, is the sound of voices, the shift in voices of power, and the sheer increase of willingness and

---

7. Gaines has discussed this interaction and theme, "what the whole thing is about," in interviews (*CEG*, 239–40, and *PT*, 132–6). The latter conversation occurred when the novel had progressed to chapter 6, and Gaines had "no idea" what Grant would say or whether Jefferson would be executed. Comparison of his comments and the finished novel makes a study in literary process and necessity.

ability to speak, to communicate genuinely with other human beings. In all four sections, multiple details of dialogue and small action, of diction and symbolic image, like slight turns in a dance, reveal the characters resisting, moving away, coming back, coming together, gradually changing themselves and their relationships. Gaines has spoken of the many "little tricks" required to make a plot work, which, if well mixed in the "gumbo," are scarcely noticed (*PT*, 135). If noticed, however, tricks and details make much of the power and pleasure of characterization and theme, especially in this novel. Noticed they must be, in their mix, by close, detailed reading.

In the first section (chapters 1 through 8), Jefferson is not seen or heard directly but at third or fourth remove—as Grant heard his story from Tante Lou, Lou from Emma or the lawyer at the trial, they from Jefferson himself. His only quoted words are his babbling to Gropé that the killer "wasn't me" (5). What Jefferson was and is, according to his public defender, is a "fool" (repeated eight times), a "thing" (repeated four times in one paragraph), and finally a "hog." Though the defender asks the jurors to "look" at or "see" him (words that appear twenty-one times), no indications are given that they saw anything, literally or metaphorically, and Jefferson himself is not seen, even by indirect report, to react to anything he sees or hears within the courtroom.

Why is Jefferson not seen for so long if he is so important? At one level, simply because after the trial no one in contact with Grant, the narrator, sees him until chapter 9. The sheriff reports on him briefly but only as he sees him, as a "contented hog" (49). At another level, for quite a while Jefferson must be "not seen" on the page, as the legal personnel have not seen him, as even his own people have not, neither in his simplicity of mind nor in his real potential for reflection and understanding. And at the level of structural meaning, Jefferson, because of his plight, has the potential to seize the reader's interest from the community that will survive him and perpetuate whatever changes he has precipitated. Aspects of the theme, of the changes needed, must be focused first in them, and especially in Grant, the neediest of them all.

Chapters 1 through 8 reveal community relationships, all more or less skewed and unhealthy, chiefly by how little these people have to say to each other and how they say it. Long, deadly silences alternate with clipped comments and answers and a very few passionate speeches by Grant, all in patterns of resistance, deception, manipulation, and capitulation. Voices are hard, bitter, or angry; only those of Vivian and a few minor characters (Inez, Claiborne, Thelma) are not. The latter have little to say, and Vivian is more a challenging listener at this point than a speaker. Only to her does Grant freely voice his true feelings in one of the few developed dialogues of this section. With the other women in his life, he evades real dialogue, so as to avoid Emma's coercion by pity and "concession" ("he don't have to") and Tante Lou's by commands and threats. White-black relations are exposed in Edna Guidry's meaningless chatter without true interest or friendship, her sheriff husband's inquisitorial or pharisaical efforts to "play" with Grant and trap him in "too smart" or disrespectful speech, and the visiting superintendent's racist lessons on hard work and "nutrition" to children he inspects like slaves on the block, of whom he speaks as a "crop," of the same limited and passing value as the corn in the fields they will work.

These are the voices of Grant's plantation, home, and school life, which he must either commit to or leave. The best of his childhood was lived in its context, surrounded by encouragement to work for a future of less degraded status but also by the limiting, demeaning expectations of whites and of Creoles like his teacher. His basic solution was to "move against" its restrictions by becoming "too smart," "too educated" (21), an angry black perfectionist who wanted things to be as they ought to be. Since he could not "move against" occupational restrictions, he tried "moving away" to California.[8] Returned by an inner compulsion, he is still "moving away" and "against," as revealed in his small actions and speeches: his absence from Jefferson's trial, avoidance of Miss Emma, slamming car doors and hitting ruts as he drives to Pichot's, deliberately correct grammar and delayed "sir," going to the Rainbow Club to eat, and not going to church. Unable to quit his job or to alter the deprivations the system imposes on his students, he displaces his anger and moves away from and against the students by "tuning out" their Bible recitations, leaving the room to go outside, terrorizing them with his slashing ruler, unmerciful scolding, rough demands, and insensitivity to the tears he causes. Out of context, the most meaningless Bible verse is "Jesus wept" (34); ironically, Grant's greatest need is to be made to weep, and the plot is his context for that achievement. For the sympathy, the "feeling with" implied in tears, he must balance "away from and against" by "moving toward" others. Bound by old affection, he moves ever so slightly toward his aunt, but otherwise only toward Vivian. One perceptive reader noted Grant's *similarity* to Tante Lou (demanding, punitive elders to the young yet desirous of their advancement) and Vivian's role, symbolized by her name, as his way to *life*.[9] Even

---

8. Cf. Paris, chapter 2, on the three "solutions" of moving against, away, or toward. For discussions of Grant's inner conflicts, see CEG, 273–4; Vancil, 489–90; Beavers, 229; Valerie Babb, "Old-Fashioned Modernism: 'The Changing Same' in A Lesson Before Dying," in CRF, 254.

9. Eugenie Coakley to Mary Ellen Doyle, May 16, 1998. In possession of Mary Ellen Doyle.

as he begins to teach and learn from Jefferson, Grant must begin to learn about and from his community, all of whose members clearly have their own needs to learn from him and his pupil.

As Grant and Jefferson represent the extremes of its young adults, the community's elders are represented chiefly by his Aunt Lou, Miss Emma, and Reverend Ambrose. The two women are depicted in profoundly ambivalent metaphors of great stones, boulders, and huge old stumps of oak and cypress, objects that either have never given life or have ceased to do so. The immobility of their bodies is likened to that of their minds; to resist them is to be in some sense crushed beneath their disapproval. Yet boulders and stumps are also the oldest or deepest-rooted parts of the land, which prevent erosion; stumps can yet bring forth new shoots. Thus, the elders have encouraged schooling to free their young from subservience to whites—but not to themselves. Grant angrily resists their manipulation yet grudgingly admires their determined use of similar tactics to get what they want from whites. Love is expressed by services, especially provision of home and food. Home, not in town, is where one eats—just one part of the code of respectful behaviors as rigidly imposed as any by whites. Miss Emma's love will come to the prison in a food basket; much later we will learn that she had never kissed Jefferson in his young life. Though determined and demanding, the women are really more flexible than Grant; to obtain dignity for Jefferson, they will surrender a bit of their own at the big house's back door. Emma can stoop to conquer, can say "sir" and "please," yet defy Pichot's advice, correct his version of the crime, and state six times his family obligation to her, a classic example of elderly servants' skill in manipulating powerful whites. In her fixed staring into a yard where Grant sees only jimsonweed and crabgrass, Emma is more alive than he, alive in her suffering, in her mental action of remembering, thinking, imagining, and planning for her godson's well-being. When Jefferson learns through Grant how to imagine and care for her, and Grant learns through him to reimagine himself and his students, then Emma and Lou will learn to express compassion in words and gestures more than in fried chicken and teacakes.

Reverend Ambrose does not appear directly in chapters 1 through 8; he is, nevertheless, structurally placed in opposition to Grant. He was "there" at Jefferson's sentencing; he will willingly visit the jail. For Grant, he is a relic, a reminder of the faith and worship that he, Jefferson, and other young people have rejected at the cost of damaged family relations. Gaines has admitted that most local schoolteachers did respect ministers, that Grant's negative attitude toward Ambrose is "one of my problems" (CEG, 308). In this novel, however, the conflict of values and methods works to a purpose. Grant's barely veiled contempt must be converted into a genuine respect for the spiritual power that enables the minister to use the "white man's faith" against white injustice, and to "be there" when he cannot. Ambrose, in turn, must be converted to understanding and valuing Grant's intuitive skill in humanizing Jefferson, itself a form of salvation. The change in this relationship will be essential for Jefferson and the community.

The future of any community is its children; the hope of the black community is in educating its children despite every obstacle placed in the way of success. Hence the urgent importance given to the teacher and his relationships with both the students and their families. The school in this novel has been called a prison, of which Dr. Joseph is the warden.[10] The school scenes in chapters 1 through 8 do indeed parallel those to come in the jail, are clearly meant to explain Jefferson, who apparently was Grant's student, is now again, and is first "seen" as one of the failures he expects nearly all his students to be. Even more, the scenes explain Grant's fierce conflict between desire to get away and avoid his own failure and desire to achieve, both in the school and the jail, the success his mulatto teacher had declared impossible (Cf. CEG, 198, 308). The arrival of wood for the winter presents the "vicious circle," old men who were and are, and young boys who will be, literally, hewers of wood. Grant's memories of his own schooling and of his bitter, hopeless teacher, Matthew Antoine, reveal that he once had better hopes for himself and his people but is now in danger of transmitting that same hate and defeatism to another generation.

In these first eight chapters, the only really hopeful, mostly happy, yet still imperfect relationship Grant has is outside the community of the quarters, with Vivian. Her power for him is in her individuality. Yet she can cross his boundaries, understand his dilemma. Gaines said, "Vivian is there to keep Grant there . . . long enough to really deal with Jefferson," to affect the next generation; he made her a mother to give her maturity (CEG, 302). As the only voice Grant can really "hear," Vivian speaks for commitment to their students, for patience with her divorce process, and for his willing action for Jefferson, also "for us" (32). Grant needs that action, Vivian intuits, to discover for *himself* what being a man is, and he must teach Jefferson successfully in order to respect himself as a teacher. In the process, Vivian herself will learn a lesson on the nature and qualities of genuine lasting love. In addition to all this, Vivian reveals initially the need for better relationships between Creole and black, Catholic and Protes-

10. Philip Auger, "A Lesson about Manhood: Appropriating 'The Word' in Ernest Gaines's Lesson," *Southern Literary Journal* 27 (1995): 76.

tant, younger and older women, plantation and town communities. The junction of all these lines will be Tante Lou's kitchen, then Jefferson's cell.

No lines, of course, are less likely to meet than those separating black and white, dividing equally the teacher and the convict from those whose power can make both their lives unlivable. Nothing in chapters 1 through 8 predicts that the races will meet across that Great Divide. Herman Beavers noted that while Jefferson's defense lawyer was making a genuine effort to save his life, he failed by using the old modes of racial hierarchy and degradation instead of a new rhetoric to make the jurors see anew.[11] On the plantation, in Pichot's kitchen, in Grant's schoolroom are heard all the old voices, all the old rhetoric. The black may reach an immediate goal, but the degrading relationships do not change. Given the nearly absolute corruption by nearly absolute power, little hope is offered for change in any of the relationships in this small community, for any lesson that will enable these people, black or white, to learn to live and let live in freedom of mind and spirit. Chapter 8 ends, surely with authorial deliberation, on the note of Matthew Antoine's defeatist advice to Grant, "Just do the best you can. But it won't matter" (66).

Enter Jefferson, the semiliterate condemned man who will teach and liberate all the other people. In his preparation for death, Jefferson, with Grant, will redirect the whole community toward life. All lessons in manhood, humanity, and community depend on their achievement. From chapter 9 to chapter 19, the plot is structured to define all relationships further and show their progressive alteration. As in the first section, there is little action as such, except for Jefferson's "hog" eating and Vivian's and Grant's lovemaking and serving cake and coffee. The rest is repeated "going": eight times to the jail by Grant and Emma, Grant alone, or the elders alone; Grant to the Rainbow Club and home, to Vivian's school; Vivian to Grant's home; Lou and Emma to Edna Guidry's home. In these places, the only action that truly matters is that which is *not* done (communal eating); what is *said* is important. Action and character development are "going somewhere" only because the talk is going somewhere—slowly, painfully, and very, very gradually. The chief indicator of progress is the voices of characters who move from silence or blaming or dishonest evasions to something like real communication. And the power to speak follows on the willingness to look directly at another human and to "read" what is in the face and eyes.

The beginnings could hardly be less promising. Hope for Jefferson is chilled by the intensity of his and Grant's resistance. Because their relationship is cen-

11. Beavers, 174–5.

tral and essential to changes in others, their portraits are deliberately paralleled, especially in chapters 10 through 12. Both use nonseeing and nonspeaking as punitively as their elders have ever done with them. Grant chauffeurs Miss Emma to the jail three times in freezing silence, refusing to look at her in the rearview mirror or even to let on that he sees the people along the road; Jefferson also refuses to look at or speak to her. Grant resists visiting at the price of humiliation; Jefferson resists being visited and wallows in his "hog" humiliation. Grant brings Jefferson a comb; Jefferson will not use it. Grant delivers Emma's food; Jefferson will not eat it. Jefferson wants to talk about "when they go'n do it" (73); Grant, like Emma before him, evades any mention of the execution, obviously the one thing Jefferson needs to talk about in order to vent his feelings and change them. The only hope offered in these early visits is in the unspoken awareness of truth that passes between the two men: "My eyes would not dare answer him. But his eyes knew that my eyes knew" (73). Ironically, the one character foil to all the nonlookers and nonspeakers in this section is a white man, Deputy Paul Bonin, who uses his eyes to direct Grant to a compassionate embrace of Miss Emma and his voice to clarify for her the discourteous double-talk of Deputy Clark and to establish a link by names to Grant and to prisoners.

Both Grant and Jefferson, by implication, are contrasted to black heroes of the past; both need to clarify the concept of heroism and accept its possibility in themselves and in the ordinary people of their community. This "conversion" occurs, as in *A Gathering of Old Men*, through the voices of old men telling their stories and provoking memory and communal feeling in a younger man. As Grant listens to the old men in the Rainbow Club describe Jackie Robinson's exploits, he remembers the community's earlier excitement over Joe Louis, the maneuvers of black and white teachers to obtain for him a story in *The Dubliners* about Irish folk, and the stories of black folk heroes heard in his own community. He begins to see the heroism in common human history, but he doesn't yet want to think about the common man in the cell uptown or their joint potential and responsibility to learn heroism.

The first ordinary people in whom Grant has to recognize heroism, through his very efforts to make Jefferson honor it, are his elders. And a corollary lesson is the fine distinction between honesty and "lies"; on these hallmarks of heroism depends the truth of love. In chapters 9 through 19, manipulation and semi-sincerity turn into outright dishonesty and pretense, making voices more strident and avoidances more pronounced. Miss Emma's sickness is a planned charade that Grant sees through, but her feeling for his humiliation is sincere, and her one truth ("They ain't nobody else" to teach Jefferson) ultimately wins his true compassion, his compliance and perseverence in the task. In the film of *A Lesson Before Dying*, usually faithful to Gaines's dialogue, this speech is given to Tante Lou, who delivers it with savage irony expressive of shame and disgust at Grant's insensibility to a need greater than his humiliation, and of a compulsion to teach him. His response is still angry, disgusted submission. In the novel, the speaker is not explicitly designated but seems clearly to be Miss Emma, whose tearful "I'm so sorry" is sincere and elicits Grant's surrender in a newly compassionate response to the truth of need. Tante Lou does indeed speak like any sheriff to a "boy" who "better . . . get out of here if you know what's good for you" (77, 79), but it is love for her friend and community, even for Grant and his character, that prompts her.

Grant can be just as insensitive and dishonest as his elders. His report from the jail is unlovingly delayed, minimally honest (they did talk, and Jefferson did "eat"); mostly it is lies about *how* they talked and ate. He could have reported enough truth to prepare them gently for their own next visit, could have held out some hope of change. When confronted later with his lies, he admits Jefferson "treated me the same way he treated her" (123). Actually, he has not yet heard how Jefferson treated Emma; he does not want to hear or to join in the sympathy given her by Lou or Ambrose. Yet he has told Jefferson the truth about his plan to lie lest the truth of Jefferson's behavior should kill Miss Emma; Vivian has told him the truth that his "je t'aime" includes not only her but "them" (94)—presumably both elders and children, the whole community of his origins. Her "Je t'aimerais toujours" (95) uses the conditional form of the verb: "I *would* love you," expressive of both her desire and the condition of character under which she intuits the possibility of lasting love.

Vivian is Grant's only accepted teacher in this part of the novel and is far more realistic and other-centered than he. Yet she too has something yet to learn about truth and deception, about what love and commitment really are and demand. Her love is real but not wholly honest or mature. She would agree to "forget . . . everybody else" and "go somewhere" (93) to spend the night if she could be sure her estranged husband would not catch her. Her commitments still harbor some obvious uncertainties and incongruities: Mass at nine and sex at eleven by the Catholic and still-married woman, her urging of church attendance on Grant as both an act of faith and "something to do on Sunday" (105), and her stated intent to keep her religion if she can or leave it if she has to. However, in their lovemaking are mutual respect and tenderness that preclude mere exploitation, that prepare for deeper understanding of themselves and others and for commitment to each other and to the least-appealing members of their community. The setting of the lovemaking is in the symbolic fields, where the ground is clean, where Grant's ancestral roots lie and Vivian digs in her heels, where they have just chewed the sweetness from sugar cane and the richness from pecans; all these symbols contribute to an atmosphere of innocence, in both senses of the word. Their conversation in the kitchen, over coffee, cake, and dishwashing, is that of a "casual" couple; after the lovemaking, it concerns the possible conception of "Paul and Paulette" (is choice of the kind deputy's name mere coincidence?). This dialogue's sincerity is intensified by the absence of "I said . . . she said" construction; it is a pure exchange of realistic, hopeful, gradually maturing love (108–10). Their new level of commitment in truth begins at once to change other relationships as Grant insists on introducing Vivian to Tante Lou and her women friends, not just as "a girl back of town" whom he likes to see "sometime" (100), but as "the woman I'm going to marry one day" (113). The dialogue of the women is a clipped "short answer test," but its topic is significant, and the elders' affirmation of Vivian's "quality" (116) is the beginning of a conversion in Creole-black and Catholic-Protestant relationships within this community.

Honest feeling and speech, gentle courtesy, and mutual recognition of equality and adulthood have been the hallmarks of Grant's relation with Vivian, as they have not been with either Jefferson or his elders, and distinctly not with any whites. To help him value these traits further and teach them to Jefferson and his own black people, Paul Bonin begins to function as a character. This improbable new relationship had begun indirectly, with Grant's observation of the deputy's unrequired, unexpected courtesy to an elder black. Observation and walking "beside" instead of "behind" lead Grant to conclude that Paul is "the most likely to be honest with me" (125), and so to seek true information about Jefferson. Man to man, they exchange names, handshakes, and parallel desires to avoid emotional involvement with Jefferson. By contrast with the meaner white men around them, Paul will teach both Grant and Jefferson that strength, sensitivity, and honesty are all elements of manhood and not incompatible with whiteness. The reduction of Paul to a silent, barely seen doorkeeper in the film adaptation of the novel is an unfortunate omission of one of the novel's main thematic lessons. What his presence and voice teach Grant and Jefferson is critical to their joint growth in humanity, especially in Gaines's superb conclusion.

Jefferson, however, can learn only as fast as Grant does. Despite his own best instructors, the teacher is a slow learner. In chapters 17 and 18, their mutual lesson advances slowly in proportion to their increasing dialogue. Grant controls his anger at insults to himself and Vivian; he begins to voice to Jefferson his obli-

gation to reciprocate a woman's love. But when Emma returns, Jefferson still refuses to look at her, speak to her, or eat. Grant declares he will talk about
anything Jefferson wants, but when Jefferson chooses "that chair" as his topic,
Grant begins to talk about the Christmas program (138). Perhaps he could tell
the truth with his eyes, but he has yet to learn to speak forthrightly as well as
compassionately. When Paul asks his assessment of the situation, Grant can only
say, "I don't know." Jefferson is still "bowed . . . stooped . . . hanging low" (137).
At the end of this series of jail visits, Grant is ready to "drop everything" because
"nothing is changing." But at the emphatic end of chapter 18, Vivian voices the
truth, "Something has" changed (141).

What has changed at the midpoint of the novel is seen in the context of the
whole community assembled for the Christmas program. Dedication of the event
to Jefferson has brought out "many people who had never attended" any program
before, and Grant describes them by name in all their variety. They have come
early, walking or riding a wagon in the rain and mud, wearing their "going-to-
town" clothes (143). The children, their teacher notes with approval, have
found a seasonal pine tree rather than just "anything else they could find" (141),
and they have contributed all the coins they made from picking pecans to buy a
gift for Jefferson. That fact recalls his earlier comment to the superintendent that
pecan money is usually family support; presumably the families have agreed to
sacrifice it. Extensive details of the program indicate Grant's own efforts to recognize and develop talent for "dramatic performance," composition, and delivery
(147–8). His tone is not mocking; the nativity scene is relayed with a humor
that still respects the children's efforts and includes even Reverend Ambrose's
prayers. The two views of Miss Rita show Grant's growing tolerance for limitations, along with admiration for patient care of the limited young. In short, Jefferson's plight has affected the community, which affects Grant's attitude to him
and to his students, which paves the circular way for the convict and the community to directly affect each other. Grant at his best is seen to be sensitive, appreciative of his people, and made more so by his efforts in Jefferson's cell. He is still
essentially isolated, discouraged by the annual sameness of program, bad grammar, and old clothes; he does not yet eat with the people but stands alone. Yet
the lone gift under the pine tree is having its effect on everyone.

With the announcement of Jefferson's execution date in chapter 20, all relationships are set into rapid motion through chapter 28, as if a projector were
switched into fast forward. People who typically do not speak to each other, who
dislike or disapprove of each other, love but vehemently disagree with each
other, come together in variant combinations, nearly all seeking to rescue Jeffer-

son's human dignity or his immortal soul. Urgency, however, creates more conflict than ever. Each new event inaugurates a new fight on what is believed to be his behalf; each fight is followed by a more explicit "lesson," given and received under the pressure of his approaching end. Battles and lessons structure this most powerful third of the novel. Several lessons are built around tools of learning: radio, pecans, gumbo, notebook. Gainesian "tricks," especially subtle, easily overlooked parallels and contrasts, abound. The effectiveness of all lessons is seen, finally, in the way people increasingly look at each other and truly listen to what each one has to teach.

The first crisis bringing unlikely togetherness is the announcement of the date of Jefferson's execution. Reverend Ambrose and Grant can meet with Guidry in Pichot's parlor (but have nothing to say to each other and are excluded from the service of coffee) because they must take the news to Emma. Guidry refers to her as the "old woman . . . who attended the trial," Ambrose as "His nannan" (157). Action now becomes an even more purposeful and revealing pattern of "going to": Guidry calls the doctor with real kindness for Miss Emma and only ironic care for the doctor's shoes in the muddy quarters; Ambrose goes to Emma for her support; Grant goes away for "a long walk in the opposite direction," wanting Vivian alone, "absolutely no one else" (159). When he does go to Emma's, where most of the people of the quarters already have gone, no one wishes to speak to him. Vivian goes herself to Grant, and in a low-keyed contrast to the lovemaking in the fields, they lie "very close together with all our clothes on" (162). That new experience of love gives him strength to go with her back to Emma, who now asks him to come together with Ambrose to help Jefferson. Vivian improves her relationship with the old women by her compassionate attention, yet it devolves upon Grant, in lesson one of this section, to make Vivian understand black women's urgent need for a "stand" by men like Jefferson and himself. In teaching her, he enforces the lesson on himself and prepares to teach Jefferson. He grasps intuitively the truth that it is "up to Jefferson" to break "that circle" of staying and running (167); he does not yet see that Jefferson's strength will break his excuse for not staying and standing too. Thus the community, like the February day in Louisiana, is between winter and spring, life and death, is "overcast" and "chill," yet being readied for "new planting." Like the trees, some persons are in blossom or full leaf, others still "bare, gray and leafless" (154). Among the latter would seem to be, still, both Grant and Jefferson. Yet on their changes depends the "salvation" of the whole community, while the community, in turn, must act to make those changes bear fruit.

Jefferson's execution date has focused all mental energies, including his own.

It belongs to his developing manhood that he begins to think his own thoughts without or beyond the promptings and pleas of Grant or the elders. His progression is marked, like ascending height lines on a wall, by his increased readiness to share those thoughts, first in dialogue with Grant, then (as reported) with others, and finally with himself in the diary and, by its delivery to Grant, with Paul and the community of Grant's readers.

The sequence of Jefferson's progress—and everyone else's with his—is marked by the sequence of visits to the jail. Using Gaines's embedded dating, it is possible to gauge their spacing, the urgency of the community, and the moral miracle of Jefferson's final six weeks of life.[12] Shortly after the execution date is set, three visits are made within a week: on Friday by Grant, on Monday by the elders, and on Wednesday by Grant again. On Friday, Grant finds that Jefferson has reflected and is ready to talk about execution, minimally but humanly. A "whole gallona ice cream" (170) may be "hog" quantity, but it is human food, something pleasant he has never had enough of and can now have, even if it is the last thing in his life. His smile is not bitter, not ironic. He looks at Grant "not as he had done in the past" but "with an inner calmness" (171). He begins to think of people and things outside his cell: notices good weather, asks about Gable's baby. Reflective memory of his plan to hunt with Gable on the day of the Gropé killing begins his assumption of responsibility for being instead at the murder scene. And Grant promises the radio, his own first unsolicited thoughtful act for another.

The radio becomes a major symbol of connections, quickly or painfully won, in the entire community. It not only connects Grant to Jefferson and Jefferson to his recent, familiar life and to the world outside the jail, it also extends his concerned community beyond the quarters to the owners and customers at the Rainbow Club who contribute to the purchase. Grant, we realize, is doing the same: he tells Thelma, "I ate before I came" (breakfast?); when she "knows" to provide a full plate, he notes, "I ate the food hungrily because I had not had dinner" (173–4). Here, ironically, he engages in one of the "lies" whose neces-

12. Guidry announces on a school day "in late February" (152) that the execution is scheduled for the "second Friday after Easter . . . April 8" (156–7). From there, one can date Easter as March 27 and the announcement probably between February 20 and 23. Grant's ensuing visit to the jail is a Friday, either February 24 or March 4 (169), the elders' visit on Monday February 27 or March 7 (178), and Grant's return on Wednesday, March 2 or 9 (183). That leaves two or three full weeks to include the climactic visit in the dayroom (chapter 24) and presumably others before Grant's final visit on March 24, the day before Good Friday (221), and two more full weeks for the visits and the developments recorded in Jefferson's diary.

sity Reverend Ambrose will soon teach him. The radio, however, as Jefferson's sound barrier against his elders, creates a pitched battle between them and Grant. He intuits clearly that they are trying to force Jefferson, in modern parlance, to "be where they are" instead of accepting him "where he is" and letting him begin to feel and act and talk again as a human, a prerequisite to any form of salvation. This, lesson two, Grant teaches them in the full reciprocal fury with which frustration has armed him. Yet this verbal explosion is also the first truly free and honest dialogue in the "community" of Jefferson's "teachers."

The fight notwithstanding, the small success of the radio has affected Grant's humanity, too. When, in two days, he returns to the cell, carrying another symbolic community gift, nuts from the children, he directly requests Jefferson's cooperation with his nannan and Reverend Ambrose. Most crucially, he begins to call Jefferson "partner" and opens the way to friendship and free communication of thoughts and feelings in speech and journaling. When Jefferson's responses— "All right . . . All right . . . All right". . . "Yeah" . . . "No"—break through to a human-to-human response, a full sentence of "thank you" to the "chirren" for the "pe-pecans," Grant feels "like someone who had just found religion . . . like crying with joy" (186). He has found one sort of faith; in due time, he will cry. A community get-together, small but real, has occurred.

The most important visit to the jail, that of Grant with the three elders, occurs sometime in the following two or three weeks and occasions the central lesson of the novel: Grant's lesson to Jefferson on the nature of heroism. This time Grant not only asks Jefferson's friendship for himself and Emma but distinguishes between friendship and obedience—a crucial point in this culture of unending submission to elders. Grant's speech seems very long, almost a manufacturing of the "very good speech" Gaines once intended to devise for Jefferson just before his death (CEG, 239–40); it is, in fact, Grant's "unloading" on Jefferson's limited powers of listening and comprehension his own desperate need to find in himself the capacities for heroism he insists Jefferson has. The hero has "dignity . . . heart . . . love for your people . . . identity"; he "does for others . . . would do anything" to "make their lives better" (191–2); no phrases could better express Grant's own urgent wish. Heavy as it is, this speech is plausible in context; Grant *speaks to* the young convict "from [his] heart"; others *talk at* him. While the others would accept few words and more eating, Grant calls for a larger response of human potential. He gets it when Jefferson looks up at him, smiles back, cries— and eats Miss Emma's gumbo, the central and possibly the single most significant action in the entire novel. Jefferson's first tears foreshadow Grant's to come; the meaning the teacher intuits, "I am still part of the whole" (194), will be true for both. Both will cry out of love for the elders and for the whole community.

After this visit, Grant's relationship with Jefferson has actually moved to a deeper level than his relationship with Vivian; it is more intense, more self-giving, more into real thought and emotional sharing, more reflective on the meaning of what he does. Though he does not see that it really *is* more important to him now than "being able to make it well in bed" (197), his success in reaching Jefferson has given him a joy that even sex with Vivian has not yet given. But before Grant can complete Jefferson's instruction, really relate to him or Vivian, the elders or the whole community, he has to receive fierce lessons from both the woman he loves and the minister he despises (or at least does not "revere"). In visits to the jail, he has expanded Jefferson's awareness of his own potential; now in rapidly succeeding fights and lessons, he is taught his own limitations with all the severity, physical and verbal, that he has ever wished to use on his students.

Grant has painfully acknowledged to Jefferson that he is not a hero. At the Rainbow Club, he proves it. This scene is all inappropriate action with no real dialogue, only insulting verbal challenges. By contrast to Jefferson, innocent bystander at a murder, Grant initiates the brawl by going to the mulattos' table, by his "Shut up," and by hitting first; he aggravates it by first seizing a chair as a weapon. In yet more ironic contrast to Jefferson and to Ambrose's wish, he is "on my knees . . . waiting for it to happen, the way a condemned man must wait" (201); then, "trying to find an opening . . . so we could kill each other" (202), he is on the verge of being first to die by a chair. That he is rescued by Thelma's broom and Claiborne's knockout does not make this a farce. The only ludicrously ironic aspects are Grant's repeated "all right . . . all right . . . all right," which are parallel to Jefferson's when he had no voice, and his "Damn it, I can stand up" (203).

Grant's subsequent confrontation with Vivian is lesson three, as crucial to him as his lesson is to Jefferson. Her tough, unyielding assessment of his conduct contrasts with his childish, illogical defenses and pleas: couldn't help it—Jefferson can't walk out—what would you have done?—I didn't start it—all that other stuff—do you still love me?—do you want to know what happened today—aren't you proud? Vivian forces confrontation of the questions of both their identities as adults and lovers, and the definition of love. Always ahead of Grant in thoughtful comprehension, she insists he recognize (as she evidently does now) how far beyond "That bed . . . The cane field . . ." (210) real love must extend. He has poured on Jefferson his frustrated "need to know" (193); now

Vivian pours on him her demand for "answers" (210). His impulse to take "the easy way out—leave" is countered by his long look into the outer darkness, where there is "nothing . . . that I cared for" (210); a reader notes, however, that his list of not-this-place, not-that-person does *not* name the jail or Jefferson. In the end, he is on his knees again, like a penitent, like a child, yet never so much a man. This kneeling is a sign of submission to truth; it acknowledges what he really "cared for" and the truth that love is "caring about"—precisely the lesson he had tried to teach Jefferson that afternoon.[13]

It remains for Reverend Ambrose, with all his educational and theological limitations, to impose lesson four, on kneeling as a form of standing, the core meaning of education, and the fine moral distinctions of truth and lying. This battle contrasts with the barroom fight; here the opponents circle warily while sparring verbally, as if to win points without landing a blow. Grant's observation of the "small, tired little man" (213) has a note of compassion; Ambrose's "He listen to you" has a note more of humility than the jealousy Grant had assumed. By repeatedly limiting his teaching role to "reading, writing, and arithmetic," Grant evades and denies what he is really teaching Jefferson and needs to commit to teaching others. Ambrose also evades that truth by adhering to his limited view of salvation, which he assumes Grant's "teaching" will prevent. With no intuition of Jefferson's real state, he has had and will have no mercy in his determination to persuade him to pray for mercy. Grant, for his part, insists that he does not "owe anybody anything" and that kneeling "hasn't helped me" (216), forgetting the very moral he has been preaching to Jefferson and how recently he knelt in sorrow before Vivian. Ambrose hears the faith Grant can truthfully express, "I believe in God" (214), but he cannot value its honesty or accept its limits; he is too "sure he's sure" and that Grant is "just lost" (217). Grant will not try to elicit a faked expression of faith or repentance from Jefferson, not even to console Emma, yet Ambrose is right that he is not "educated" if he does not know his people or how to "help relieve the pain" (218). Their views of truth and lying are not flatly contradictory: Grant must acknowledge what others have done by stretching the truth and concealing their pain; Ambrose must learn to honor Grant's basic integrity, his one great strength. When both have learned their lessons, they may be able to come together, in the jail if not the church,

13. The film, for some puzzling reason, puts this confrontation (or a semblance of it) much earlier in the sequence of events, at the end of a typical TV bedroom scene. It transposes and combines other scenes and speeches into this one, and so obscures the full effect of Gaines's structure and dialogue, of Vivian's powerful instruction on love and control, as well as the evidence of her own learning. The Vivian of the film has little or nothing to learn.

each with his own form of "education," to teach the uneducated man and be taught by him.[14]

It is Grant's simple integrity that finally frees Jefferson to assert his own humanity, to assume control of his own behavior and manner of dying. In the last visit Grant describes directly, Jefferson is really conversing, not just saying "All right." He quotes Ambrose enough to reveal that the minister has communicated at least the notion of a loving God to "be there" at his death, has induced reflection on the values of this life and the possibility of eternal life. Grant cannot truthfully say he prays or believes in eternity, but he acknowledges the benefit of faith in others and his own sense of loss. He touches Jefferson's central loving relationship, that to Emma, with apparent awareness that it is the best sign of any other love that may exist. In the end, Jefferson may see himself as an "old stumbling nigger," but no longer as "hog." He can and will "take the cross"; he can fearlessly ask honest information about what "it go'n feel like" and still declare himself genuinely "all right" (225). The men have reversed roles; Jefferson is "you-man," (a symbolic as well as phonetic spelling), "the one" who teaches, urges Grant to look up at him, and offers him food.

Jefferson's final achievement is rendered in his diary, that part of the novel that has garnered most critical attention and unreserved praise. It has been considered chiefly as an act of writing that both develops and reveals Jefferson's character. Philip Auger notes that writing in itself runs counter to the whites' assessment of Jefferson; by it he takes his life in "new and different" directions. By the power of language, he escapes one "prison house," achieves his manhood, finds a new "word" and produces a "biblical" text to guide others. Babb and Beavers stress the power of writing for self-knowledge, self-worth, and self-assertion; through his words Jefferson grasps his thoughts and feelings, names and claims his own history, evaluates it, and asserts his resources to end it bravely. Reviewers praise the style, the authentic equivalent of oral vernacular speech.[15]

Perhaps nothing Gaines has written has so poignantly revealed and elevated a character of such lowly and unpromising beginnings. Gaines revealed an inter-

14. For analyses of this scene and others involving Ambrose and of Gaines's progressing views of religion, cf. Beavers, 176–7; Babb, "Old-Fashioned Modernism," in *CRF*, 257–59; Gaines, qtd. in *CEG*, 186; Marcia Gaudet, "The Failure of Traditional Religion in Ernest Gaines' Short Stories," *Journal of the Short Story in English* 18 (1992): 81–9; and William R. Nash, " 'You think a man can't kneel and stand?' Gaines's Revision of Religion in *A Lesson Before Dying*" (paper presented at the annual meeting of the College Language Association, Winston-Salem, N.C., April 21, 1996).

15. Auger, 75–83; Babb, "Old-Fashioned Modernism," 260–2; Beavers, 174–6; reviews in *Time* (March 29, 1993): 65–6, and *Choice* 31 (October 31, 1993): 287–8.

esting fact of his composition process that produced the diary. When he saw that a "great statement" by Jefferson "just before he sat in the chair" would be obviously phony, he still needed a way to let readers inside the character despite his anger and evasion. So he invented the diary, not as a device to make a universal statement, but to elevate Jefferson to himself, to show him that he had expressed and could express humanity (CEG, 299–300, 305). And though the diary is not precisely like the "camcorder" used in the short stories of *Bloodline* (see chapter 3), since Jefferson is actually writing and not simply registering impressions inwardly, it functions in very nearly the same way, with the same immediacy and intensity of revelation. Jefferson's sentences employ the past tense to record his recollection of recent words and deeds of his visitors. He uses the present tense, however, to express the puzzlement, fear, hope, and love that he feels as he writes: "i aint got but just a few days lef an i hope i see my nanan jus one mo time . . . the lord kno mr wigin i hope i can see her one mo time on this earth for i go is that love mr wigin when you want see sombody bad bad . . ." (229). As he gets closer and closer to his end, his entries get shorter, more and more immediate, and as intense as any of the thoughts or feelings of any of the protagonists of the short stories. One lives his last hours with him as they pass:

> my lite on but they aint no mo lite on in the place an the place is quite quite but nobody sleepin
> they got a moon out ther an i can see the leves on the tree but i aint gon see no mo leves after tomoro. . . .
> its quite quite an i can yer my teefs hitin an i can yer my hart . . . now i got to be a man an set in a cher. . . .
> day breakin
> sun comin up
> the bird in the tre soun like a blu bird
> sky blu blu mr wigin (233–34)

From the perspective of Grant's action for Jefferson, giving him the notebook is an extremely shrewd psychological move. By it, he has given him a second voice, enabled him both to go outside himself and to let someone else in. The diary reveals the depths of humanity released in Jefferson: his capacity to notice simple sensory beauty and to reflect on serious questions, to be in touch with his own emotions and moved by those of others, to measure the authenticity in his jailers' kindness and to appreciate that of his visitors, to accept and express love, to acknowledge his own measure of responsibility for his situation, and finally to face the door in his bad dreams and go to death with simple courage. His thoughts come at random, his language is "broken," yet his ideas are formed; we have his "thinking." Never has he been so "whole" in comprehension and character.

The diary also penetrates as deeply into Grant as he has urged Jefferson to go into himself. The progression of "grades" Grant is giving to the diary signals that he is visiting Jefferson voluntarily and often during the final weeks and is discussing with him what he has written. It is evidently Grant who has arranged visits not only by his students, but also by the adults of the quarters, signaling the great improvement in his attitude toward both groups. The children are afraid of the jail but not of Jefferson or their teacher; he has taught them to face reality bravely. He has brought Vivian, so the reconciliation that he began on his knees is complete. While Jefferson does not know of the strain between Grant and the three elders and so does not refer to it, it is evident that Grant has influenced him to accept Reverend Ambrose's ministry as much as he can and to allow Miss Emma to demonstrate her love for him not only in her cooking but in the embraces new to both of them. That has to have helped Grant's own relationships with them and Tante Lou; it implies an appreciation likely to be mutual. Most of all, Grant's actions, the counsel he has given Jefferson, and the bond he has clearly forged with him, all reveal the humanity that he has found in himself as well as elicited from his best student.

Throughout the jail visits, blacks and whites have ever so slightly come toward each other. Guidry has allowed the dinners in the dayroom, as well as the radio, with decreasingly rude assertions of his authority. By contrast to Guidry, Deputy Clark, who enjoys being rude, and the white clerk who sells Grant the radio, Deputy Paul, by tacit mutual agreement, has become Grant's ally in managing or evading the prison system of searches and communication. Most importantly, he has informed Grant of what other whites did not tell him; in so doing, Paul has enacted the role of a black servant, the one who overhears whites in power and passes the word to the community. Now, in the visits recorded in the diary, the presence of the children and especially of the folk from the quarters reveals that Guidry apparently has an open-door policy (not even Deputy Clark could do the old-style searches of such a crowd). Pichot and Morgan are there, still grossly betting, but Pichot has recognized Jefferson's strength of character enough to double his bet and give him a knife to sharpen his pencil—which Guidry allows. The people from the quarters are all there; Jefferson's list in the diary is essentially the same as Grant's at the Christmas program; it includes "ole bok ole bok ole bok" and Creole Catholic "mis felia wit her beeds an jus prayin" and "god kno who all" (230). An entire community—white, Creole, and black, young and old, privileged and poor—has come together across all barriers in at least a few days of compassion and good will. Auger comments on the role of these people; they bring into Jefferson's prison cell all the forces of change—affirmation, education, and religion.[16] Most of all, they bring the force of simple attention, affection, and deep concern. No reader wonders why Jefferson is overpowered to free-flowing tears "cause they hadn never done nothin lik that for me befor" (231); his tears are likely to be shared because the reader "hadn never [read] nothin lik that befor."

Up to chapter 30, the community most affected by Jefferson has included blacks from the quarters or the Rainbow and whites from the Pichot house or the jail. On execution day, the community is extended to all the town within reach of the courthouse and within reach of human feeling. Some whites evade awareness, some harden their emotions; blacks are chilled or silent or stunned. Whites and blacks alike are gruesomely fascinated or genuinely horrified by the sight of the chair and the sound of the generator that can be heard for blocks. One white laughs nervously, another cries shame, a third notes the likeness to the crucifixion of Christ, a fourth to the execution of the thieves with him, presumably justifying the present event but recalling the "Good Thief." Amid the merely curious or sincerely grieved, the approving or aghast, are the relatives and friends of the condemned. The latter group seems to include the jail officials: the sheriff, who cannot look directly at his wife and wishes "this day had never gotten here" (238); the added deputies, whose name, Guerin, suggests they may be Cajuns and thus improbable friends of this convict; and definitely Paul, whose "I'll be there" (245) is less a fact than a promise. Bizarre as it may seem, Jefferson's achievement of humanity in facing his execution has become a lesson for and a measure of similar achievement in the community at large, in people previously unknown to him and also unknowing, uncaring.

Yet Grant, despite his new bond with Jefferson, is "not there" at the execution, as he was not at the trial. The almost unbearable poignancy of the final chapter of the novel (in contrast to the film) is in his prolonged wrestling with that fact until Paul Bonin brings him "there" by a description as searing as any in literature. The profound thematic implication of the novel's finale is in the fact that it is not Ambrose nor, at another remove, Tante Lou who brings him, but Paul. The elders are "there" yet "not there" in the chapter; they have been, as always, strong boulders, tree stumps whose new shoots of life have appeared in the Bayonne courthouse. Ambrose has "been there" and returned, again the one

16. Auger, 79.

brave enough to tell Emma, as Lou is to be with her. Now the trio has withdrawn. Wrestling with the present and especially the future is the task of younger men, black and white, bound in friendship by common experience of pain and possibility, bound by common necessity to tell what they have learned to those still younger.

Action is completed in dialogue and in a new, racially reversed pattern of "going to": Paul goes to Grant; Grant receives him as an equal, receives the final lesson about potential achieved, his own included: "You're one great teacher" (254). Paul requests friendship and offers his hand; Grant accepts both relationship and gesture. Grant invites Paul to come "one day" to tell the children of Jefferson's heroism; Paul accepts the "honor" (256). Then Grant can go to the children.[17]

Gaines was too wise an artist to convert Grant to a totally transformed character. He will still need to contend with his aunt and search for freedom and faith. Vivian will still need to encourage all that is new and best in him. He will need Paul's friendship to safeguard his own memory and "conversion" and to "spread the word" to his students. Yet the final scene clearly implies that Grant is deeply committed to Vivian and to his students. The lover and teacher who was "drifting," who had felt dead for lack of emotion and mentally enslaved for lack of faith, who made his students kneel for Jefferson though he could not, who had formerly made them cry without compassion, now breaks through to his own humanity: "I was crying." Gaines achieved his goal, that Jefferson be "the savior of Grant, so Grant could save the children" (CEG, 300). With the community to back the teacher, he can take "the burden" willingly. Elders, young people, children—the whole community can hold on to a new hope.

But that is not all for Grant. As he gave Jefferson a voice through writing, so he finds his voice to teach the lesson he learned from Jefferson. Just as Jane Pittman taught her interviewer by telling her story, and he passed the lesson on in written form for his students and other readers, so Grant must do. As narrator of the novel, he is his own protagonist, editor, and interpreter.

The first-person narrative mode is, I contend, a chief fiction of the novel, central to understanding how it accomplishes its project of reestablishing communal ties. Grant and his storytelling techniques are obviously Gaines's creations, but by making him narrator, Gaines has given an additional dimension to him and to the story. Grant is no Huckleberry Finn who could not write his own story,

---

17. In a first version, Gaines had Paul go into the school and give a talk. His agent caused him to reconsider and recognize that Grant, not a white man, must first go to the children (CEG, 305–6).

requiring a reader's suspension of disbelief. His narrative style is neither "porch talk" nor a stream of consciousness, private memory nor what I have called "camcorder" narration of events and their impact as they are occurring (chapters 3 and 8). This narrator is an educated man crafting an after-the-fact account of the most crucial six months in his life (October through April, 1948), sparing neither himself nor anyone else in what he reveals, telling the story so as to reveal the changes wrought in his and others' characters and essential relationships. John Lowe told Gaines he had thought Grant's name might have alluded to the general who "forced himself to write his memoirs" for the sake of his family. Though Gaines denied he had that link in mind, Lowe captured an aspect of Grant as narrator, his need to tell the story (CEG, 301–2). He may be writing for his own catharsis of grief or for self-possession; he is also, surely with some conscious intent, recording a story that must be preserved as part of communal history. His intent and his own changed character, what he now thinks and the "lessons" he learned, are implied everywhere by the manner of his after-the-fact narration.

About Jefferson's trial, the concern of the entire community, black and white, Grant had the same knowledge, the same expectation as everyone else, much the same anger as the black community; yet the tone of the first chapter is objective, almost journalistic. "I was not there, yet I was there" (3). He has assembled the details of the murder that Jefferson gave his lawyer or the lawyer reconstructed from probabilities, as well as the speeches he has reconstructed from all who heard and repeated them. This reportorial mode is employed not only because the reader needs basic factual information at the start, but also because Grant was then maintaining and is now revealing his determined emotional detachment and strong will to "stay out of it."

From that point through chapter 28 and in chapter 31, Grant tells directly what he remembers or found out, and what he thought about Jefferson's story and his own involvement. Because he was not "there" any more than he had to be, Grant as narrator is dependent on what he "learned later" from various sources: his aunt, the deputy, Inez in Pichot's kitchen. His aunt and Emma must be his sources for their visit to Mrs. Guidry; probably Paul, or possibly even Guidry himself, recounted his conversation with Jefferson about visiting in the dayroom. At first, Grant is receiving unsought information more or less forced upon him by his elders. But the shift in his level of involvement is reflected in his beginning to ask what he cannot otherwise know, such as Paul's explanation of the choice of execution date. Paul, in fact, becomes his main source for assessing changes in Jefferson. Chapter 30 makes it evident that Grant has, in the end, plunged into his community to acquire every scrap of information he missed by not "being there."

Besides seeking out and presenting what he missed, Grant also tells what he might well be inclined to omit: his own humiliations. He details the barroom fight and the ensuing lecture from Vivian. Her lesson he might include out of love, but he also details the confrontation with Reverend Ambrose, omitting none of his own inconsistencies and giving the long last word to the preacher. None of these three episodes directly affects Jefferson, yet all of them reveal how Grant was shaped to be his teacher and to connect the community to him. By their deliberate inclusion without negative critical diction about his "teachers," Grant implies not only that he was nearly a murderer himself and that he was forced to accept moral chastisements, but that he has accepted their justice and learned his lessons. To his own credit or not, Grant tells the whole truth.

As narrator, he also implies or emphasizes certain truths and meanings by the way he arranges his memoir. The account of Jefferson's cruelty to the elders, overheard only "a couple of days" after it took place (120), is interjected into his account of his own battle with them, thus stressing that he had not sought it at the time or wanted to know or share their pain. But now he does know and share. Again, he juxtaposes the black woman giving money to buy the radio with the "powdered-faced" white woman who stalls, objects, and insults him as she sells it. He carefully analyses the "kind of love" in Thelma's generous "here"; the other woman's motives are all too obvious (174–6). Often he uses a chapter ending as a striking marker for an emotion, a thematic meaning, or progress in the development of relationships: after Emma's plea to Pichot, "The sun had gone down, and it was getting colder" (23); after her first visit to Jefferson, "With his eyes . . . [Paul] told me to put my arms around her. Which I did" (74); after his protest against humiliation at the jail, Emma's tearful "I'm so sorry, Mr. Grant. . . . But they ain't nobody else" (79); after Vivian's question about breaking "that circle" of defeat, "It's up to Jefferson, my love" (167); and finally, at the end of his last recorded jail visit, " 'Care for a 'tato, Mr. Wiggins?' . . . 'Sure,' I said" (225).

That this account is more than Grant's self-absorbed memoir is indicated by some of his explanations, as if to readers unfamiliar with the culture of southern Louisiana. He made a point, he says, of asking the families of his students to do something for the school because "they expected it of me" (17). He explains the "bricklaying genes" (201) of the two mulattos and the reasons for their status, prejudice, and hostility; this implies a distinction of his own anger at the time of the barroom fight from his thoughts about it at the time of writing. Grant the narrator knows what Grant the character had forgotten but relearned, what he is now teaching his readers—and presumably his students.

Grant the narrator's new thoughts and feelings are reflected in his tone. He knows enough not to make the fight comical (except slightly, in Claiborne's agitated response), but he projects a warm humor in his description of the Christmas program: the children's grammar, the glitches in their performance and stage management, even Reverend Ambrose's pointed prayers. Though he says he was unhappy with the people's unchanging limitations and way of life, tone distinguishes his past boredom or ambivalence from his present respect and appreciation of what they did, despite their poverty, to unite and extend the season to the one who could not be there. David Vancil notes that Grant's humor is often ironic, even bitter. He cites the repeated use of the Christian elements of redemption as examples.[18] Grant's irony, however, reflects his new awareness of the complexity of faith and love. His lengthy reflections on the analogous dates of Christ's and Jefferson's executions are filled with his continuing anger at the blasphemy of men who played God by killing and choosing the date and time, but also by his sense of ironic aptness of the choice, given the heroism and love with which both men died, each without "a mumblin' word" (223), but with a still-echoing voice and word of dignity, love, and promise.

The Christmas program is but one example of Grant's use of expansive descriptions to reveal varied and changing relationships. He could easily have summarized his two-hour wait in Pichot's kitchen and the conversation that finally occurred; the same for the school superintendent's visit. Instead he develops each event into a chapter, enlarging a reader's awareness of what humiliations were leveled out to any black who dared to learn, to become a man. When Grant and Ambrose are called to Pichot's parlor, he records, as he obviously noted them, numerous details of furniture, clothes, movements, and glances; all are etched in his memory and signal his high-strung attention at the time when the execution date shook the usual racial barriers between men and the exclusion of blacks from white space, when he himself was forced to think about the execution. By contrast, when Vivian visits his home, he describes the bedroom and kitchen with details of furniture, pictures, cabinets, brooms, ax, pots and pans. He includes the way they eat and wash dishes, the weather and scenery on their walk—houses, gardens, railroad cars, derrick and scales, trees in the cemetery. This is the "rustic" scene and culture in which he and Vivian propose to marry. Writing this after they have lived and loved together through Jefferson's ordeal,

18. Vancil, 489–90.

he implies the quality and permanence they have achieved together, their final acceptance of the place and people.

Amplified descriptions are matched with attention to "minor" details. The sensitized narrator recalls that Jefferson first talked to him about the weather, a "nice day . . . No clouds anywhere. Just blue" (170), a day he ironically hoped for at his death. Grant has now read the end of his diary, "sky blu blu blu mr wigin" (234), and notes that as he himself waited for news of the death, it was "a nice day. Blue sky. Not a cloud" (247). Grant the "new" teacher, as if to enforce his new hope, calls attention to the student most like Jefferson, Louis Washington: poor, unkempt, ungrammatical, yet perceptive of Grant's inconsistencies, who places questions right on target. And Grant, the "new" friend to all, notes that at the end he met Paul as an equal, waited for him to come to him, granted his requests, accepted his double handshake.

No details of Grant's narration are more telling than his regular use of motifs: the "being there" and "not there," going to, going away, and staying, silence and speech, looking or refusing to look, seeing or not seeing, crying or not as measure of sensitivity. Symbols are placed naturally, but too clearly to be other than the work of a narrator conscious of their meaning. Bayonne's major industry is a "slaughterhouse, mostly for hogs" (25); "a low ashen sky loomed over the plantation, if not over the entire state of Louisiana" (107). At school, the U.S. flag "hung limp" (33); Bible verses were meaningless rote recitations. Ruts in Pichot's yard were made by years of blacks' driving labor vehicles through the side gate; like the ruts in his own character, Grant is neither aiming for them nor avoiding them. Loveliest of all symbols of new life, the butterfly doubles its significance for Grant: it is Jefferson's spirit taking flight and his own spirit finding reason to "light on a hill . . . that offered it nothing" and then to fly "down into the quarter" (252). Surely this is the narrator's way of saying, "I learned. I stayed."

The switch in chapters 29 and 30 from Grant's direct narration may be one of Gaines's most successful authorial decisions. Its success, however, is best appreciated when one realizes that the two chapters are, nevertheless, still Grant's narrative production. Paul gives him Jefferson's diary after the execution. Grant may have read it during his visits, but because his final farewell was on Thursday, its last pages are new to him. Having read or reread the whole, Grant as narrator interrupts his account to put the diary in the sequence of Jefferson's writing it. So appreciative, indeed, has Grant become of Jefferson's character that he has to present his final weeks, and especially his final day, in the young man's own words, deficient as they are in the grammar he once harshly demanded of his students. So sensitive is he to his own changed feelings during these weeks, and humbly aware of their impact on others, that he can hardly reveal them directly as he has done before. Let them be seen, if at all, through Jefferson. Commenting on the strategic placement of the diary, John Lowe suggested that it "doesn't exactly affect Grant" but makes the book's balance shift from him to Jefferson. Gaines said he had to "get into" Jefferson but then remove him from the book so that Grant could pick up the story (CEG, 300). That seems exactly the point: the diary *has* affected Grant, so much so that he has to pick up the story after Jefferson's death and tell it in both their words. Placement may have "just so happened" in the author's experience, but it serves a purpose in the narrator's. He seems to have reread his own experience in light of the diary, as Lowe rightly said a reader rereads the book (CEG, 305).

Chapter 30, the preparation for the execution, has puzzled readers, seeming to be a switch into omniscient narration. It has also been called a "communal narrative" akin to that used in other Gaines works with multiple narrators.[19] It is, as discussed above, a narration about the community, but close reading reveals that this chapter, too, is Grant's first-person narration. He has drawn his account from all possible contacts, each of which can be identified: a black laborer, Aunt Lou, Vivian, Reverend Ambrose, black employees at a department store and a Bayonne café, a convict on jail duty, and Paul. The one scene hard to account for is the conversation of the sheriff and his wife at breakfast—until one notices the reference to "Lillian, their colored maid," the omnipresent but overlooked listener at every upper-class white dining table. Once again, Grant has been "not there, yet there"; this time, however, he has made it his business to "be there" later, to inquire and to know all. Formerly alienated from his community by education, he has reconstituted himself as a member by gathering stories from all witnesses and storytellers on the circuit, including the least privileged, those who serve in the most menial positions. If his tone is again objective and reportorial, he has withdrawn his own emotion not to shield it but to let the situation be revealed and judged in the varied emotions of the entire town, black and white.

In his final, summary chapter, Grant returns to first-person narration so a reader may hear, as only he did, Paul's moving account, and be, as he was, "converted" to whatever service of humanity or eventual faith in God is needed or possible. He also must, with integrity and in brief, poignant understatement, reveal his response as no one else can. On the reader's response may depend, in some measure, the future of his students, of all children, of the human community.

---

19. Babb, "Old-Fashioned Modernism," in *CRF*, 263.

In this last novel, Gaines raised once more his foremost, recurrent issues and largely resolved them. Not fully, of course, because the issues remain in the American and human community. But the one question at the hub of all others, that of defining and exemplifying manhood, has been answered. The novel dichotomizes not man and woman but hog and human. The same trait of "standing" that defines manhood in Jefferson has been required of all his protagonists, is required of and available to any person willing to face his or her moment of challenge. Manhood equals simple, integral humanity. Learning that lesson and acting on it create "quality" in every Jefferson, every Irene Cole and Louis Washington, Emma and Ambrose, Grant and Vivian. On that lesson depends quality and unity in every human community.

Conclusion

AT SIXTEEN, ERNEST GAINES began his career with what he "thought was a novel"; he began again, seriously and professionally, with the short story, hoping to make his fame and bread with that form. When practicality intervened and he began to labor to create the extended yet unified genre of the novel, his love and talent for the short story continued to generate creativity in his work. Various and original uses of the short form were melded into the novel and made to serve his related concerns for theme and technique.

Gaines's thematic development has been a progression from simple questions about the definition of manhood to penetrating explorations of possible answers, to a final, defining portrait of humanity as unselfish concern for the happiness of others combined with courage to make good choices in a crisis and to act for specific goals. Humanity is expressed most profoundly in love and relationships, in choices and actions of labor and providing, of protest and risk and even rebellion against visible evils. Developing such humanity takes a lifetime of many related events, so Gaines needed the length of the novel to explore his ideas. Yet humanity "happens" in multiple small experiences, so his theme was also well served by his penchant for the short tale, either complete in itself or a formally structured part of a longer work.

In Gaines's fiction, humanity also "happens" when people can freely speak their truth from mind and heart, regardless of risk. And so he wanted to release the voices of his characters, to let them express their own inner selves, from youngest to oldest, weakest to strongest among them. For that, he needed to capture the varieties of their sounds, to find his narrative voice in their voices. For that, too, he could draw most effectively on the story form he had heard all his life, the short oral tale or report or reminiscence. In that form, he could play original variations on voices, internal and external, formal and folk, barely articulate and most expressive. He could give to Sonny Howard a voice of juvenile consciousness sufficient to express one day's trauma, and eventually give to Grant Wiggins a voice strong enough and "knowing" enough to unfold the prolonged and complex development of an entire community. In developing his narrative voice, Gaines moved from the uneven, static quality of *Catherine Carmier* to the dynamism of *A Lesson Before Dying*, which is all voice, one voice with the varied tones of a definite personality, repeating the voices of other personalities telling their stories and becoming less or more human as they speak.

In the voices of his people, Gaines also found his implied authorial voice. In developing it, he progressed from the omniscient yet uncertain voice of his first novel to the firm sound of his last, where open-endedness about life beyond death is matched with a sureness about the definition and value of human life itself. It is no great exaggeration to say that Ernest Gaines has remained at heart, in imagination and metaphor, on a Louisiana gallery or ditchbank in summer, at a firehalf in winter, telling or listening to other voices tell tales, many short tales that combine into the history of his people and give meaning to their story and the related story of the whole human race.

Almost without exception, readers cite the same two novels as Gaines's weakest: *Catherine Carmier* and *In My Father's House*—the two that use omniscient narration and no "tales" in their composition. With even more unanimity, three novels are cited as his best: *The Autobiography of Miss Jane Pittman*, *A Gathering of Old Men*, and *A Lesson Before Dying*. Of these, one can say that the first two draw much of their superiority precisely from their composite character, their formal unity in variety of episodes, persons, and voices, represented in short tales and in narration. *A Lesson Before Dying*, though it is an extended single action, is strongly marked throughout by short accounts rendered in varied voices, most notably in Jefferson's very "oral" diary and in the various reports of the morning of his execution day. Like portions of the other two novels, these chapters could be "lifted" and, with little alteration, made to stand on their own. Yet they unquestionably fit in place where they are in the structure of the whole.

"Sketches, sketches, sketches," "little short chapters," tales and the voices of tellers: these are the hallmark and the unique strength of Ernest Gaines's fiction. Not surprising, then, that having achieved the freedom with sufficiency he sought as a young artist, he has said that he now has in mind several novellas (CEG, 327–8), the form that stands between short and long. It allows especially for one developed personality and voice, for one moderately extended action— and perhaps a few artfully embedded sketches. The novella would be a logical and fruitful development from all Gaines has done until now. Readers have something new to anticipate.

Bibliography

PRIMARY SOURCES

Note: Gaines's published work is listed here by genre and in chronological order. Second publications of novels are paperbacks; the edition used is cited in the first footnote referencing a particular work. Generally, the paperback is the edition referenced.

Short Fiction

"The Turtles." *Transfer* 1 (1956): 1–9.

"Boy in the Double Breasted Suit." *Transfer* 3 (1957): 2–9.

"Mary Louise." In *Stanford Short Stories*. Edited by Wallace Earle Stegner and Richard Scowcroft. Stanford: Stanford University Press, 1960, 27–42.

"The Sky Is Gray." *Negro Digest* 12 (August 1963): 72–96. Reprinted in *Bloodline*.

"Just Like a Tree." *Sewanee Review* 71 (1963): 542–68. Reprinted in *Bloodline*.

"A Long Day in November." *Texas Quarterly* 7 (1964): 190–224. Reprinted in *Bloodline*. Reprinted with some revisions as a children's book. New York: Dial, 1971.

"My Grandpa and the Haint." *New Mexico Quarterly* 36 (1966): 149–60.

Bloodline. New York: Dial, 1968. New York: Norton, 1976; New York: Vintage, 1997.

"Chapter One of *The House and the Field*, A Novel." *Iowa Review* 3 (1972): 121–5.

"Chippo Simon." *Yardbird Reader* 5 (1976): 229–37.

"In My Father's House." *Massachusetts Review* 18 (1977): 650–59. Reprinted in *Chant of Saints*, edited by Michael S. Harper and Robert B. Stepto, 339–48. Urbana: University of Illinois Press, 1979.

"The Revenge of Old Men." *Callaloo* 1 (May 1978): 5–21.

"Robert Louis Stevenson Banks, aka Chimley." *Georgia Review* 37 (1983): 385–89.

Novels

Catherine Carmier. New York: Atheneum, 1964; San Francisco: North Point Press, 1981.

Of Love and Dust. New York: Dial, 1967; New York: Norton, 1979.

The Autobiography of Miss Jane Pittman. New York: Dial, 1971; New York: Bantam, 1972.

In My Father's House. New York: Knopf, 1978; New York: Norton, 1983.
A Gathering of Old Men. New York: Knopf, 1983; New York: Vintage, 1984.
A Lesson Before Dying. New York: Knopf, 1993; New York: Vintage, 1994.

Nonfiction

"Miss Jane and I." *Callaloo* 1 (May 1978): 23–38.
"Auntie and the Black Experience in Louisiana." In *Louisiana Tapestry: The Ethnic Weave of St. Landry Parish,* edited by Vaughn B. Baker and Jean T. Kreamer, 20–29. Lafayette: Center for Louisiana Studies, University of Southwestern Louisiana, 1982.
"Bloodline in Ink." *College English Association Critic* 51 (winter 1989): 2–12.
"A Very Big Order: Reconstructing Identity." *The Southern Review* 26 (1990): 245–53.

Film Adaptations

The Autobiography of Miss Jane Pittman. Adapted by Tracy Keenan Wynn. Directed by John Korty. CBS, January 31, 1974.
"The Sky Is Gray." Adapted by Charles Fuller. Directed by Stan Lathan. PBS, 1980.
A Gathering of Old Men. Adapted by Charles Fuller. Directed by Volker Schlondorff. CBS, May 10, 1987.
A Lesson Before Dying. Adapted by Ann Peacock. Directed by Joseph Sargent. HBO, May 1999.

SECONDARY SOURCES

Aubert, Alvin. "Ernest J. Gaines's Truly Tragic Mulatto." *Callaloo* 1 (May 1978): 68–75.
———. "Self-Reintegration through Self-Confrontation." *Callaloo* 1 (May 1978): 132–5.
Auger, Philip. "A Lesson about Manhood: Appropriating 'The Word' in Ernest Gaines's *Lesson.*" *Southern Literary Journal* 27 (1995): 74–85.
Babb, Valerie Melissa. *Ernest Gaines.* Twayne United States Authors Series, no. 584. Boston: Twayne, 1991.
Beavers, Herman. *Wrestling Angels into Song: The Fiction of Ernest J. Gaines and James Alan McPherson.* Philadelphia: University of Pennsylvania Press, 1995.
Bryant, Jerry H. "Ernest J. Gaines: Change, Growth, and History." *Southern Review* 10 (1974): 851–64.
———. "From Death to Life: The Fiction of Ernest J. Gaines." *Iowa Review* 3 (1972): 106–20.

————. "Politics and the Black Novel." *Nation* (April 5, 1971): 436–8.

Burke, Virginia. Review of *In My Father's House*. *Library Journal* 1 (June 1, 1978): 1195.

Burke, William. "*Bloodline*: A Black Man's South." *College Language Association Journal* 19 (1976): 545–58.

Byerman, Keith. *Fingering the Jagged Grain: Tradition and Form in Recent Black Fiction*. Athens: University of Georgia Press, 1985.

Callahan, John F. "Hearing is Believing: The Landscape of Voice in Ernest Gaines's *Bloodline*." *Callaloo* 7 (winter 1984): 86–112.

————. *In the African-American Grain: The Pursuit of Voice in Twentieth-Century Black Fiction*. Urbana: University of Illinois Press, 1988.

Curet, Bernard. *Our Pride: Pointe Coupee*. Baton Rouge: Moran Publishing Corporation, 1981.

David, Idolie Olinde. "Historical Sketch of Early Pointe Coupee." New Roads, La., Public Library, n.d., Typescript.

Davis, Thadious M. "Headlands and Quarters: Louisiana in *Catherine Carmier*." *Callaloo* 7 (spring/summer 1984): 1–13.

Doyle, Mary Ellen. *The Sympathetic Response: George Eliot's Fictional Rhetoric*. Rutherford, N.J.: Fairleigh Dickinson University Press, 1981.

Duncan, Todd. "Scene and Life Cycle in Ernest Gaines' *Bloodline*." *Callaloo* 1 (May 1978): 85–101.

Estes, David C., ed. *Critical Reflections on the Fiction of Ernest J. Gaines*. Athens: University of Georgia Press, 1994.

Fabre, Michel. "Bayonne or the Yoknapatawpha of Ernest Gaines." Translated by Melvin Dixon and Didier Malaquin. *Callaloo* 1 (May 1978): 110–24. Originally published in *Recherches Anglaises et Americaines* 9 (1976).

Folks, Jeffrey J. "Ernest Gaines and the New South." *Southern Literary Journal* 24 (1991): 32–46.

Forkner, Ben. "Ernest J. Gaines." In *Critical Survey of Short Fiction*, edited by Frank N. Magill, vol. 4: 1429–36. Englewood Cliffs, N.J.: Salem Press, 1981.

————. Review of *A Gathering of Old Men*. *America* (June 2, 1984): 425.

Fuller, Hoyt N. Review of *Of Love and Dust*. *Negro Digest* (November 1967): 51–2, 85.

Gaudet, Marcia. "The Failure of Traditional Religion in Ernest Gaines' Short Stories." *Journal of the Short Story in English* 18 (1992): 81–9.

————. "Miss Jane and Personal Experience Narrative: Ernest Gaines' *The Autobiography of Miss Jane Pittman*." *Western Folklore* 51 (January 1992): 23–32.

Gaudet, Marcia, and Carl Wooton. *Porch Talk with Ernest Gaines: Conversations on the Writer's Craft*. Baton Rouge: Louisiana State University Press, 1990.

Grant, William E. "Ernest J. Gaines." In *Dictionary of Literary Biography*, Vol. 2, *American Novelists since World War II*, edited by Jeffrey Helterman and Richard Layman, 170–75. Detroit: Gale, 1978.

Griffin, Joseph. "Calling, Naming, and Coming of Age in Ernest Gaines's A *Gathering of Old Men.*" *Names* 40 (June 1992): 80–97.

———. "Ernest J. Gaines's Good News: Sacrifice and Redemption in *Of Love and Dust.*" *Modern Language Studies* 18: 3 (1988): 75–85.

Hicks, Jack. *In the Singer's Temple: Prose Fictions of Barthelme, Gaines, Brautigan, Piercy, Kesey, and Kosinski.* Chapel Hill: University of North Carolina Press, 1981.

———. "To Make These Bones Live: History and Community in Ernest Gaines's Fiction." *Black American Literature Forum* 11 (1977): 9–19.

Jackson, Blyden. "Jane Pittman through the Years: A People's Tale." In *American Letters and the Historical Consciousness: Essays in Honor of Lewis P. Simpson,* edited by J. Gerald Kennedy and Daniel Mark Fogel, 255–73. Baton Rouge: Louisiana State University Press, 1987.

Jansen, William Hugh. "The Esoteric-Exoteric Factor in Folklore." In *The Study of Folklore,* edited by Alan Dundes, 43–51. Englewood Cliffs, N.J.: Prentice-Hall, 1965.

Jeffers, Lance. Review of *A Gathering of Old Men.* *Black Scholar* (March 1984): 45–6.

Jones, Eldred Durosimi, ed. *Insiders and Outsiders.* Vol. 14 of *African Literature Today.* London: Heinemann, 1984.

Jones, Gayle. *Liberating Voices: Oral Tradition in African American Literature.* Cambridge, Mass.: Harvard University Press, 1991.

King, Martin Luther, Jr. *Why We Can't Wait.* New York: Harper and Row, 1963.

Laney, Ruth. "The Last One Left." (*Baton Rouge*) Advocate Sunday Magazine. October 30, 1983: 6–7.

"The LSU Rural Life Museum." Guidebook. Rural Life Museum. Baton Rouge, La.

Lowe, John, ed. *Conversations with Ernest Gaines.* Jackson: University Press of Mississippi, 1995.

McCluskey, John, Jr. "A Brooding Novel, Important Questions." *Obsidian* 6 (1980): 239–43.

McMurtry, Larry. Review of *In My Father's House.* *New York Times Book Review* (June 11, 1978): 13.

Millican, Arthenia Bates. Review of *The Autobiography of Miss Jane Pittman.* *College Language Association Journal* 15 (1971): 95–6.

Nash, William R. " 'You think a man can't kneel and stand?' Gaines's Revision of Religion in *A Lesson Before Dying.*" Paper presented at the annual meeting of the College Language Association, Winston Salem, N.C., April 21, 1996.

Papa, Lee. " 'His feet on your neck': The New Religion in the Works of Ernest J. Gaines." *African-American Review* 27 (1993): 187–93.

Paris, Bernard J. *Imagined Human Beings: A Psychological Approach to Character and Conflict in Literature.* New York: New York University Press, 1997.

Price, Reynolds. "A Louisiana Pageant of Calamity." *New York Times Book Review* (October 30, 1983): 15.

Puschmann-Nalenz, Barbara. "Ernest J. Gaines: 'A Long Day in November' (1963)." In *The Black American Short Story in the 20th Century: A Collection of Critical Essays*, edited by Peter Bruck, 157–69. Amsterdam: Gruner, 1977.

Ramsey, Alvin. "Through a Glass Whitely: The Televised Rape of *Miss Jane Pittman*." *Black World* (August 1974): 31–6.

Review of *Catherine Carmier*. *Times Literary Supplement* (February 10, 1966): 97.

Review of *A Lesson Before Dying*. *Choice* 31 (October 1993): 287–8.

Review of *A Lesson Before Dying*. *Time* (March 29, 1993), 65–6.

Review of "Long Day in November." *Hornbook* 48 (1972): 153.

Roberts, John W. "The Individual and the Community in Two Short Stories by Ernest J. Gaines." *Black American Literature Forum* 18 (1984): 110–3.

Rowell, Charles H. "The Quarters: Ernest Gaines and the Sense of Place." *Southern Review* 21 (1985): 733–50.

————. "That Little Territory in and around Bayonne: Ernest Gaines and Place." Paper presented at the annual meeting of the Modern Language Association, Los Angeles, December 1982.

Sacks, Sheldon. *Fiction and the Shape of Belief*. Berkeley: University of California Press, 1966.

Schraufnagel, Noel. *From Apology to Protest: The Black American Novel*. Deland, Fla.: Everett/Edwards, 1973.

Shelton, Frank W. "Ambiguous Manhood in Ernest J. Gaines's *Bloodline*." *College Language Association Journal* 19 (1975): 200–9.

————. "*In My Father's House*: Ernest Gaines after *Jane Pittman*." *Southern Review* 17 (1981): 340–5.

Simpson, Anne K. *A Gathering of Gaines*. Lafayette: Center for Louisiana Studies, University of Southwestern Louisiana, 1991.

Smith, Rick, and Ruth Laney. *Ernest J. Gaines: Louisiana Stories*. Videotape. Distributed by Louisiana Public Television.

Stoelting, Winifred L. "Human Dignity and Pride in the Novels of Ernest Gaines." *College Language Association Journal* 14 (1971): 340–58.

Tallant, Drury. "French Influences on River Lake Plantation." Private collection of Mrs. Madeline Caillet. N.d. Typescript.

Thomas, H. Nigel. "The Bad Nigger Figure in Selected Works of Richard Wright, William Melvin Kelley, and Ernest Gaines." *College Language Association Journal* 39 (1995): 143–64.

Tomlinson, Barbara. "Characters Are Coauthors: Segmenting the Self, Integrating the Composing Process." *Written Communication* 3 (1986): 421–48.

Vancil, David E. "Redemption According to Ernest Gaines: Review of *A Lesson Before Dying*." *African-American Review* 28 (1994): 489–91.

Vinson, Audrey L. "The Deliverers: Ernest J. Gaines's Sacrificial Lambs." *Obsidian II*, 2d ser., 2, no. 1 (1987): 34–48.

Vinson, James, ed. *Contemporary Novelists*. New York: St. Martin's Press, 1976.

Walker, Alice. Review of *A Gathering of Old Men*. *New Republic* (December 26, 1983): 38.

Walker, Robbie. "Literary Art and Historical Reality: Ernest Gaines's Portrayal of the South in Transition." *Griot* 2 (summer 1983): 1–9.

Ward, Phil. "Artistic Story Compels Quick Reading, Thought." (*Baton Rouge*) *Advocate* Sunday Magazine. October 30, 1983, 16.

Washington, Mary Helen. "Commentary on Ernest J. Gaines." In *Memory of Kin: Stories about Family by Black Writers*, edited by Mary Helen Washington, 38–42. New York: Doubleday Anchor Books, 1991.

———. "The House Slavery Built." *Nation* (January 14, 1984): 22–4.

Watkins, Mel. Review of *In My Father's House*. *New York Times* (July 20, 1978): C 19.

Werner, Craig Hansen. *Paradoxical Resolutions: American Fiction since Joyce*. Urbana: University of Illinois Press, 1982.

Wertheim, Albert. "Journey to Freedom: Ernest Gaines's *The Autobiography of Miss Jane Pittman*." In *The Afro-American Novel Since 1960*, edited by Peter Bruck and Wolfgang Karrer, 219–35. Amsterdam: Gruner, 1982.

Wideman, John. "*Of Love and Dust*: A Reconsideration." *Callaloo* 1 (May 1978): 76–84.

Personal Interviews

Aaron, Willie, Carrie Hebert, and Rosie Ruffin. Residents of River Lake Plantation Quarters. July 22, 1986.

Caillet, Madeline. Owner of River Lake Plantation. July 22, 1986.

Gaines, Lionel. Brother of Ernest Gaines. July 23, 1986.

McVay, Horace. Great-uncle of Ernest Gaines. July 23, 1986.

Turner, Bruce. Archivist, Dupre Library, University of Southwestern Louisiana. July 21, 1986.

Index